School-based management and school effectiveness

The concern for school effectiveness has attracted international interest for some years as school systems worldwide have become subject to wide-ranging reform programmes. This book links together school effectiveness research with studies of school-based management, to develop understanding of the relationships and connections between school-based management, school effectiveness and school improvement.

The studies in this book describe and analyse how effective principals (headteachers) and teachers perceive and undertake school reform and educational change; how a sense of values, vision and school culture can improve leadership; and ways in which delegating financial management to schools may improve the quality of teaching, learning and the curriculum. It offers suggestions on future directions for educational administration, school effectiveness and school improvement as fields of study and research.

Examples and empirical data are drawn from an international context – from Australia and New Zealand, Canada, the USA and the UK – and address themes in both practical and theoretical terms. The contributors are all established leaders in their field, with wide experience of working with principals (headteachers) and teachers in practical problem-solving settings.

Clive Dimmock has lectured in educational management and administration at University College, Cardiff, and is currently Senior Lecturer in Educational Management at The University of Western Australia in Perth. He is an experienced trainer and conference presenter on principals' leadership programmes in the UK and Australia, and also acts as consultant to government and non-government school systems in both countries. His research interests focus on educational leadership, school effectiveness and school improvement, and he has published numerous papers on these themes in international journals.

Educational management series
Edited by Cyril Poster

Managing the primary school
Joan Dean

Schools, parents and governors:
a new approach to accountability
Joan Sallis

Management skills in primary
schools
Les Bell

Special needs in the secondary
school: the whole school
approach
Joan Dean

The management of special
needs in ordinary schools
*Edited by Neville Jones and Tim
Southgate*

Creating an excellent school:
some new management
techniques
*Hedley Beare, Brian Caldwell
and Ross Milikan*

Teacher appraisal: a guide to
training
Cyril and Doreen Poster

Time-constrained evaluation
Brian Wilcox

Performance-related pay in
education
Edited by Harry Tomlinson

Evaluation in schools: getting
started on training and
implementation
Glyn Rogers and Linda Badham

Managing change in schools
Colin Newton and Tony Tarrant

Managing teams in secondary
schools
Les Bell

Managing evaluation in
education
*Kath Aspinwall, Tim Simkins,
John F. Wilkinson and M. John
McAuley*

Education for the twenty-first
century
Hedley Beare and Rick Slaughter

Parents and schools: customers,
managers or partners?
Edited by Pamela Munn

Education 16–19: in transition
Eric MacFarlane

Opting for self-management
Brent Davies and Lesley Anderson

Managing external relations in
schools
Edited by Nick Foskett

School-based management and
school effectiveness
Edited by Clive Dimmock

School-based management and school effectiveness

Edited by Clive Dimmock

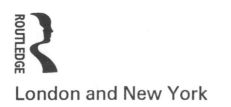

London and New York

First published 1993
by Routledge
11 New Fetter Lane, London EC4P 4EE

Simultaneously published in the USA and Canada
by Routledge
29 West 35th Street, New York, NY 10001

© 1993 Clive Dimmock

Typeset in 10 on 12 point Garamond by
by Michael Mepham, Frome, Somerset
Printed and bound in Great Britain by
Mackays of Chatham PLC, Chatham, Kent

British Library Cataloguing in Publication Data
A catalogue record for this book is available from the British Library
    ISBN 0–415–08313–3
        0–415–08314–1 (pbk)

Library of Congress Cataloging-in-Publication Data
has been applied for
    ISBN 0–415–08313–3
        0–415–08314–1 (pbk)

Contents

List of figures

List of tables

Contributors

Raymond Bolam is Professor of Education at University College, Swansea. He was formerly Director of the National Development Centre for School Management Training and Senior Lecturer in Education at the University of Bristol. Ray has published extensively in the areas of management training for school leaders, in-service education and the management of educational change. He has undertaken consultancies to many governments and international agencies, including the OECD, UNESCO and the British Council.

Brian Caldwell is Reader and Associate Dean (Research), Institute of Education, The University of Melbourne. His areas of interest include leadership, especially in systems where substantial authority and responsibility have been decentralized to the school level. He has written widely on the concept of school self-management and has served as consultant and speaker on the theme on five continents in recent years. He is President of the Australian Council for Educational Administration.

Glenda Campbell-Evans lectures in the Policy and Administrative Studies Department of Edith Cowan University in Perth, Australia. She is Director of the Centre for Educational Leadership, the aim of which is to serve the professional development needs of practising and aspiring administrators in Western Australia. Dr Campbell-Evans' research interests include the role of school administrators, the influence of values in decision making and the socialisation of beginning principals. She is a consultant in these areas in both Australia and Canada.

Judith Chapman was formerly Director of the School Decision Making and Management Centre within the Faculty of Education, School of Graduate Studies, Monash University, Australia, before her appointment as Professor of Education at The University of Western Australia. After teaching and administrative experience in secondary schools in Australia and Europe she undertook postgraduate study in educational administration in the USA where she worked for the Educational Planning Service. Among her publications are two edited books, *School-based Decision-making and Management* and *Democracy and Bureaucracy: Tensions in public schooling* (with J. Dunstan).

In recent years Dr Chapman has undertaken major research and consultancy projects on behalf of international and national authorities, and she is currently principal consultant for the OECD activity entitled *The Effectiveness of Schooling and Educational Resource Management.*

Peter Cuttance was Director of Education and Head of the Education Review Unit in the Department of Education, South Australia before moving to his present position in the New South Wales Department of Education. Formerly, Dr Cuttance was Senior Research Fellow in Education at the University of Edinburgh, and consultant to the Scottish Education Department. He has been a visiting research scholar at universities in Finland and Denmark, and has extensive experience of teaching at school and university level. His research interests and publications focus on school effectiveness, the performance of public and private schooling, performance indicators in education, evaluation methodologies and statistical methods.

Clive Dimmock has lectured in Educational Management and Administration at universities in Britain and Australia. He is currently Senior Lecturer in the Department of Education at The University of Western Australia in Perth. His research interests focus on educational leadership, the quality of teaching and learning, restructuring, and school effectiveness and school improvement. He has published many articles in prestigious journals on these issues. Dr Dimmock has worked as a consultant to school systems in Australia and England and Wales.

Philip Hallinger is Associate Professor in the Department of Educational Leadership in Peabody College of Vanderbilt University and Director of the Center for the Advanced Study of Educational Leadership (CASEL). He has served as a regular and special education teacher, vice principal, administrator of a school for special needs students, and director of the Westchester Principals' Center, a professional development centre serving over 1200 school administrators outside New York City. Dr Hallinger has written numerous articles in prestigious professional journals and is recognized internationally for the development of the Principal Instructional Management Rating Scale. His areas of interest include principal and superintendent leadership, administrative problem solving, and leadership development.

Charles Hausman is a doctoral student (PhD) in the Department of Educational Leadership at Vanderbilt University and Research Assistant in CASEL. His areas of interest include school improvement, organizational theory and behaviour, the principalship, and quantitative methodology as a tool to study these areas. He has founded a positive peer pressure organization for adolescents, coordinated two international conferences on educational leadership development, helped to develop a computer simulation for training school leaders and co-authored an article on restructuring schools for *Educational Administration Quarterly.*

Shirley Hord is currently Senior Research Associate at the Southwest Educational Laboratory in Austin, Texas, where she conducts research and designs professional development activities in educational change, school improvement and school leadership. In her previous role as Director of Research on the Improvement Process at the Research and Development Center for Teacher Education at the University of Texas at Austin she researched on the role of school leadership in school change. She is a fellow of the National Center for Effective Schools Research and US representative to the Foundation for the International School Improvement Project.

Brian Knight is an Honorary Research Fellow of the University of Exeter and an educational consultant. Formerly, he was headteacher of Holyrood Comprehensive School in Chard, Somerset. Among his publications are *Managing School Finance* (Heinemann), *Local Management of Schools, Managing School Time, Public Relations and Marketing for Schools* (co-author) and *Designing the School Day* (Longman). Brian Knight has lectured and consulted in the UK, Australia and South Africa.

Kenneth Leithwood is currently Professor of Educational Administration and Head of the Center for Leadership Development at the Ontario Institute for Studies in Education. His most recent books include *Understanding School System Administration* (with D. Musella) and *Developing Expert Leadership for Future Schools* (with P. Begley and B. Cousins). Dr Leithwood's interests are in the nature and development of leadership for change.

Joseph Murphy is Professor and Chair in the Department of Educational Leadership in Peabody College and a Senior Research Fellow with the National Center for Educational Leadership. He has served on several national commissions for educational enhancement and published extensively in professional journals. His work focuses on the issue of school improvement, with particular interest in the role that administrators can play in that process. Recent books include: *Understanding the Principalship: A metaphorical analysis from 1900–1990* (with Lynn Beck), New York: Teachers College Press (in press); *Restructuring Schools: Capturing and assessing the phenomenon*, New York: Teachers College Press (1991); and (Editor) *Reform of American Public Education in the 1980s: Perspectives and cases*, Berkeley: McCutchan (1990).

Cyril Poster is currently a freelance education management trainer and consultant, and editor for the Routledge education management series. Since he retired from the post of Deputy Director of the National Development Centre for School Management Training at the University of Bristol, he has worked with many local education authorities in England and Wales, and in particular for the past four years with the West Midlands LEA, Dudley. He was for four years honorary general secretary of the International Community Education

Association, and has written extensively about community education and education management.

David Reynolds is at the School of Education in the University of Wales College of Cardiff, United Kingdom. He has published widely on school effectiveness, the sociology of the school and educational policies. His books include *The Comprehensive Experiment* (with M. Sullivan and S. Murgatroyd), *School Effectiveness* (with P. Cuttance) and *Educational Policies: Controversies and critiques* (with A. Hargreaves). He is currently working as a consultant to the OECD project on 'The Effectiveness of Schooling and of Educational Resource Management' and is a member of ISERP (The International School Effectiveness Research Project) working on the identification of effective schooling practices internationally.

Rosanne Steinbach is a Senior Research Officer in the Center for Leadership Development at the Ontario Institute for Studies in Education. Her research interests are in the areas of cognitive development, administrative problem solving, and the nature and development of administrative expertise.

Preface

Throughout Australia and New Zealand, Canada, England and Wales and the United States policy makers and politicians are formulating and implementing policies to restructure and reform school systems. In most cases restructuring involves wholesale change, affecting the distribution of powers and responsibilities between all groups with vested interests at school, district and central office levels. Parents, students and even the home are involved in restructuring; and whereas many changes in the past have avoided the classroom, the latest waves of reform are all embracing. Given the comprehensiveness of these reforms the restructuring phenomenon is more accurately described as multiple change occurring simultaneously. In a complex web of change some forces and trends are to be recognised acting in different directions from others. Consistency may at times be difficult to detect, and certainly more apparent than real.

Notwithstanding elements of centralization within restructuring, the prevailing thrust of reform is towards school-based management. In essence, the aim is to devolve more powers and decentralize responsibilities to the school level. While more decision making over the allocation of resources used by the school is transferred to the school level, school-based personnel are generally held more accountable for their performance and for student outcomes achieved.

This book focuses on school-based management and its links with school effectiveness knowledge and school improvement practice. It recognizes that government policies for school-based management and their implementation tend not to be predicated on bodies of theory or research evidence. It assumes that there is an urgent need to examine purposes and practices at the school-site level, which is seen as increasingly critical in shaping the quality of service delivery. Trends towards school-based management have gathered momentum accompanied by an equally strong concern for quality of teaching and learning, and performance of schools more generally. Increasingly, it is necessary to relate school-based management to school effectiveness knowledge and school improvement practice to obtain a more complete understanding of the network of ideas and forces shaping the operation of school systems.

In writing the book the authors attempt to achieve a number of aims. First, the book places emphasis on the need for more informed discussion and recognition of the effects of school-based management. The book is unequivocally research driven. All chapters report empirical research findings, some relying on primary data, others on secondary sources. A second aim is to bring together a number of studies and perspectives of school-based management drawn from six countries and three continents – Australia and New Zealand, Canada, England and Wales and the United States. There are surprisingly few collections of multinational work on restructuring outside the major projects undertaken by the international agencies. Third, the multinational perspective allows for the generation of similarities and differences between the practices of school-based management. The studies contained in this volume raise the fallacy of assuming school-based management to be represented by just one model. There is a need eventually to recognize and develop a categorization of different models within the generic term *school-based management*. A fourth aim of the book is to link the characteristics of school-based management with research findings on school effectiveness and school improvement. Ultimately, a convincing justification for school-based management rests on the extent to which research evidence reveals its associations and linkages with creating more effective schools, especially in terms of improved academic and affective student learning and development. Fifth, for practitioners, the book is intended to provide many useful ideas for school improvement. Finally, at a more theoretical and conceptual level, the book supports future research by providing frameworks and ideas for conceptualizing and clarifying complex processes and their interrelationships within the domains of school-based management, school effectiveness and school improvement.

In addressing these aims the book should appeal to a wide audience comprising policy makers, practitioners, academics and researchers. Whether operating in school, district, or central office; whether interested as a principal, teacher, parent, district superintendent or LEA adviser; whether concerned as an academic, researcher, or postgraduate student – the book aims to inform thought and practice on issues of school-based management, school effectiveness and school improvement.

THEMES OF CHAPTERS

In Chapter 1 Clive Dimmock explores the effects and implications of school-based management for those working in schools, and relates these to the existing knowledge base of school effectiveness. He argues for the development of greater understanding of the direct and indirect ways in which school-based management affects the quality of the curriculum, teaching and learning. In developing such research it is suggested that a conceptual framework based on the concept of *linkage* has potential and promise. There follows

an application of the concept of linkage to a school-based curriculum management model aimed at improving student learning.

The following three chapters report empirical studies. In Chapter 2 Hallinger, Murphy and Hausman continue the theme of linkage between
school-based management and curriculum and instruction, recognizing the
dearth of research linking the political and structural changes of restructuring
to classroom processes. Accordingly, their survey of teachers' and principals'
perceptions of how restructuring might affect curriculum and instruction is
designed to draw out the connections between new emergent governance
structures and processes and teaching and learning.

Chapter 3 focuses on the relationship between principals and school improvement. Leithwood and Steinbach research the questions whether and in
what ways the practices used by principals to foster school improvement
differ. While it appears that distinct patterns of principals' practice are discernible the key to understanding how principals act is how they think: in
particular, their problem-solving processes. The authors elaborate key variables for distinguishing differences in principals' mental processes when
problem solving.

In Chapter 4 Hord and Poster continue the theme of principals and school
improvement. Two case studies – one of an American elementary school
principal, the other of an English primary school headteacher, and how each
secures significant school improvement – are detailed. While comparisons
between the strategies employed by both principals reveal similarities and
differences, when both are compared with an established taxonomy of effective principal behaviours there is a close fit.

The following three chapters each focus on a particular functional area of
school-based management. In Chapter 5 Campbell-Evans explores from a
value orientation the principal's role in securing school effectiveness within a
school-based management context. While acknowledging the importance of
leadership, vision, participation and culture, each of which is fully elaborated,
it is argued that effective practice in school-based management seeks the
interrelationships and linkages between these, and that values provide an
appropriate underpinning.

A second functional area of school-based decision making, delegated financial management, is the theme of Chapter 6. Drawing on research evidence
from many education systems Brian Knight attempts to answer the key
question of whether financial delegation within school-based management
promotes school effectiveness and, in particular, improves student learning.
Does delegated financial responsibility to schools tend to lead to better quality
teaching and learning? What are the linkages, if any, between these two sets of
variables? While acknowledging the incompleteness and embryonic nature of
much of the research data, Knight is able to form some tentative conclusions.

In Chapter 7 Peter Cuttance describes the school development planning
and review process as designed in one education system. Few studies to date

report on school development planning, a process which aims to secure school improvement and which lies at the heart of most restructuring and school-based management reforms. The purposes of school development plans are explained along with the selection of objectives, statements of outcomes and performance levels, training and development to support school development, and approval and review of school development plans. Cuttance places school development planning and reviews within a broader perspective of systemic reviews.

Chapters 8, 9 and 10 raise issues and concerns of a broader nature. In Chapter 8 Brian Caldwell covers a large canvas while focusing on emergent structures and the changing role of school principals in Australian and New Zealand education. Many of the changes described, such as the concerns for quality, equity and empowerment, have their parallels in other education systems. One of the most significant changes in restructured schools in the 1990s, however, will be a new kind of leadership role for principals in self-managing schools. A number of 'megatrends' and likely scenarios for the 1990s are 'played out' and implications for principals derived.

Both Chapters 9 and 10 address the state of the art in the development of knowledge and research in school effectiveness and school improvement. In Chapter 9 David Reynolds recognizes the lack of linkage between what he calls school effectiveness knowledge and school improvement practice. In surveying each of the two communities, each with their different paradigms, Reynolds is able to suggest ways in which each could gain from the knowledge base of the other. In developing a new paradigm built on the foundations of the existing two there is a real prospect of advances in knowledge and its application to benefit the quality of schooling experienced by children.

Underpinning Judith Chapman's contribution in Chapter 10 are two broad themes: a concern to improve understanding of school-based management, school effectiveness and school improvement in an Australian and international setting, while mindful of the elusiveness of the concept of school effectiveness; and a review of existing research in the three areas which leads her to argue for a more integrated coherentist approach to leadership, school-based decision making and school effectiveness.

In Chapter 11 Raymond Bolam presents an overview of the foregoing chapters. It proves to be a rich tapestry of interwoven themes and issues around the configurations of restructuring and school-based management, school effectiveness and school improvement.

USAGE OF TERMS

In a volume containing the writings of American, Canadian, Australian and British authors it is understandable, excusable and even desirable that different terms are used to convey essentially the same ideas or meanings. For example, in North America and Australia it is customary to refer to the *principal* as school leader, while in Britain the term *headteacher* is used. Similarly, different terms are used between and even within countries to refer to *school councils, governing bodies, school boards* and *school-based decision-making groups.* Sometimes there are subtle but significant differences in meaning (in powers, functions, membership, roles and so on) that may not be explicitly conveyed by the terms themselves; for example, in Western Australia a school council is a more empowered body than a *school-based decision-making group*. Contributors to this book have used terms and expressions commonly understood within the cultural boundaries of their research contexts and points of reference. The reader is urged not simply to make allowance for such variations and attendant differences of meaning, whether they be semantic or substantive, but to endorse such linguistic and cultural variations, as a means of developing a wider and more global perspective on issues of concern addressed in the book.

ACKNOWLEDGEMENTS

In bringing this book to fruition I wish to express my gratitude to Cyril Poster, editor of the Routledge educational management series, for his wisdom and patience. I am grateful to Mike Lally, a colleague in the Department of Education at The University of Western Australia, who encouraged the initial concept of the book and supported the effort required to produce it. Tribute is due to the academics, scholars, students and practitioners of educational administration who contributed chapters to this volume. Finally, for her computer typesetting skills and administrative help I am indebted to Jenny Foo.

Clive Dimmock

Foreword

It is a pleasure to welcome a book by Clive Dimmock into the Routledge education management series. He is well known in England and wales, particularly for his work at the former University College of Cardiff and for his work in and for the British Education Management and Administration Society (BEMAS). Since he moved to the other side of the world, to the University of Western Australia, he has maintained many of his previous educational connections and has made many new ones. This edited book, with contributions from Canada, the United States, the United Kingdom and Australia itself, is evidence of that diversity.

The theme is all important today; and there are many who think it should have been more important in the halcyon days of the 1960s and 1970s. As one who was a school principal in those decades I like to think that I and those similarly placed in schools in the countries of the contributors to this book concerned ourselves very much with the effectiveness of our institutions. What we lacked, and what this book demonstrates so clearly now exists, is a corpus of experience and research against which to match our effectiveness. Today the cry on all sides is for accountability. What is frequently forgotten is that imposed accountability may be no more than a paper exercise designed to satisfy *them*, whoever they may be. True accountability needs to be in the bloodstream of our educational institutions and to address itself primarily to its clients, the students and their parents, and to those elected bodies – School Councils, boards of governors, district committees – whose main purpose must be seen as facilitating the work of the school so that it can be as effective as circumstances allow.

This is not a book of wholly homogeneous contributions, as Ray Bolam implies in his masterly overview. If differing, even controversial, points of view can be detected in the contributions, that is all to the good, for the book deals with live issues, not a comfortable set of acknowledged facts.

Cyril Poster
Series Editor

Chapter 1

School-based management and linkage with the curriculum

Clive Dimmock

Connections between the quality of school-based management and curriculum are typically assumed. Underlying much of the emphasis on school-based management and principals' professional development is the belief that improvement in the management of schools will necessarily generate better quality curricula, teaching and learning. Yet this relationship, when investigated more closely, is by no means self-evident. The notion that school-based management *per se* automatically improves curriculum quality deserves to be challenged (Malen *et al.*, 1990).

This chapter argues the importance of developing greater understanding of the direct and more subtle ways in which school-based management actually affects the quality of the curriculum. It also recognizes the importance of knowing how school-based management might contribute to enhancing the quality of the curriculum. Restructuring, and the trend towards school-based management, provide the context for the discussion to follow. Two underlying sets of reasons, one educational, the other economic and political, are presented as the rationale for school-based management. Both have as their goal improvement in the quality of education. It is argued that greater understanding of the relationships between management and curriculum is predicated on building a clear picture of the characteristic features of effective school-based management, and on developing conceptual frameworks which facilitate investigation of the relationships. The concept of linkage is offered for its potential analytical qualities in examining the relationships between management and curriculum. A conceptual framework built around linkage is then applied to curriculum management.

SCHOOL-BASED MANAGEMENT AND QUALITY OF EDUCATION

Many school systems throughout North America, Europe and Australasia are undergoing restructuring. Although emergent patterns of power relations are complex, with decentralizing shifts of responsibility for some functions to the school level, and recentralizing of control of others to central offices and ministries, the pervading impression of the restructuring movement focuses on school-based management. The compelling momentum for this restructuring, from an educator's viewpoint, is driven by the desire to improve the quality of education. Underlying this concern for quality are two quite distinct sets of reasoning (Chapman, 1990).

One line of reasoning, based largely on school effectiveness research, suggests that improvements in student achievement are most likely to be gained in schools which are relatively autonomous, possess a capacity to resolve their own problems, and in which strong leadership, particularly by the principal, is a characteristic (Finn, 1984; Prasch, 1984). Reinforcing this, Duignan (1990) argues for a curriculum, client-based approach, with the focus on school-based decision making, allowing schools control over resources by which to fine-tune curricula for the benefit of students.

Another path sought for improvement in the quality of schooling stems from economic and political imperatives. Chapman (1990) attributes this to the link, perceived by politicians, between education, economic performance and productivity. She argues that 'in many countries the recent educational debate has been conducted in a context of alarm regarding the state of the economy and national competitiveness', and that, 'in some countries education has received much of the blame for the nation's relatively poor economic performance' (p. 241). Against this background of concerns, politicians and policy makers have become more stringent in allocating resources to education and have exacted top-down policies, such as new accountabilities owed by the school to the centre and local community, based on targets and expected outcomes, student system-wide testing, and monitoring and appraising of school performance.

Substantial differences are revealed when both motivations for improving the quality of education are closely examined. The educational motivation for school-based management depends on initiatives taken from within the school itself to improve its performance, through the quality of management, teaching and learning. In the case of political motivation, the initiative is largely driven by system-level pressures, with externally imposed outcomes as targets for schools to meet. In assessing the likely impact of each of these initiatives on the organization and functioning of schools, two conclusions may be drawn. First, research evidence of successful educational change supports the notion of practitioner involvement in all stages of the change process, even if the change is predominantly top down (Fullan, 1986; Huberman and Miles, 1984). The involvement of school personnel in key stages of the politically driven initiative has typically been minimal. Second, the setting and achieving of targets, and the expectancy and creation of new accountability relationships, depend, for their successful implementation and attainment, on changed structures and work practices at the school level. The inescapable conclusion is that the intended improvement in the quality of schooling, whether inspired by educational motives or political imperatives, is based on reforms in school-based management and school-level practices.

A focus on school-based management therefore seems a *sine qua non* for improving the quality of education. The term school-based management may, however, be applied to a number of different arrangements, all of which concentrate management functions at the school level. The actual distribution, pattern and exercise of these functions at the school level may vary considerably. Consequently, it is important to understand the key processes and structures of schools which display those characteristics considered critical in attaining and delivering improvements in the quality of education. From the evidence available, what are these characteristics? Only a tentative picture can be traced, given the limits on the present state of knowledge. There are relatively few empirical studies reporting the efficacy of school-based management, and its influence on the quality of education (Brown, 1990). There are, however, considerably more conjectural accounts of the processes thought to be necessary for effective school-based management.

BUILDING THE PICTURE OF EFFECTIVE SCHOOL-BASED MANAGEMENT

The characteristics of effective school-based management most likely to promote quality curricula may be gleaned from two sources: research on school effectiveness, and descriptions of processes and structures in schools which have successfully embraced school-based management. It is instructive, therefore, to elicit those features common to both school-based management and school effectiveness. Descriptions of effective school-based management focus on six features (Brown, 1990):

* autonomy, flexibility and responsiveness
* planning by the principal and school community
* adoption of new roles by the principal
* a participatory school environment
* collaboration and collegiality among staff
* a heightened sense of personal efficacy for principals and teachers

A discussion of each of these may highlight their likely impact on teaching, learning and curriculum.

A key issue is whether school-based management possesses features in common with those identified by the effective schools research. The school effectiveness literature identifies certain attributes of schools which seem to correlate positively with enhanced learning outcomes. Among the managerial attributes are strong principal leadership, school planning, and monitoring and evaluation of school activities (Beare *et al.*, 1989). The relevant question is whether these are features of school-based management. According to the respondents in Brown's (1990) survey, principals claimed that their leadership capacity had been enhanced by their additional authority. Consequently, more planning was undertaken by principals and staff, and principals claimed that they had more control over the resources supplied to their schools. Some schools even had 'monitoring procedures in place, either direct testing for learning outcomes or measures of parental and student satisfaction, or both' (Brown, 1990, p. 245). School-based management seems to foster many of the features associated with school effectiveness. School-based management, however, does not guarantee effectiveness, or improvement in the quality of the curriculum.

A number of studies suggest that schools perform well when the environment within which they function allows them a large amount of autonomy (Garms et al., 1978; Goodlad, 1984; Guthrie, 1986). Simply allowing schools autonomy, however, does not guarantee improvement in performance. More improvement is likely to occur in the way schools respond to the opportunities afforded by greater autonomy. Autonomy itself is relative, since no government school is completely unfettered in its policies and practices. There are always constraints, some of which are set by the district and centre. There is the suggestion that schools function well when their 'autonomy' is bounded by closely aligned district policies (Peterson et al., 1987).

Another characteristic of school-based management thought to enhance performance relates to flexibility and responsiveness (Brown, 1990). In a Canadian study of school communities, Brown cites the work of Mintzberg (1979), Brooke (1984), and Kochen and Deutsch (1980) as lending support to the argument that flexibility, or the capacity to change, facilitates quick and appropriate responses by service agencies, such as schools, to the needs of their clients. Flexibility is also seen as possibly generating innovation and creating more rewarding work environments and a better motivated staff. After testing some of these propositions in a survey of Canadian principals, teachers and parents, Brown (1990) concluded that school-based management had increased the flexibility of decision making. Flexibility, for example, was manifested in the practice of virement. Responsiveness also featured, although it was found to be based 'not on client needs but on the perception of student needs by school personnel' (Brown, 1990, p. 237). In terms of school performance, the key question centres on whether resource flexibility matches student needs.

There is evidence in Brown's study that school-based management fosters more planning by the principal and the school, and that more resources are available at the school level to align with those plans. Moreover, there is some evidence that increased resources are channelled to activities thought to be linked with learning outcomes, such as professional development and textbooks. As Brown admits, however, it is not possible to claim that increased resource allocation necessarily increases 'productivity in the form of learning outcomes' (Brown, 1990, p. 243).

In a comprehensive review of the implications of school-based decision making, Chapman (1990) writes of a new conception of the principalship. Principals have found themselves 'working with new values, new decision-makers and a new set of management decisions and responsibilities' (Chapman, 1990, p. 227). Principals become coordinators of a number of different groups, all of which have interests in the school. Dual accountabilities to both school council and central office provide principals with new challenges. Working with inexperienced council members, encouraging participative decision making and power sharing constitute a different kind of work environment for principals. The key question, however, is how these new roles and responsibilities for principals are likely to affect school improvement and the quality of education.

While assuming a more public and educative role outside, principals experience changed work practices inside school. Chapman (1990) argues that 'principals must form, liaise and interact with consultative groups', and 'attend to the interpersonal dynamics that such intensive interaction produces' (p. 229). Teachers experience the challenge of cultural change presented by school-based management as much as principals. It is the influence of the principal, however, which is critical in shaping the nature and extent of teacher participation in decision making. Participation is likely to be high among staff where the principal encourages participation, values individual contributions, and the decision-making process is affected as a result. When these conditions exist, participation seems to result in increased trust between senior management and teachers. How does a participatory and trusting climate contribute to improved quality teaching and learning, and curricula in general? It is likely to promote opportunities for greater collaboration among staff with resultant curriculum benefits. More authoritarian principals, on the other hand, are likely to confine power to a few people, with resultant staff resentment, even if democratic structures are in place.

A more participative school environment may enhance the sense of personal efficacy felt by principals and teachers. The construct of self-efficacy refers to the individual's expectations of coping with, and being able to control, the environment (Bandura, 1986; Wood and Bandura, 1989). An individual's expectations regarding ability to exert personal control over the environment have been shown to facilitate adaptive behaviour, promote constructive behaviour change, and lead to improved performance. High levels of personal and professional efficacy also increase the likelihood of the individual successfully coping with environmental challenges, and through persistence, adopting effective problem-solving behaviours (Bandura and Wood, 1989). It is possible that school-based management, in so far as it facilitates a more participative school environment, could lead to an increased sense of control over school activities for teachers and principals, and a greater sense of individual contribution to the school. However, it is not clear whether it is a change in the school environment which nurtures teachers' and principals' sense of self-efficacy, or whether the changed environment simply allows more opportunities for the exercise of control over school management by those who already possess strong feelings of self-efficacy.

Although there is relatively little research to date on whether school-based management benefits the curriculum, Chapman's (1988) study is one of the few to address this issue. She tentatively argues that teachers are more likely to confront issues, to consider alternatives, and to justify practices under school-based management. Consequently, there is likely to be more personal interaction between principals, teachers, students and parents. In the second-ary school, a further outcome may be closer interdepartmental relations, fostering a more coordinated, whole-school curriculum perspective. Increased teacher participation may also generate greater commitment to curriculum policy decisions, which Chapman (1990) believes may improve educational outcomes in two ways. First, more information and knowledge dissemination is likely to lead to improved understanding and clarity of policies, decisions and reasons for change. Second, feelings of increased trust, greater sense of self-efficacy, and commitment to decisions are thought to improve curriculum development and educational outcomes. However, Chapman's (1988) study found no link between participation and improved teacher practice. Indeed, participation may detract from teaching performance by distracting teachers from their classroom duties. Future research might, therefore, consider this aspect.

A parallel and potentially rewarding line of investigation of the relationship between school-based management and curriculum quality may be provided through linking participation with collaboration and collegiality. If a partici-patory school decision-making environment is conducive to teacher collaboration and collegiality, then the critical question is whether there are benefits to student learning when teachers work together. While more syste-matic inquiry of collegial influences has yet to take place, the work of Little (1982, 1990) and Bird and Little (1986) provides important evidence of the potentially positive effects of collegiality on curriculum quality, especially on teaching.

The work of these aforementioned authors presents a balanced view of the benefits to students when teachers work together. Little (1981), for example, cites a study of six urban high schools in the United States where teachers attributed school-wide academic gains and improved classroom performance to having worked together once a week for two years to tie their curriculum and instruction to principles of mastery learning. Compelling evidence is provided by Bird and Little (1985), who report teacher claims of substantial student gains in mathematics and improved classroom behaviour after they had collaborated on changes to the curriculum, including testing and student placement. According to Little (1990) the benefits of teacher collaboration for students are 'the quality of program in which students participate, the sense of program coherence and faculty cohesiveness that students detect, and the consistency in expectations that students encounter' (p. 167). Little admits, however, that there are also many examples of unsuccessful teacher collaboration. Furthermore, productive teacher peer relations is one of a number of 'interwoven and cumulative' influences shaping 'students' learning, attitudes and actions' (Little, 1990, p. 167).

Nevertheless, Little argues that collegiality has the potential to benefit both experienced and beginning teachers. The isolation of the classroom (Little, 1990), experienced by many teachers, is broken. Further benefits result in teachers' better preparation for classroom work; teaching which displays greater instructional range, depth, and flexibility; teachers who are more influenced by, and gain respect for, each other; and a more rewarding and satisfying work environment for teachers. It seems reasonable for Little (1990) to argue that the quality of teaching and student learning is likely to benefit from collegiality in at least four ways:

- when teachers talk about teaching, the complex relations between their actions and student learning are clarified;
- teachers' shared planning and preparation of programmes makes for consistency and coordination of approach throughout the school;
- teachers are more willing to engage in classroom observation of each other's lessons, and to provide feedback;
- teachers are more likely to train together and to train one another.

The kind of school-based management that fosters a participatory work environment is also instrumental in promoting teacher collegiality. Although the relationship between teacher collegiality and improved student learning remains to be systematically tested, supportive evidence is beginning to accumulate. The vital ingredient seems to be that collegiality is characterized by close, constructive, and congenial individual and group relations (Little, 1990). The ability of principals and school managers to foster such a climate is critical.

SCHOOLS AS NON-COLLABORATIVE CULTURES

Relatively few schools may have created the work environment described above. Little (1990), for example, claims that:

Emerging visions of the teaching profession and of the school as a professional environment are in tension with inherited traditions. On the whole, tenacious habits of mind and deed make the achievement of strong collegial relations a remarkable accomplishment: not the rule, but the rare, often fragile exception. (pp. 166–7)

Corroborative evidence for the nature of the interplay which exists between teacher experiences and school environment is provided by Lieberman and Miller (1990). These authors apply the following descriptors to capture the true nature of teaching:

- style is personalized;
- rewards are derived from students;
- teaching and learning links are uncertain;
- the knowledge base is weak;
- goals are vague and conflicting;
- control norms are necessary;
- professional support is lacking;
- teaching is an art. (pp. 153–6)

A view of schools as organizations subject to rational forces is supplanted by a perspective of life in schools governed by 'rhythms, rules, interactions and feelings' (Lieberman and Miller, 1990, p. 162). The school work environment is determined by daily, weekly, termly and yearly patterns and cycles (rhythms). The strong influence of formal and informal rules helps to explain the inviolability of individuals and their classrooms and the resistance to collective plans and rational decision making (rules). The importance of interactions promotes the 'centrality of children in teachers' lives', the 'unrealized potential of colleagueship and of the power of a principal to make a school better or worse' (Lieberman and Miller, 1990, p. 162). Teachers' feelings are affected by the absence of standards by which to gauge their work. Their sense of relative control over their classrooms and powerlessness over the rest of the school environment helps explain the privatized world of many teachers.

SCHOOL-BASED MANAGEMENT AND CURRICULUM: THE NEED FOR RESEARCH

Reviews of the literature on school-based management, school effectiveness, the social organization of schools, and on the social context of teachers, reveal substantial differences between potential managerial and organizational arrangements on the one hand, and reality on the other. While some schools have created invigorating work environments, displaying responsiveness, flexibility, participation and collegiality, the majority of schools remain resistant to, or find difficulty in, forging new organizational arrangements and work practices. The key problem is how the existing practices and cultures in many schools can be transformed into realizing the potential benefits offered by school-based management. A starting point for this transformation is an improved understanding of the link between managerial and curriculum work in schools.

There is a need to improve our knowledge of existing work patterns and practices in schools. As Bell (1990) argues, our approach to school management has been preoccupied with structures and processes of management, as though they were ends in themselves. Instead, the focus needs to shift to how school-based management can maximize student learning. How can learning be facilitated through school-based management of the curriculum? In answering this question a more substantial data base is needed to clarify existing curriculum management practices (Malen *et al.*, 1990). Further questions relate to how school-based management can nurture a quality curriculum. What is the meaning attributed to *quality curriculum*? What are the management processes, teaching practices and school cultures conducive to creating and supporting improved teaching and learning?

To facilitate such research there is a need to identify and develop appropriate constructs and conceptual frameworks to expose and elicit the patterns of interaction between school management and curriculum. Such constructs and frameworks should be selected for their potential contribution to data collection and analysis, and ultimately for their efficacy in generating understanding of, and improvement in, managing and delivering a better quality curriculum.

THE CONCEPT OF LINKAGE

In investigating the relationship between school management and the quality of the curriculum, the concept of coupling as applied to education by Weick (1976) provides a useful starting point. Weick used the concept of *loose coupling* to convey the image that the constituent parts of an educational organization, for example a school, are responsive but retain their separate identities. Many writers (Hannaway and Sproull, 1978; Deal and Celotti, 1980) have since supported this view that schools consist of constituent parts which are only weakly coordinated and controlled. Orton and Weick (1990) provide a comprehensive explanation as to why schools tend to be loosely rather than tightly coupled. The concept of linkage developed in this chapter incorporates not only Weick's notion of loose–tight coupling, but other dimensions too. *Linkage* is therefore preferred to coupling because of its broader scope.

Although the concept of linkage (coupling) has a rich imagery, is frequently cited by authors, and appears to offer a potentially powerful insight into managerial and organizational life in schools, there has been relatively little development of the concept (Dimmock, 1991). Bossert (1986) supports the need for greater recognition to be paid to the concept of linkage when he states:

> If the primary function of school management is to foster an effective instructional programme, research must address how the formal organisational milieu of the school affects schooling outcomes. This will happen only when studies explicitly examine the linkages among management activities, the use of resources by teachers and students in the classroom context, and instructional practices. (p. 122)

In developing the concept of linkage it is useful to review ways in which the concept has been applied and developed in education since Weick's seminal work describing educational organizations as 'loosely-coupled' (1976). Several writers have since added the dimensions of *direct–indirect*, and *formal–informal* to *tight–loose*. Murphy *et al.* (1985) introduced the concept of the tightly coupled curriculum, in which the curricular materials, the instructional approaches, and the assessment instruments are tightly aligned with the basic learning objectives for students. Murphy *et al.* (1986) distinguish direct from indirect organizational control mechanisms in the instructional leadership arena. Direct controls influence the behaviour and activities of principals, whereas indirect controls modify organizational structures, processes and tasks which in turn affect behaviour and activities. These authors also distinguish between formal and informal mechanisms of control. Formal controls are planned outcomes of the formal organization of the school, while informal controls evolve, independently, within the school's formal organizational structure.

A distinction between bureaucratic and cultural linkages was made by Wilson and Firestone (1987). Bureaucratic linkages refer to the formal enduring rules, procedures, and authority relations designed to control the behaviour of teachers, while cultural linkages include the 'system of collectively accepted meanings, beliefs, values, and assumptions that organizational members (teachers) use to guide their regular, daily actions and interpret their surroundings' (p. 19). The extent to which one type of linkage can compensate for the other is worth considering. If a strong unifying cultural linkage exists in a school, with staff sharing common values and beliefs, is there less need for bureaucratic linkage? Wilson and Firestone argue that principals need to use both bureaucratic and cultural linkages – the mechanisms that coordinate people's activities – to build commitment among teachers to the goals of the school.

In the most exhaustive review of the coupling literature to date, Orton and Weick (1990) identify eight most frequently recurring types of loose coupling. These authors distinguish loose coupling between the following:

- individuals
- sub-units
- organizations
- hierarchical levels
- organizations and environments
- ideas
- activities
- intentions and actions

This development of the concept is helpful in two ways. First, it provides a framework for understanding different types of linkage and, second, it portrays linkage as a *dialectical* rather than a *unidimensional* concept (Orton and Weick, 1990, p. 205). Typically, the unidimensional interpretation of the concept portrays systems or organizations on a scale 'that extends from tightly coupled to loosely coupled' (p. 205). This usage of the concept gives it limited analytical power. The dialectical interpretation, however, offers scope for understanding the nature of the diverse, complex and subtle interactions taking place in organizations such as schools.

The eight dimensions of coupling identified by Orton and Weick (1990) provide a useful basis for developing a conceptual framework by which to gain further insights into the linkages between school-based management and the curriculum. The analytical potential of the framework is demonstrated by applying each of the eight dimensions to appropriate school situations. The first dimension concerns relationships between individuals. Teachers have traditionally enjoyed a large amount of independence in their classroom behaviour and have justified their considerable classroom autonomy by appeal to their professional status. The loose coupling among teachers in a school militates against the achievement of collegiality. On the other hand, principals' respect for the professionalism of teachers can lead to teacher empowerment. Considerable autonomy allows many teachers to determine their policies and programmes within a framework of national or district policy. *Looseness* exists in the way teachers are innovative in the classroom, in their use of materials, style of teaching, method of lesson presentation and assessment of students' work. This view is supported by Deal and Celotti (1980), who found that professionals in schools operated independently of one another, as demonstrated by the divergent images held by staff working within the same school setting. Participants in more tightly knit, coordinated organizations would tend to share a common perception of the organization's rules and work practices. Deal and Celotti, however, found there was little agreement among principals within the same districts, and little consensus among teachers within the same schools, as to which instructional approaches to adopt. This suggests that establishing tighter structures and processes may prove difficult.

The second dimension of linkage refers to sub-units, the school classroom being one of the most frequently studied (Deal and Celotti, 1980; Murphy and Hallinger, 1984; Weick, 1976). Deal and Celotti (1980) found that the classroom operated as a relatively autonomous unit. This buffered pattern of classroom life shielded its instructional and organizational characteristics from the formal influence of teaching colleagues, principal, district office and the community. This may be attributed to individualized teacher classroom instruction and management as well as to the physical setting of many classrooms, each enclosed within its four walls and tightly shut door. Loose coupling also exists between subject departments in secondary schools in relation to their lack of collaboration in curriculum design and coordination (Hoyle, 1986; Weick, 1976).

The third dimension of linkage is between organizations. Typically, there is relatively little contact between schools, and between schools and non-school organizations, such as business firms. Hannaway and Sproull (1978) noted that schools characteristically function without much coordination or control from national- and/or district-level policy. These authors attributed this loose linkage between organizations to the nature of the technical tasks, focused as they are on their own cohort of students, to ambivalent and problematic school goals, unclear instructional technology, and fluid participation of students (March and Olsen, 1976).

The fourth dimension of linkage concerns a lack of connectedness between the senior administrative staff and teachers in the same school. Weick (1976, p. 17) noted that 'the typical coupling mechanisms of authority of office and logic of the task do not operate in educational organizations'. In addition, research evidence (Bossert *et al.*, 1982) suggests a lack of connectedness in schools between senior managers, particularly principals, and teachers responsible for the delivery of the curriculum. This is confirmed by Wildy (1990) who, in her small sample of highly performing academic schools in Western Australia, found little or no linkage between the work of principals and deputies, and the instructional core. Senior teachers assumed the role of instructional leaders, exerting instructional leadership in a direct sense, while principals and deputies were engrossed with routine administrative tasks, few of which were associated with instructional leadership.

The fifth dimension of linkage is between an organization and its environment. Linkage between schools and their environments has traditionally been loose outside of North America. In former highly centralized systems school councils or governing bodies have rarely existed. Policies and decisions made at ministry level were often implemented by schools without the involvement of local school communities. Local community concerns were rarely considered when setting educational goals, priorities and policies. Schools owed relatively little accountability to governments and communities for the quality of education they provided and mechanisms were lacking for monitoring school performance. In these ways schools were loosely linked to their communities. The introduction of community schools catering for the educational and recreational needs of adults as well as children represents a direct linkage between the school and the wider community. Previously centralized systems currently experiencing devolution, such as those in Australia, are at various stages of instituting school decision-making groups and school councils with the intention of fostering closer school–community linkage. The introduction of new activities at the school level may foster school–community linkage. School development planning and goal-setting constitute tasks which require the close collaboration of principals, teachers, parents and others.

The sixth dimension of linkage is between activities, actions, events or sequences within organizations. In schools where there is little collaborative decision making, there is generally loose linkage between activities. The allocation of facilities and resources is not aligned closely to reflect the priorities of the educational programme. Cohen *et al.* (1972) focused on the loose coupling between problems and choice. Their 'garbage can' model depicts a process where problems and choices are 'uncoupled'. Decision making is presented as a non-rational activity, with choices made 'only when the shifting combinations of problems, solutions, and decision-makers happen to make action possible' (p. 16). Decisions are often taken with inadequate information, or with little regard to the information available. The general absence of evaluation and accountability on the part of principals and teachers helps explain the loose linkage between sequential processes of problem identification through to analysis, and between managerial processes and resultant outcomes.

The seventh type of linkage is between ideas expressed in the form of values, missions and goals. Loose linkage may occur between the ideas, ideologies and goals of a school. Orton and Weick (1990) cite the work of Bussigel *et al.* (1986), who found that goals in some medical schools were 'incompatible, inconsistent, and only indirectly related. The relationships between these goals were vaguely articulated' (Orton and Weick, 1990, p. 209). Few schools engaged in goal-setting prior to the late 1980s, and even fewer did so collaboratively. Nowadays, schools in many countries are expected to engage in school development planning. Loose linkage between the parts of a school may lead to inconsistent or incompatible goals, especially when they are poorly communicated to staff. It is hardly surprising, therefore, that goals are often discounted, ignored or misunderstood by teachers.

Finally, another dimension of linkage is between intentions and actions, and between policy and practice. The exclusion of staff from participative decision making, and poor levels of communication between staff, can lead to loose coupling between intentions and actions in schools. A lack of planning may also create loose coupling between intentions (goals, policies and priorities) and actions. There may be loose linkage between planning and implementation. Educational programmes, instructional activities and classroom management may not align with educational goals and priorities. The planned curriculum may not coincide with the taught curriculum and the taught curriculum may not align with the curriculum experienced by students (Hill, 1990).

DEVELOPING THE CONCEPT OF LINKAGE

The original conception of schools as loosely coupled organizations (Weick, 1976) was more a statement of fact than a prescription of what ought to be. The efficacy of loose coupling for the effective functioning of schools is only briefly discussed by Weick. It has been argued elsewhere (Dimmock, 1991) that, with the advent of restructuring and school-based management, the effectiveness of loosely coupled schools is seriously challenged. Faced with new activities to be undertaken, such as school development planning, the formation and operation of school decision-making groups, the introduction of participative decision-making processes, the appraisal of staff, and greater emphasis on school-level curriculum planning within system frameworks, it is logical to assume tighter linkages in each of the eight dimensions recognized by Orton and Weick. This is supported by studies on effective schools

(Dimmock, 1991; Murphy *et al.*, 1985; Peterson *et al.*, 1987) which emphasise the importance of tight linkage and interaction between principals and teachers, especially in the area of instructional leadership.

Although Orton and Weick's eight dimensions develop the concept of linkage into a more comprehensive and useful framework there is scope for developing the framework further to give it greater descriptive, and possibly explanatory, power. Most applications of the concept, hitherto, have referred either to organizational structures or to relations between them. Two of the eight dimensions recognized by Orton and Weick, however, are qualitatively different and point to development of the concept in a new direction. The notion of linkage between ideas, goals and ideologies introduces a values dimension as a basis on which the operation of schools and their constituent parts may be studied. A second promising development is linkage between intentions and actions, where loose linkage may exist, for example between planning and implementation. This introduces the possibility of using the concept to address more socio-psychological questions, such as what determines principals' and teachers' reactions to planned change, as in the introduction of school-based management? It also offers possible avenues into understanding the important but hitherto neglected connection between principals' practices and teachers' perceptions of the values and meanings underpinning principals' behaviours. This is important since the influence of principals' practices on students is likely to be heavily moderated by teachers. Unless teachers have a common and integrated perception of the goals and values which the principal is attempting to communicate, their behaviour will not be consistent and mutually reinforcing across the school. The nature of the messages which teachers receive from their principal may form a basis for future comparisons between stated and perceived goals and values, and between verbal and symbolic communications of principals. It also provides an indication of the consistency with which these communications impact on individual teachers. It is important to research whether *effective* or *expert* principals are better attuned than typical principals to behaviours that influence teachers. A complex network of linkage between principals' values and thought processes, principals' behaviours, staff perception of those behaviours, staff behaviours, and student outcomes requires investigation.

The remaining section of this chapter provides an application of the concept of linkage which, *inter alia*, illustrates these new dimensions. It focuses on an approach to curriculum management aimed at improving student outcomes, within a context of school-based management described earlier in this chapter.

CURRICULUM MANAGEMENT, STUDENT OUTCOMES AND LINKAGE

Current trends to school-based management, national curricular guidelines, school-site curriculum planning, and system-level setting of performance targets, have placed a premium on student outcomes as the measure of school performance. The concept of linkage has potential for explicating a model for managing a quality curriculum, based on student outcomes.

Responsibility is placed on the principal and teachers of each school, using available resources in the most efficient and effective way, to secure the best possible student learning outcomes. The achievement of high student learning outcomes is dependent on the school providing a quality curriculum for every student.

Managing for a quality curriculum involves the promotion of student learning, the fostering of quality teaching, the creation of a climate that supports learning, and an appropriate curriculum structure and content. A model illustrating a student outcomes approach to curriculum management is shown in Figure 1.1.

The starting point in this process is for a school to consider the gap between the actual and desired levels of student achievement. Appropriate assessments enable the school to gauge present levels of student achievement across age and ability ranges. Teaching staff, and the school community in general, would then agree on the desired level of learning to be achieved over a given period of time. The intention, for example, might be to secure a 5 per cent improvement in learning for all students over the following two years. This aim would form part of the school development plan. In this example, linkage is conceptualized between actual and desired learning outcomes. If the improvement in learning outcomes is a priority expressed in the school development plan, then the plan might need to be endorsed by the school community. Linkage is implied in collaborative decision making by the staff, and by the staff and the wider school community, in adopting the aim as policy. The values and goals of participant groups in the decision-making process may be studied for their degree of linkage. The relationship between the stated intention of the plan and its practical implementation may be conceptualized as a linkage.

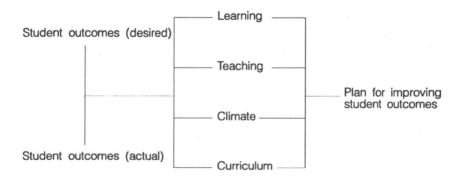

Figure 1.1 Curriculum management for improving student outcomes

Following this, it is then necessary to identify the critical variables which influence, or link with, student outcomes. The aim of those responsible for managing the curriculum is to improve the quality and performance of those variables in order to achieve the desired improvement in student learning outcomes. Figure 1.1 identifies four critical variables deemed to influence student outcomes: learning, teaching, school climate, and curriculum structure and content. A school is most likely to achieve improved student outcomes when there is a focus on learning by staff and students. In staff development and discussion, for example, emphasis is given to the school-wide adoption of an appropriate learning theory. An example of a learning theory is Gagné's *phases of learning* (Gagné, 1974). A resolution needs to be taken collaboratively by staff to apply the principles of the learning theory in classroom practice. Linkage is achieved between principles of learning theory and classroom practice, and between teachers. If the whole staff can agree to apply the same theory then there is systematic reinforcement across the school. The learning improvements desired are most likely to be secured when there is consistency in approach across subjects and lessons and between teachers (Murphy *et al.*, 1985).

Teaching is closely aligned with learning. Gagné's model, for example, views teaching and learning as integrated activities. According to Gagné, approaches to teaching should be based on sound principles of learning. The likelihood of achieving improved student learning is enhanced when all teachers practise the same principles of teaching, irrespective of their personal teaching style. Examples of teaching principles include: informing the learner of the objectives, directing attention, stimulating recall, promoting transfer of learning, and eliciting performance and providing feedback (Gagné, 1974). These principles of teaching can be introduced whatever the method or style of teaching adopted. Linkage is exemplified through consistency across subjects, lessons and teachers, and between theory and practice of learning and teaching.

Teachers' adherence to teaching techniques which empirical research shows to be positively correlated with improved learning outcomes is more likely to secure the improvement required. A meta-analysis of effective teaching techniques (Fraser *et al.*, 1987) shows conclusively that the following methods are among those with strong positive impact on student learning:

- reinforcement and reward for correct performance,
- instructional cues, engagement and corrective feedback,
- personalized and adaptive instruction based on individual student guidance.

Linkage is applicable in conceptualizing the relationship between teachers and their adoption of effective teaching techniques, in the alignment of both teacher and student in focusing on the same learning tasks and objectives, and in the degree of consistency across the whole teaching staff. The degree of alignment between decisions taken collaboratively by staff to adopt a particular set of learning and teaching behaviours, and their subsequent implementation in classrooms, constitutes linkage between intentions and actions. Promoting staff discussion and securing agreement to adopt the same learning and teaching strategies provides a common language for all staff, including the principal. Through improved communication it is possible for values, goals, intentions and practices to be more readily shared.

A school culture and climate which support and promote learning as the most important goal of the school constitute a third cluster of variables. A host of factors pertain to culture and climate, including values, expectations and the quality of relationships, particularly between teachers and students. Values and expectations are expressed in many ways. The extent to which students spend time on a task in the classroom, and are protected from interruptions, are indicators of values. The allocation of resources to staff development, especially where professional development is closely aligned with the instructional and curriculum needs of the school, is another indicator of school values. Recognition that schools have many sub-cultures and climates implies a degree of linkage between them. Linkage may be useful in comparisons of student and staff sub-climates and how they interact. The degree of alignment between the values of the individual teacher, the department and the whole school may be conceptualized in terms of linkage. It is likely that the greater the difference between the individual teacher's values and practices and those of the department and school, the more likely it is that the teacher will experience low levels of job satisfaction and high levels of stress. Linkage is exemplified in the connections between resource allocations and values, as well as the relations between climate, teaching and learning.

A fourth set of variables which influence student outcomes concerns the content and structure of the curriculum. The provision of a quality curriculum may be judged against the following set of criteria: breadth, balance, coordination, relevance and differentiation. A *broad* curriculum includes content from all areas of experience and knowledge; a *balanced* curriculum places an appropriate weighting on each area of experience and knowledge; a *coordinated* curriculum achieves continuity and sequencing of work across units, subjects and courses, both vertically, between stages, and horizontally, between subjects at the same stage; a *relevant* curriculum matches with the needs of students; and a *differentiated* curriculum is sufficiently diversified to reflect differences in student abilities.

Linkage between these dimensions is helpful in defining and evaluating the quality of a curriculum. There are linkages, for example, between curriculum breadth and balance, and linkage is implicit in the concept of coordination, incorporating vertical as well as horizontal continuity and sequencing of material. Relevance and differentiation can be seen in terms of linkage in matching the curriculum to the individual student's abilities and needs.

In securing improved student learning the model of curriculum management outlined in Figure 1.1 suggests a focus on improving the learning, teaching, climate and curriculum structure and content in school. A necessary initial stage is for the school to evaluate its current performance in respect of each of these four. When staff work collaboratively the review process is more comprehensive, and agreement on which areas to improve, together with commitment to a programme of improvement, is more likely. When viewed holistically, linkage is endemic to the model. Student outcomes are seen as responsive to, and therefore connected with, learning, teaching, climate and curriculum. Close linkage also exists between each of these four variables in the model. Important processes, such as staff collaboration, can be explained in terms of linkage. They are vital to the successful implementation of evaluation and other curriculum management functions.

CONCLUSION

This chapter has explored some of the complex relations between school-based management and the curriculum. A conceptual framework built on the notion of linkage may offer useful insights into the connections between management and curriculum. In attempting to understand both the direct and more subtle ways in which school management may influence teaching, learning and the curriculum, it is helpful to take account of the following. First, the distinguishing features of school-based management need clarification; second, the elements likely to influence student learning outcomes require identification; and third, understanding of the connections between management, student learning and the curriculum may be enhanced by invoking appropriate conceptual frameworks using linkage.

School-based management may take many forms, but it is generally suggested that autonomy, flexibility and responsiveness, planning, participatory and collaborative decision making, and self-efficacy are associated features. Prevailing cultures and power relations, however, may confound the introduction of some or all of these features in many schools.

Improvement of student learning across the age and ability spectrum is a worthy focus for school-based curriculum managers. It is suggested that four sets of factors exert a strong influence on student learning: the method by which students are expected to learn; the quality of teaching; a supportive learning climate; and a quality curriculum defined according to its breadth, balance, coordination, relevance and differentiation. In the pursuit of improved student learning outcomes, management of the curriculum focuses on evaluation of present school performance in these four areas, with the goal of securing improvements in practice. These improvements may, in turn, benefit student learning outcomes.

The critical challenge is to connect the features associated with school-based management with the factors affecting student learning. If the functional connections can be achieved so that autonomy, flexibility, responsiveness, planning, participation, collaboration and self-efficacy have maximal impact on learning, teaching, climate and curriculum structure and content, then improved student learning may be achieved. Greater understanding of the precise ways in which these connections may be developed awaits further investigation. It is likely that future study of these connections will be enhanced by invoking the concept of linkage in a dialectical form, embracing the many dimensions advocated in this chapter.

REFERENCES

Bandura, A. (1986) *Social Foundations of Thought and Action: A Social Cognitive Theory*, Englewood Cliffs, NJ: Prentice Hall.

Bandura, A. and Wood, R.E. (1989) 'Effect of perceived controllability and performance standards on self-regulation of complex decision-making', *Journal of Personality and Social Psychology* 56: 805–14.

Beare, H., Caldwell, B. and Millikan, R. (1989) *Creating an Excellent School: Some New Management Techniques*, London: Routledge.

Bell, L. (1990) 'Educational management: An agenda for the 1990s', *Educational Management and Administration* 19(3): 136–40.

Bird, T.D. and Little, J.W. (1985) *Instructional Leadership in Eight Secondary Schools* (Final report to the National Institute of Education), Boulder, CO: Center for Action Research.

—— (1986) 'How schools organize the teaching occupation', *Elementary School Journal* 86(4): 495–511.

Bossert, S. (1986) 'Instructional management', in E. Hoyle and A. McMahon (eds) *The Management of Schools: World Yearbook of Education 1986* (pp. 112–24), London: Kogan Page.

Bossert, S.T., Dwyer, D.C., Rowan, B. and Lee, G.V. (1982) 'The instructional management role of the principal', *Educational Administration Quarterly* 18(3): 34–64.

Brooke, J.Z. (1984) *Centralization and Autonomy: A Study in Organizational Behaviour*, New York: Holt, Rinehart & Winston.

Brown, D.J. (1990) *Decentralization and School-Based Management*, Basingstoke: The Falmer Press.

Bussigel, M., Barzansky, B. and Grenholm, G. (1986) 'Goal coupling and innovation in medical schools', *The Journal of Applied Behavioural Science* 22: 425–41.

Chapman, J.D. (1988) 'Teacher participation in the decision making of schools', *Journal of Educational Administration* 26(1): 39–72.

—— (1990) 'School-based decision-making and management: Implications for school personnel', in J.D. Chapman (ed.) *School-Based Decision-Making and Management* (pp. 221–44), Basingstoke: The Falmer Press.

Cohen, M.D., March, J.G. and Olsen, J.P. (1972) 'A garbage can model of organizational choice', *Administrative Science Quarterly* 17: 1–25.

Deal, T.E. and Celotti, L.D. (1980) 'How much influence do (and can) educational administrators have on classrooms?', *Phi Delta Kappan* 60: 471–3.

Dimmock, C. (1991) 'School-based management and school effectiveness: Developing the concept of linkage', in I. McKay and B.J. Caldwell (eds) *Researching Educational Administration: Theory and Practice* (pp. 153–66), Hawthorn, Victoria: Australian Council for Educational Administration.

Duignan, P.A. (1990) 'School-based decision-making and management: Retrospect and prospect', in J.D. Chapman (ed.) *School-Based Decision-Making and Management* (pp. 327–45), Basingstoke: The Falmer Press.

Finn, C.E. (1984) 'Toward strategic independence: Nine commandments for enhancing school effectiveness', *Phi Delta Kappan* April: 518–24.

Fraser, B.J., Walberg, H.J., Welch, W. and Hattie, J. (1987) 'Syntheses of educational productivity research', *International Journal of Educational Research* 11(2): 145–252.

Fullan, M. (1986) 'The management of change', in E. Hoyle and A. MacMahon (eds) *The Management of Schools: World Yearbook of Education 1986* (pp. 73–86), London: Kogan Page.

Gagné, R.M. (1974) *Essentials of Learning for Instruction*, Hinsdale, IL: Dryden.

Garms, W.I., Guthrie, J.W. and Pierce, L.C. (1978) *School Finance: The economics and Politics of Education*, Englewood Cliffs, NJ: Prentice Hall.

Goodlad, J.I. (1984) *A Place Called School*, New York: McGraw-Hill.

Guthrie, J.W. (1986) 'School-based management: The next needed educational reform', *Phi Delta Kappan* December: 305–9.

Hannaway, J. and Sproull, L.S. (1978) 'Who's running the show? Co-ordination and control in educational organizations', *Administrator's Notebook* 27: 1–4.

Hill, J.C. (1990) 'The principal as curriculum supervisor', *Principal* 69(3): 6–9.

Hoyle, E. (1986) *The Politics of School Management*, London: Hodder & Stoughton.

Huberman, A.M. and Miles, M.B. (1984) *Innovation Up Close: How School Improvement Works*, New York: Plenum Press.

Kochen, M. and Deutsch, K.W. (1980) *Decentralization: Sketches Towards a Rational Theory*, Cambridge, MA: Oelgeschler, Gunn & Hain.

Lieberman, A. and Miller, L. (1990) 'The social realities of teaching', in A. Lieberman (ed.) *Schools as Collaborative Cultures* (pp. 153–63), Basingstoke: The Falmer Press.

Little, J.W. (1981) *School Success and Staff Development: The Role of Staff Development in Urban Desegregated Schools*, Boulder, CO: Center for Action Research.

—— (1982) 'Norms of collegiality and experimentation: Workplace conditions of school success', *American Educational Research Journal* 19: 325–40.

—— (1990) 'Teachers as colleagues', in A. Lieberman (ed.) *Schools as Collaborative Cultures* (pp. 165–93), Basingstoke: The Falmer Press.

Malen, B., Ogawa, R.T. and Kranz, J. (1990) 'What do we know about school based management? A case study of the literature – a call for research', in W.H. Clune and J.F. Witte (eds) *Choice and Control in American Education: Vol. 2. The Practice of Choice, Decentralization and School Restructuring*, Lewes: Falmer Press.

March, J.G. and Olsen, J.P. (eds) (1976) *Ambiguity and Choice in Organizations*, Bergen: Universitetforlaget.

Mintzberg, H. (1979) *The Structuring of Organizations: A Quantum View*, Englewood Cliffs, NJ: Prentice Hall.

Murphy, J. and Hallinger, P. (1984) 'Policy analysis at the local level: A framework for expanded investigation', *Educational Evaluation and Policy Analyses* 6: 5–13.

Murphy, J., Peterson, K.D. and Hallinger, P. (1986) 'The administrative control of principals in effective school districts: The supervision and evaluation functions', *The Urban Review* 18(3): 149–75.

Murphy, J., Weil, M., Hallinger, P. and Mitman, A. (1985) 'School effectiveness: A conceptual framework', *The Educational Forum* 49(3): 361–74.

Orton, J.D. and Weick, K.E. (1990) 'Loosely coupled systems: A reconceptualization', *Academy of Management Review* 15(2): 203–23.

Peterson, K.D., Murphy, J. and Hallinger, P. (1987) 'Superintendents' perceptions of the control and co-ordination of the technical core in effective school districts', *Educational Administration Quarterly* 23(1): 79–95.

Prasch, J.C. (1984) 'Reversing the trend towards centralization', *Educational Leadership* 42(2): 27–9.

Weick, K.E. (1976) 'Educational organizations as loosely coupled systems', *Administrative Science Quarterly* 21: 1–19.

Wildy, H. (1990) 'School-based management and its linkage with school effectiveness: A study of three secondary schools in Western Australia', Unpublished Masters Dissertation, The University of Western Australia, Perth.

Wilson, B.L. and Firestone, W.A. (1987, September) 'The principal and instruction: Combining bureaucratic and cultural linkages', *Educational Leadership* 19–23.

Wood, R.E. and Bandura, A. (1989) 'Social cognitive theory of organisational management', *Academy of Management Review* 14(3): 361–84.

Chapter 2

Conceptualizing school restructuring
Principals' and teachers' perceptions

Philip Hallinger, Joseph Murphy and Charles Hausman

In schools throughout the world, initiatives to restructure education are taking root. They have gained momentum from widespread dissatisfaction with the outcomes of schooling and the educational conditions believed to be responsible for these outcomes. Consequently, efforts are under way in Australia, New Zealand, the United States, Canada and Great Britain to transform fundamentally the basic components of educational systems (Elmore, 1990a; Murphy, 1990).

This process of reinventing public schooling is occurring simultaneously on three fronts. Measures are being formulated and strategies are being implemented to:

- decentralize the organizational structure of schools (for example, school-based management);
- empower teachers, parents and students to reshape and direct the education system (for example, the ascendancy of school choice plans, an enhanced voice for teachers and parents in site-level decision making, new roles and responsibilities for teachers); and
- transform the teaching–learning process that unfolds in classrooms: for example, the replacement of the entrenched psychological model of teaching with a sociologically oriented perspective of instruction, the acknowledgement of the importance of professional craft knowledge (Elmore, 1990b; Murphy, 1991; Rowan, 1990; Smith and O'Day, 1990).

To date, the bulk of attention in the restructuring movement has been devoted to organizational and governance issues. Considerably less attention has been invested in conceptualizing how the core technology of curriculum and instruction should be revised in conjunction with restructuring efforts. The deficiency is twofold. Few researchers are attempting to develop links from proposed structural and political alternatives to classroom processes. Even fewer investigators are undertaking to develop new views of organization and governance based on the most appropriate conditions of learning (Elmore, 1991; Evertson and Murphy, 1992; Lieberman, 1988; Rowan, 1990). Our purpose in this chapter, therefore, is to shed some light on issues of how school restructuring might affect curriculum and instruction and, more specifically, to draw connections between teaching and learning and emerging governance structures and processes.

A second conclusion that we have reached in our study of restructuring is that, in the dialogue about transforming schools, the voices of teachers and administrators are either conspicuous by their absence or drowned out by the din created by academicians, policy makers and business persons (Murphy *et al.*, 1991). In this article we therefore build on the beliefs and speculations of teachers and administrators to paint our portrait of the direction that school restructuring may take. We note both areas of agreement and disagreement in their perceptions. We discuss the implications these differences hold for efforts to redesign education.

RESEARCH DESIGN

Because limited information is known about teachers' and principals' views on restructuring, we undertook an exploratory study using qualitative methodology. Since our aim was to discover their beliefs and perceptions, we used in-depth interviewing. Finally, because our objective was to probe deeply into teachers' and principals' perspectives and to develop rich descriptions of their views on restructuring, we selected a small sample with whom we could work more intensively. We acknowledge the limitations that accompany the choices made in the procedures employed in conducting our research, specifically those that accompany the small sample size. We present our results within the context of these limitations.

SAMPLE

Fourteen teachers (13 women and one man) from the state of Tennessee participated in the study. Six were elementary school teachers, two taught at the middle school level, and six taught at high schools. Participants' ages ranged from 26 to 50, with teaching experience spanning from 3 to 20 years. Twelve of the teachers had earned Masters' degrees. Since our goal was to paint a picture of how the 'average' teacher conceives of restructuring, we selected participants who were neither 'super' teachers nor experiencing serious difficulties.

Fifteen principals (two women and 13 men) from public schools in New York, Illinois, and Tennessee also participated in the study. Six were elementary school principals, four were administrators at the junior high or middle school level, and five were high school principals. Participants ranged in age from 34 to 58 and in experience as principals from 3 to 23 years. Since our intent was to elicit divergent perspectives on restructuring, we conducted interviews with principals from northern and mid-western industrialized states as well as from a rural southern state. We also selected principals who were beginning restructuring efforts in their districts as well as principals who were still grappling with initiatives from the earlier wave of educational reform.

INSTRUMENT

A scheduled interview protocol was developed to assess teachers' and principals' perceptions of restructuring (Goetz and LeCompte, 1984). The instrument consisted of 22 open-ended questions drawn from our review of the restructuring literature (Murphy, 1991).

Staff members were initially asked to respond to a series of open-ended, non-cued questions regarding their general feelings about restructuring, their beliefs about whom they thought might be affected, and their thoughts about the changes that would have to take place in their specific schools in order for restructuring to occur. We then moved to more focused questions about teaching and learning and sought their views about areas of potential change at both the classroom and the school levels. These included: the teaching–learning process in general, teachers' relationships with students, school learning climate, budget development and allocations, curriculum, professional development, student schedules, expenditures of time by teachers and other school professionals, specific teaching practices, organization of students for learning, management of student behaviour, outcomes for students, students' interactions with other students, and students' interactions with teachers. Finally, we provided two role-playing scenarios in which each respondent, as a member of the school-based decision-making group, was charged with developing strategies to establish a learning orientation in the school, to encourage student responsibility for learning, and to improve student learning outcomes.

The framework of the protocol was designed to guide participants to analyse restructuring first in the most general terms, to collect their thoughts on who would be affected, what broad changes would occur, what general alterations at the school and classroom levels they would expect, and then to focus on specific changes at the school and classroom levels. Redundancy was a deliberate feature of the interview protocol. We asked questions that involved the same persons in different contexts. We also addressed similar issues at multiple levels – school, classroom, small group – to learn how principals and teachers view restructuring at varying organizational strata.

DATA COLLECTION AND ANALYSIS

Each of the 29 interviews lasted between 1 and 2 hours. Audio recordings were made of all interviews. These were transcribed and then checked against the taped discussions. Transcriptions were analysed qualitatively following procedures outlined by Miles and Huberman (1984). A descriptive matrix comparing and contrasting perceptions on restructuring issues was developed. Coding and analytic induction were employed to develop the themes presented in the remainder of this chapter.

RESULTS

Elsewhere, we have reported separately on teachers' (Murphy *et al.*, 1991) and principals' (Hallinger *et al.*, 1992) perceptions of restructuring. Here, our goal is to build on these findings with the intent of revealing where the views of these two groups of educators are consistent and where differences of opinion exist. The findings are organized under the following headings: general conceptions of restructuring, potential impact of restructuring, prerequisites for successful implementation, and changes at the classroom and school levels. In general, observed differences in the participants' responses did not conform to patterns related to the level of the school in which they worked, geographic location, district context, or years of experience in education. A small sample size may account for the limited variance in perceptions.

GENERAL CONCEPTIONS OF RESTRUCTURING

In this portion of the interview, the questions were structured with as few cues as possible. Our intent was to elicit respondents' perceptions of restructuring unbiased by our beliefs. An overwhelming majority of participants from both groups expressed the belief that restructuring schools was an outstanding idea. They envisioned significant inclusion of teachers in the decision-making process leading to teacher ownership and school improvement through more effective problem solving. The principals mentioned that teachers' ownership of proposed changes could potentially increase their motivation, initiative and commitment. This suggests their belief that school improvement requires greater effort on the part of teachers.

While the teachers were unanimous in their support for restructuring, two principals viewed the idea as a good one but with caveats, and two others clearly opposed the concept. The two principals with reservations saw no need to implement an all-purpose solution where there was no perceived problem. One of these individuals, who claimed to be working in a school that had already begun efforts to restructure, viewed the fact that decision making is slowed down as more people become involved, as problematic. Advocates of restructuring argue that the extra time devoted to decision making should result in better decisions that are also more likely to be successfully implemented.

The two principals who clearly opposed the concept of restructuring cited different reasons. The first saw the necessity of having an individual who had the final authority to make decisions and was, therefore, ultimately accountable to the superintendent and board of education. Although this point was of greater significance to this principal, a majority of the administrators agreed that if parents and teachers are given the authority to make decisions, they must be held accountable for the results. One respondent expressed this general sentiment by stating 'the old theory that if something goes wrong, hang the coach, should not apply'. The second principal opposed to restructuring believed it would lead to increased stress on administrators, erode administrative power, and put the building administration at 'odds somewhat with the central office which pays lip service to restructuring but doesn't really let go of some of that central authority'.

Although the teachers viewed restructuring as a good idea, they expressed considerable scepticism about the system's ability to change. They noted the serious shortcomings of the present educational system and claimed that it functioned only because of 'a few good teachers', most of whom were not visible to the community or even to their colleagues. They blamed the bureaucratic infrastructure for the current crisis in education. Their comments in this regard were consistent with the argument that bureaucratic regulation of schooling clashes with teachers' views of themselves as autonomous professionals (Carnoy and MacDonell, 1989; Lieberman, 1988).

Despite their generally positive responses, the principals cited reservations regarding the practical implications of the restructuring concept. All of the principals noted that some portion of the faculty would have to allocate time for decision-making committees. Several were concerned that this would reduce the teaching effectiveness of those teachers. Furthermore, four of the 11 principals who believed in the merits of restructuring and two administrators who were less supportive argued that many teachers do not want the responsibility of decision making. In their view, a relatively small percentage wanted the type of extensive involvement in decision making envisioned by reformers. They contended that even fewer teachers would be interested once the time commitment necessary for true involvement in decision making became clear.

POTENTIAL IMPACT OF RESTRUCTURING

Most of the comments of teachers and principals concerning the general nature of restructuring focused on governance issues, decision making and professional roles. The primary impetus behind school restructuring, however, has been the need to improve teaching and learning in schools. We were therefore interested in discovering the potential impact of school restructuring as viewed by school professionals. Would restructuring, as they conceived of it, affect parents, teachers or students? Would its impact be felt most strongly in school governance, teaching and learning, teacher morale, parent satisfaction or some other area of school functioning?

Impact on teachers

The consensus among both groups was that school restructuring would have its greatest impact on the role of teachers, who would assume more responsibility in a restructured decision-making process. Despite their uncertainty over the extent to which teachers really desire this increased involvement, the principals, like the teachers, saw this greater sense of responsibility and ownership as leading to more teacher collaboration and participation. Several principals also forecast that these new roles would lead to higher teacher self-esteem which would carry over and positively influence students.

Although the majority of both groups predicted positive changes for teachers, they expressed serious concerns about possible increases in pressure. The administrators anticipated pressure on teachers 'to perform or get out' of restructured schools. One individual went as far as to cite the necessity of eliminating tenure. Several school leaders also commented on the unanticipated impact of the tensions that accompany participation in decision making. One principal summarized this perspective remarking, 'The people who now feel that shared decision making is what they want, don't have to deal with the political pressures, the board pressures, the central office pressures, etc.' They also anticipated that, as teachers played a larger role in the decision-making process, they would become more independent thinkers and struggle to break away from union control. These potential sources of tension exemplify the administrators' tendency to view the educational enterprise through a more political framework than teachers.

A potential contradiction was apparent in the conceptions of time allocation voiced by both groups. While the teachers desired increased involvement in school decision making, they also called for more uninterrupted instructional and planning time. Several principals expressed the reservation that increased allocation of time for decision-making committees by teachers would reduce classroom effectiveness. One principal stated, 'The more you pull a teacher out of the classroom, the less the students get.' This is a dilemma that awaits creative resolution.

Two additional potential problems were noted by the teachers. First, they alluded to the additional paperwork that could accompany restructuring efforts. This is congruent with the second potential problem that was identified, namely, teachers' inclination to attribute the shortcomings of the educational system to its bureaucratic infrastructure. Ironically, the principals saw restructuring as a tool to reduce the teacher paperwork load through greater school-level autonomy, fewer mandates from the state, federal, and central office levels, and additional clerical support. Does increased paperwork stem from centralization or decentralization? Tyack (1990) comments:

> To the degree that school governance is now characterized by fragmented centralization, we may have the worst of both worlds: many accountants to higher state and federal authorities but few people really accountable to

students or parents. Eliminating overlapping jurisdictions and unnecessary paperwork may require both more centralization and more decentralization, depending on the particular function. (p. 187)

Impact on administrators

Principals and teachers viewed the effects of restructuring on administrators almost exclusively in terms of power. The principals forecast fewer decisions made alone and a loss of control and power. One principal stated bluntly, 'I think the administrator, if he has any insight into anything, could see the handwriting on the wall. He has two choices, change or get out.' This is congruent with one group of teachers who wanted the role of administrators de-emphasised and their influence greatly reduced. Although they predicted a reluctance on the part of principals to change, they believed that the decision-making reins should be handed over to the teaching corps and that principals should maintain their administrative duties and leave teachers alone.

In contrast, a second group of teachers believed that principals should be entrusted with more power to do their jobs – for example, discretion to fire teachers who are not performing – and that they should devote considerably more energy to working with teachers on important schooling issues – for example, the curriculum. Similarly, some principals thought that with the increased delegation of selected responsibilities, they would be able to devote more time to teacher development. They also foresaw benefits in the effectiveness of their decision making due to the exposure from additional perspectives in the decision-making process.

Impact on parents

Both teachers and principals raised concerns regarding parental involvement in school decision making. They noted in particular that it would be difficult for parents to be aware of the latest educational trends. This perspective was captured in the folk wisdom of an administrator who remarked that 'people are not experts on schools simply because they attended one'. The principals also noted that the parents involved on a school's leadership council would not represent the entire community. They feared that parental input on decisions would be based on self-interest as opposed to needs perceived by significant portions of the community. During a period in which reformers are calling for greater equity in educational financing, distribution of resources, and quality of instruction, this poses a potentially serious problem. Carnoy and MacDonell (1989) have written:

> Another downside [of shared decision making] is that the low-income pupils who could profit most from innovative, at-risk focussed programs are the ones with the least vocal, least politically powerful parents. This

makes things more difficult for those teachers and principals ... who want to see more resources going to those pupils. (p. 20)

Impact on students

In their initial responses, only six teachers and seven principals mentioned the likelihood that students would be touched by restructuring efforts. When pressed on this point, teachers noted the potential of both affective and academic benefits accruing to pupils. In contrast, the responses of the majority of principals tended to focus exclusively on affective gains.

In terms of academic outcomes, teachers described improvements in basic literacy, critical thinking, creativity, inquisitiveness and independence of thought. Similarly, those principals who did foresee cognitive gains hoped that students would become 'better problem solvers and less regurgitators'. They also spoke of restructured schools helping students to take greater responsibility for their own learning and to become lifelong learners. Although almost all of our respondents attributed these potential gains to the restructuring process, one individual poignantly stated, 'I'm not sure restructuring guarantees any outcomes. I think that it is a result of your commitment to whatever it is you are doing.'

Somewhat surprisingly, even when the focus was on student outcomes, there was hardly any mention of testing. There seemed to be an implicit belief among both groups that the assessment system would adapt to measure both cognitive and affective outcomes. In providing a suggestion on how to use this assessment data, one principal concluded: 'We have to start dealing with that [assessment results] in an atmosphere where we're not looking to blame anyone for failure, but we are looking to identify what's going on so that we can make it better.'

PREREQUISITES FOR SUCCESSFUL IMPLEMENTATION

There was surprising agreement between the teachers and administrators on the nature of the changes needed to make restructuring work. Both deemed a clear definition of restructuring and collaboration between all groups involved as fundamental to success. These beliefs were reflected in phrases such as 'commitment to these new partnerships', 'having trust in the system ... a belief that it can be done', and 'clear role definitions'.

Teachers and principals also reported that extensive training in shared decision making and effective schools research and practice was essential to prepare parents, teachers, principals, central office administrators and school board members for restructuring. The teachers identified their own need for training in administrative skills and learning how to lead. For their principals, they saw the need to learn how to lead through collaboration and consensus, or as one teacher poignantly remarked, to learn to be 'not as domineering'.

Although the principals stated similar needs, they added the need to train teachers to be better teachers. The two groups seemed to perceive each other's weaknesses more clearly than their own and to scrutinize the other to identify potential obstacles to restructuring.

As might be anticipated due to the historical lack of teacher input into fiscal matters, only the administrators identified the budget as a possible constraint to restructuring. They listed broad-based financial support as necessary, as well as the need for a contingency budget to be prepared for unanticipated problems. They also identified the development of an accountability policy given shared decision making and an ongoing means of assessment as fundamental.

CHANGES IN CLASSROOMS AND SCHOOLS

After hearing the teachers' and principals' general conceptions of restructuring, we encouraged them to project themselves into a restructured school where shared decision making had been implemented: where the staff at the school had been given considerable autonomy over such areas as budget, curriculum, scheduling and professional development. We asked them how conditions, processes and activities might change at both the school and classroom levels given this type of restructured environment. At this point, the probes were still very general, for example: 'Given school-based management and shared decision making, what changes would you envisage in the area of curriculum?' We group the themes culled from the responses into the following sections: curriculum, teacher roles and workplace, organizing for learning and managing classroom behaviour, and professional development.

Curriculum

The most consistent theme reported by both groups was their desire for a more integrated curriculum delivered more cooperatively by the teachers. With an increasing amount of information in the curriculum, they affirmed the importance of teaching the whole child and ridding education of 'curricular debris' by implementing a coherent curriculum. At the same time, many of the teachers reported that they would make available a specific course to meet the needs of their particular students, for example a home economics course at the elementary level, or an AIDS curriculum. While this is consistent with the concept of local responsiveness, it appears inconsistent with expressed interests in developing an integrated, interdisciplinary curriculum.

While the teachers unanimously foresaw a greater role for themselves in developing this curriculum, only three principals believed that teachers should be given this responsibility, and all three warned that extensive training and a great deal of time would be required for teachers to be successful in this endeavour. One principal, who opposed a teacher-developed curriculum, added, 'I do not find my staff to be knowledgeable at all about curriculum innovation or current research.'

Despite being asked to project themselves into a restructured school with the ability to initiate a wide range of changes, the principals were clearly sceptical about the system's ability to move away from a deeply entrenched state-mandated curriculum. One remarked, 'The method of instruction may change, but the curriculum will not. The curriculum has been clearly defined by the state and we have to live within those boundaries.' The teachers in general desired greater control over the curriculum with fewer mandates from the state and local authorities. Consistent with our earlier discussion, only one respondent from each group foresaw a role for parents in revamping the school's curriculum.

Teacher roles and workplace

There was surprising congruence in the views of the teachers and principals on how restructuring might affect the teaching–learning process. They envisaged an interdisciplinary curriculum that fosters more collaborative activity among teachers. This collaboration was expected to result in instruction that was more considerate of different learning styles. Furthermore, there would be less reliance on lectures and worksheets, and more hands-on lessons which would enable students to become more actively involved. Finally, they hoped for a greater diversity of student-centred instructional strategies, such as cooperative learning, which require the teacher to be 'more of a facilitator ... less a feeder of information'. The teachers clearly stated that greater teacher choice would serve as the vehicle to achieve this type of learning environment.

Both groups of participants predicted that restructuring would significantly influence teachers' allocation of time. As they projected themselves into the future, they foresaw a greater proportion of teachers' available time being devoted to instructional activities. The teachers also expressed a desire for more time to be available for personal and developmental needs. Both groups believed that this additional time would be gained through: the employment of paraprofessionals to handle a variety of non-teaching duties, such as supervising the cafeteria, playground and car park, and providing clerical assistance to teachers; more efficient and flexible scheduling; employment of parents and other community members as instructional aides; more collaborative student work; and closer coordination of work among teachers. They intended to devote this additional time to collaborative student-centred planning and instructional activities. As one teacher succinctly stated, 'Give me more teaching duties; I'd love it!' The principals also saw a direct connection between this additional time for professional activities and teachers' attitudes towards their work. They predicted better teacher attendance, more willingness to help students before and after normal school hours, and 'less time spent complaining'.

In terms of scheduling, there was a consensus among both groups that the traditional school year needs to be reconfigured by implementing shorter, staggered breaks in place of one extended summer vacation. However, there were two distinct opinions regarding the length of the school day. While the teachers neglected to address whether or not the school day should be altered, seven principals recommended that it be extended, but three others argued that this would be unrealistic because of its impact on families, school budgets and the transportation system. When asked about schedule changes, another principal reaffirmed the intensity of state influence by responding, 'In my own mind, I can't go so far as to say that we're not going to worry about state mandates.'

At the classroom level, both sets of educators would restructure schedules so that their lessons would be controlled less by the clock and organizational routines and more by the dictates of the learning activities themselves. Second, they would greatly reduce external interruptions, such as public address announcements and pullouts from regular classrooms, that encroach on academic learning time. Finally, the teachers wanted to reform school schedules so that they could spend more quality time with fewer students. Likewise, the principals supported reduced class sizes and scheduling an advisory period to enable students and teachers to develop more positive relationships.

After overcoming an initial hesitance to describe new personal relationships with students, probably due to a belief that this might reduce their authority and control, the teachers' descriptions were very similar to those of the administrators. Both groups maintained that there would be more of a partnership between teachers and students in their restructured schools. They spoke of cooperation and mutual responsibility for learning. They hypothesized that smaller class sizes and more student-centred lessons would result in more genuinely personal student–teacher relationships. The principals claimed that the teachers would serve as advisers and as role models for the students, and there would be a mutual respect for each others' feelings. This is congruent with the teachers' description of an environment characterized by trust, openness and other family-like qualities, in which the students would know that the teachers really cared about them as individuals.

Organizing for learning and managing classroom behaviour

There was very little agreement between and within these groups of educators on how best to group students for maximum learning. All but one of the teachers reported that there would be both heterogeneous and homogeneous grouping arrangements in their restructured schools. Furthermore, for every principal who provided a suggestion on grouping, a colleague expressed an opposing viewpoint. Recommendations included grouping by interests, age, ability, learning styles, interdisciplinary teams, and mainstreaming, that is integrating students of all abilities into mainstream classes. The only common theme echoed by the principals and teachers was that grouping practices must be tailored to meet students' needs, and students must be organized in a manner that enables them to learn from one another. Despite fundamental disagreements over the nature of grouping strategies, a strong belief was expressed that cooperative learning and peer tutoring would be defining characteristics of restructuring schools.

As a group, the principals supported student management approaches that 'focused on the positive rather than the negative' and were 'preventative as opposed to corrective or punitive'. Suggested steps to achieve this goal included hiring additional counsellors, earlier intervention by a larger number of social workers, and doing away with the disciplinarian position. As the latter suggests, they predicted that teachers would assume greater responsibility for managing student behaviour. Their focus was on support structures which would enable teachers to be successful at this endeavour: for example, more counsellors, decreased class sizes, increased parental support, and a school-wide discipline policy. They did not, however, mention training teachers to enhance classroom management skills. On the contrary, the teachers focused on techniques that they could rely on to improve discipline: for example, increased positive reinforcement, more positive attitudes towards teaching, sharing trade secrets with one another, and training on a discipline management plan. Not surprisingly, given their emphasis on strategies such as cooperative learning and peer tutoring, both groups foresaw greater student involvement in managing their own behaviour.

Professional development

The principals interviewed had far more highly developed visions regarding the role of professional development in their restructured schools than the participating teachers. Excluding their expressed need for training in administrative skills and human relations processes, which we discussed earlier, no major themes emerged from the teachers' responses.

The principals also noted that training would be essential to help staff, parents, students and administrators understand what restructuring involves and to learn how to participate effectively in an environment characterised by shared decision making and collaborative work relationships. Furthermore, they supported training those involved in restructuring to provide them with the tools necessary to assume new roles and responsibilities: for example, assisting teachers to develop decision-making, communication and group-process skills.

However, the administrators identified a second role for staff development in a restructured school. They were adamant about the need for restructured schools to develop ongoing professional development plans tailored to the school's vision and supported by the budget. As stated previously, they emphasised the value and need for staff development to enhance teacher performance. Staff would be more involved in the selection and delivery of professional development activities. Finally, after noting a reluctance on the part of many teachers to take time off to participate in professional growth activities, they foresaw increased collegial pressure to attend workshops with an obligation to share information upon returning.

DISCUSSION

In this chapter, we have reported the perceptions held by selected American teachers and principals regarding reforms that fall under the rubric of school restructuring. A premise of this study was that the success or failure of the movement to restructure schools would be based to a great extent on the ability of educators to conceptualize new solutions to both persisting and new problems. The findings of this study were limited to a description of the current thinking of selected teachers and administrators in the United States. While we do not assume that the data are the equivalent of information generated by a staff engaged in ongoing, creative problem solving, the results suggest directions in which the restructuring movement may move as well as some of the obstacles that may be encountered.

In this final section, we discuss three particularly salient issues that emerged from the results. These issues are:

- the connection between changes in school governance structures and changes in teaching and learning;
- the nature of teachers' participation in school decision making;
- decision making and accountability.

School governance and the teaching–learning process

A finding that was predictable, yet surprising, concerned the lack of connections made by teachers and principals between new governance structures and the teaching–learning process. This finding was predictable in the sense that there is a long history of education reforms in which curriculum innovations have been displaced in practice by governance procedures (Sarason, 1990). At the same time, this finding was surprising in that few, if any, of these educators voiced a perspective on school restructuring that was driven first and foremost by a vision of teaching and learning, whether good, bad or indifferent. This was reflected in the relatively few references made to the potential impact of restructuring on students' cognitive development. It was also apparent in the paucity of concrete examples of how restructured schools might reorganize curriculum and instruction to meet the needs of students. In sum, neither the teachers nor the principals seemed to view restructuring as a reform designed to assist students.

Given these observations, we wonder how restructuring, in practice, will serve the needs of students. Smith and O'Day (1990) note:

> Although restructuring literature stresses the critical importance of developing complex problem-solving and higher order thinking skills in our youth, achieving this goal requires a major reorientation in content and pedagogy as well as in the structure of the educational enterprise.... Site-based management, professional collaboration, incentives and choice may be important elements of the change process, but they alone will not produce the kinds of changes in content and pedagogy that appear critical to our national well being. (pp. 2–3)

Neither the principals nor the teachers in this study appeared to have a vision of how schooling might change to accommodate the changing needs of students and society. This is significant given the relatively high levels of education and sophistication of these educators and their general support for restructuring. It highlights the need for more intensive discussion on the educational components of restructuring among teachers and administrators. It also reinforces the importance of connecting practitioners to channels through which they can develop the skills needed to implement new governance mechanisms *and* new pedagogical methods.

Teachers' participation in school decision making

A second issue highlighted in the study concerned the perspectives of principals and teachers towards teachers' involvement in decision making. Teachers and administrators took quite different positions on this issue. The teachers explicitly favoured a more active role in technical decision making, though they were not convinced that such participation would be authentic. At the same time, administrators tended to question the number of teachers who wanted to participate in school decision making. Furthermore, they wondered how long that interest would last once the reality of increased meeting time, commitments and conflict set in.

This contrast in views is consistent with prior research on this issue. For example, in one study, Duke and his colleagues found that teachers viewed shared decision making as a 'formality or an attempt to create the illusion of teacher influence' (Duke *et al.*, 1980). They noted:

> This frequently heard complaint of teachers, that their involvement made little or no difference, provides a key to understanding the findings of this study. Since the teachers were less than enthusiastic about participating in shared decision-making even though they viewed the potential benefits as high and the potential costs as low, it is reasonable to conclude that they believed that the probability of actually realizing the potential benefits of participation was low. (p. 104)

Thus, it may be true that teachers are both reluctant to participate in school decision making, and also desirous of exercising more influence in the school (Duke and Gansneder, 1990).

This highlights the importance of treating influence as a dimension separate from participation in decision making. Teachers do not want to be involved in decision making without a clear designation of their role and authority in the process. The teachers in this study were sceptical that administrators would willingly share their authority in the decision-making process. They seemed to believe that school administrators would find excuses to hold on to their authority or would devise ways to mitigate the effects of new governance structures. This scepticism is consistent with the rhetoric of reform advocates who question the extent to which school administrators can be the leaders of truly radical reform. These critics have suggested that, inevitably, school administrators will be reluctant to relinquish the reins of control and, if unchecked, will prevent fundamental change from occurring (Chubb, 1988; Lieberman, 1988).

While such scepticism does not seem unreasonable given the failure of past efforts systematically to involve teachers in decision making, the data available to assess the issue of influence are preliminary and conflicting. Substantial restructuring efforts in a number of American school districts (Dade County, FL; Sarasota, FL; White Plains, NY; Santa Fe, NM) have been initiated by school superintendents (Carnoy and MacDonell, 1989; David, 1990; Hallinger and Edwards, 1992; Hallinger and Yanofsky, 1990; Tyack, 1990). Furthermore, in several of these cases the decision to adopt radical reform measures was made in anticipation of, rather than in response to, significant educational problems (Carnoy and MacDonell, 1989; Hallinger and Edwards, 1992; Hallinger and Yanofsky, 1990).

While some superintendents have assumed leadership roles in restructuring schools and school systems, principals have not been key players in the conceptualization of restructuring. Although principals remain the gate-keepers of change at the school site, they have been relatively passive recipients of this latest round of educational reform. Only after restructuring efforts are underway are principals becoming involved. The reactive quality of this response was recently illustrated in the decision of principals in Los Angeles to form a union as a means of exercising voice in the district's plan for restructuring (Bradley, 1991). For the first time, the principals in this large district will not be a part of the district's official management team.

Decision making and accountability

While accountability has long been a popular target of critics of shared decision making (Geisert, 1988), it is only recently that this issue has begun to receive close attention (Cohen, 1990; David, 1990; Smith and O'Day, 1990; Sykes, 1990; Tyack, 1990). Our findings reaffirm the intensity of accountability concerns in a shared decision-making environment. Furthermore, the data suggest that considerable energies will need to be focused on the resolution of these concerns before restructuring efforts will effect positive change.

Although the teachers in this study overwhelmingly favoured a greater voice in the decision-making process, they neglected to address how they might share accountability for decisions. Furthermore, they did not appear to view accountability as a problem that they needed to address. It may be that since teachers have been largely buffered from institutional or professional accountability in the past, the connection between increased involvement in decision making and accountability remains an abstract issue for them.

On the other hand, the principals expressed serious concerns over the prospect of mandated teacher participation in school governance in the absence of clearly defined means of assessing accountability. They resented the prospect of being on the 'hot seat' for school decisions reached jointly by a school-based council, particularly if they held but a single vote on the council. The vividness of the principals' concern for accountability stands in stark contrast to the absence of teacher engagement on this issue.

An interesting contrast also emerged in discussions of empowerment. As noted earlier, teachers doubt whether principals will share authority over school decisions, even if compelled through district policy. Although the teachers attributed considerable power to their principals, it is ironic that the principals in this study did not view themselves as owning a significant piece of the decision-making pie. In fact, they questioned the willingness of their own superordinates to change either their own leadership practices or the sphere of decisions over which the school is responsible. One principal suggested that the central office 'pays lip service to restructuring but doesn't really let go of some of that central authority'. Initial evidence suggests that this scepticism is not without justification (Chapman and Boyd, 1986; Hallinger and Yanofsky, 1990; Seeley et al., 1990), although there are also favourable reports from districts that are experimenting with original accountability policies (David, 1990). Perhaps the most interesting data related to the issues of participation and accountability in this study concerned the attitudes of teachers and principals towards parental involvement. Both the principals and teachers raised serious questions regarding the appropriateness and potential effectiveness of parental involvement in curricular and instructional decision making. Neither group of educators was convinced that parental involvement would solve more problems than it would cause. This perspective runs counter to the strong trend in the restructuring literature advocating a more significant role for parents in public schooling.

It remains to be seen which levels of the hierarchy, if any, will relinquish power. The route taken by most restructuring efforts has begun by changing governance procedures at the school site. We are pessimistic, however, about the likelihood that formalized procedures for sharing authority will achieve the desired ends in the absence of trust, a commodity that seems to be in short supply.

This chapter has highlighted differences in the perspectives of teachers and principals towards school restructuring. While the differences in their points of view are not insignificant, we would note, in conclusion, that a more fundamental discrepancy is apparent when the views of these practitioners are compared with those of the policy community that is driving education reform. This is particularly salient with respect to the issue of connecting reforms in education governance with changes in classroom practice. If school restructuring is to succeed, better connections will need to be forged between these communities. In particular, schools will need to find the resources that can assist practitioners in developing knowledge about curriculum and instruction that will meet the demands of our future society. The alternative is that schools will reduce restructuring to a new governance process that fails to influence what goes on beyond the classroom door.

Acknowledgements

Support for this research was provided by the National Center for Educational Leadership (NCEL) under US Department of Education Contract No. R117C8005. The views in this chapter are those of the authors and do not necessarily represent those of the sponsoring agency nor the universities in the NCEL Consortium – The University of Chicago, Harvard University, and Vanderbilt University.

The authors would like to acknowledge the assistance of Barbara Habschmidt in collecting the data for this study and to thank the teachers and principals who offered their time and support for the project.

REFERENCES

Bradley, A. (1991, March 20) 'Administrators in Los Angeles form a bargaining unit', *Education Week* 10(26): 1–14.
Carnoy, M. and MacDonell, J. (1989, December) *School district restructuring in Santa Fe, New Mexico*, Center for Policy Research in Education Research Report Series RR–017.
Chapman, J. and Boyd, W. (1986) 'Decentralization, devolution, and the school principal: Australian lessons on statewide educational reform', *Educational Administration Quarterly* 22(4): 25–8.
Chubb, J. (1988) 'Why the current wave of school reform will fail', *Public Interest* 90: 28–49.
Cohen, D. (1990) 'Key issues facing state policymakers', in R. Elmore (ed.) *Restructuring Schools: The Next Generation of Educational Reform* (pp. 251–88), San Francisco: Jossey Bass.
David, J. (1990) 'Restructuring in progress: Lessons from pioneering districts', in R. Elmore (ed.) *Restructuring Schools: The Next Generation of Educational Reform* (pp. 209–50), San Francisco: Jossey Bass.

Duke, D. and Gansneder, B. (1990) 'Teacher empowerment: The view from the classroom', *Educational Policy* 4(2): 145–60.

Duke, D., Showers, B.K. and Imber, M. (1980, Winter) 'Teachers and shared decision making: The costs and benefits of involvement', *Educational Administration Quarterly* 16(1): 93–106.

Elmore, R. (1990a) 'Introduction: On changing the structure of public schools', in R. Elmore (ed.) *Restructuring Schools: The Next Generation of Educational Reform* (pp. 1–28), San Francisco: Jossey Bass.

—— (1990b) 'Conclusion: Towards a transformation of public schooling', in R. Elmore (ed.) *Restructuring Schools: The Next Generation of Educational Reform* (pp. 289–98), San Francisco: Jossey Bass.

—— (1991, April) 'Teaching, learning, and school organization: School restructuring and the recurring dilemmas of policy and practice', Paper presented at the Annual Meeting of the American Educational Research Association, Chicago.

Evertson, C. and Murphy, J. (1992) 'Implications for restructuring schools', in H.H. Marshall (ed.) *Redefining Student Learning: Routes of Educational Change*, Norwood, NJ: Ablex.

Geisert, G. (1988) 'Participatory management: Panacea or hoax?', *Educational Leadership* 46(3): 56–9.

Goetz, J.P. and LeCompte, M.D. (1984) *Ethnography and Qualitative Design in Educational Research*, Orlando, FL: Academic Press.

Hallinger, P. and Edwards, M. (1992) 'The paradox of superintendent leadership in school restructuring', *School Effectiveness and School Improvement* 3(2): 131–49.

Hallinger, P. and Yanofsky, S. (1990) 'Gearing up to change slowly: Restructuring roles and relationships and the district level', Paper presented at the Annual Meeting of the American Educational Research Association, Boston.

Hallinger, P., Murphy, J. and Hausman, C. (1992) 'Restructuring schools: Principals' perceptions of fundamental educational reform', *Educational Administration Quarterly* 28(3): 330–49.

Lieberman, A. (1988) 'Teachers and principals: Turf, tension, and new tasks', *Phi Delta Kappan* 69(9): 648–53.

Miles, M. and Huberman, A. (1984) *Qualitative Data Analysis: A Sourcebook of New methods*, Beverly Hills, CA: Sage.

Murphy, J. (1990) 'The educational reform movement of the 1980's: A comprehensive analysis', in J. Murphy (ed.) *The Reform of American Public Education in the 1980s: Perspectives and Cases* (pp. 3–56), Berkeley, CA: McCutchan.

—— (1991) *Restructuring Schools: Capturing and Assessing the Phenomenon*, New York: Teachers College Press.

Murphy, J., Evertson, C. and Radnofsky, M. (1991) 'Restructuring schools: Fourteen elementary and secondary teachers' perspectives on reform', *Elementary School Journal* 92(2): 135–48.

Rowan, B. (1990) 'Applying conceptions of teaching to organizational reform', in R. Elmore (ed.) *Restructuring Schools: The Next Generation of Educational Reform* (pp. 31–58), San Francisco: Jossey Bass.

Sarason, S. (1990) 'What are schools of education for?', in A. Lieberman (ed.) *Schools as Collaborative Cultures: Creating the Future Now*, Bristol, PA: Falmer Press.

Seeley, D., Niemeyer, J. and Greenspan, R. (1990, May) *Principals speak on restructuring and school leadership*, Report #1, New York.

Smith, M. and O'Day, J. (1990) 'Systemic school reform', Paper prepared for inclusion in S. Fuhrman and B. Malen (eds) *The Politics of Curriculum and Testing*, Bristol, PA: Falmer Press.

Sykes, G. (1990) 'Rethinking teacher professionalism in schools', in R. Elmore (ed.)

Restructuring Schools: The Next Generation of Educational Reform (pp. 59–96), San Francisco: Jossey Bass.

Tyack, D. (1990) 'Restructuring in historical perspective: Tinkering towards utopia', *Teachers College Record* 92(2): 170–91.

Chapter 3

The consequences for school improvement of differences in principals' problem-solving processes

Kenneth Leithwood and Rosanne Steinbach

Do principals make a significant contribution to the improvement of schools? Based on the results of research reported over the past 15 years, the answer is that 'some do but many do not'. This research, recently reviewed by Leithwood *et al*. (1990), has begun to generate the information required to explain the substantial variation in principals' impact on schools. Our framework for organizing this information suggests that a broad array of variables in the principals' environment influences how they think and feel about their job – their internal mental processes. These thoughts and feelings, in turn, give rise to their administrative practices; such practices exercise both direct and indirect effects on a variety of student and other school-related outcomes.

In spite of impressive additions to the empirical knowledge base about constructs and relationships in this framework, little is known about principals' internal mental processes and their direct relationship to principals' practices. Efforts to explain variation in principals' contribution to school improvement will remain seriously deficient without further research on these issues. Responding to this void was the general purpose of the study reported in this chapter.

The study was conducted with a selected sample of principals in British Columbia, Canada, who were attempting to improve their schools through the implementation of a major Ministry of Education policy initiative. Called the *Primary Program* (1990) this initiative aimed to restructure the first four years of schooling through such organizational changes as student grouping by criteria other than grade, continuous assessment to measure progress and dual entry periods to kindergarten. Instructional changes were premised on a constructivist image of learning and aimed at the type of active participation of students in their own learning, evident, for example, in whole language approaches to instruction (see Watson, 1989). Anecdotal reporting to parents, greater parent involvement as partners in instruction and a concern to meet more effectively the needs of a culturally diverse population of students were among some of the other elements of the Primary Program. This Program was, itself, part of a broader set of policies (*Year 2000*, 1989) to be implemented through to the end of secondary school over a ten-year period.

Within this context, our study asked three specific questions: How do practices used by principals to foster school improvement differ? What is the nature of the thinking or problem solving giving rise to variations in principals' practices? What are the consequences for school improvement of differences in such practices? Our study also inquired about the relationships between variations in principals' thinking and practice and a small number of demographic variables.

FRAMEWORK

Principals' practices

One obvious explanation for variation in principals' contribution to school improvement is offered by research describing differences in the methods they use for this purpose (Blase *et al.*, 1986; Blumberg and Greenfield, 1980; Brady, 1985; Hall *et al.*, 1984; Hoy and Brown, 1986; Leithwood and Montgomery, 1986; Salley *et al.*, 1978). Four distinct patterns of practice are evident in this research, which Leithwood *et al.* (1990) have summarized as follows:

> Leadership style A is characterized by a focus on interpersonal relationships; on establishing a cooperative and genial 'climate' in the school and effective, collaborative relationships with various community and central office groups. Principals adopting this style seem to believe that such relationships are critical to their overall success and provide a necessary springboard for more task-oriented activities in their schools.
>
> Student achievement and wellbeing growth is the central focus of leadership style B. Descriptions of this class of practices suggest that while such achievement and wellbeing are the goal, principals use a variety of means to accomplish it. These include many of the interpersonal, administrative, and managerial behaviours that provide the central focus of other styles.
>
> Compared with styles A and B, there is less consistency, across the four dozen studies reviewed, in the practices classified as style C (programme focus). Principals adopting this style, nevertheless, share a concern for ensuring effective programmes, improving the overall competence of their staff, and developing procedures for carrying out tasks central to programme success. Compared with style A, the orientation is to the task, and developing good interpersonal relations is viewed as a means to better task achievement. Compared with style B, there is a greater tendency to view the adoption and implementation of apparently effective procedures for improving student outcomes as a goal – rather than the student outcomes themselves.
>
> Leadership style D is characterized by almost exclusive attention to what is often labelled 'administrivia' – the nuts and bolts of daily school organization and maintenance. Principals adopting this style, according to all four

studies, are preoccupied with budgets, timetables, personnel administration, and requests for information from others. They appear to have little time for instructional and curriculum decision making in their schools, and tend to become involved only in response to a crisis or a request. (pp. 12–13)

There is considerable evidence to warrant the claim that styles B and C make the greatest contribution to school improvement – especially style B (see Heck *et al.*, 1990; Leithwood and Montgomery, 1982). Indeed, these four patterns appear to represent a hierarchy in terms of their contribution to school improvement with the student growth focus (B) making the greatest contribution followed in diminishing order by the programme focus (C), the interpersonal relationships focus (A) and the building manager focus (D) (Hall *et al.*, 1984; Leithwood and Montgomery, 1986; Stevens and Marsh, 1987; Trider and Leithwood, 1988). Such differences in effectiveness are partly explained by the increased inclusivity of patterns closer to the student growth focus; this focus, for example, also includes attention to building management, school climate and school programmes but as 'means' to the student growth 'end' not as ends themselves. In the present study, we inquired about whether the initiatives principals took towards school improvement corresponded to one or more of these four styles or patterns.

Problem-solving processes

What principals do depends on what they think. More specifically, the patterns of practice used for school improvement are products of how principals think about and approach not just the overall problem of school improvement but also the multitude of smaller, imbedded sub-problems. Only recently, however, has systematic research begun to be devoted to the thinking and problem solving of educational administrators, and accumulated evidence to date is quite small; considerably more research has been reported on the problem solving and strategic thinking of managers and leaders in non-educational organizations (Schwenk, 1988). Without a better understanding of principals' thinking and problem solving, it is difficult to explain differences in their school improvement practices; nor are attempts to assist principals in acquiring more effective patterns of practice likely to be especially successful. Further, a significant number of school improvement problems are unpredictable and must be solved in contexts which are highly variable. Under such contingent circumstances, it is unlikely that any single set of specific interventions will be reliably effective. Much more important is the quality of those problem-solving processes (or thinking) giving rise to practice.

The present study inquired about principals' thinking and problem solving using theoretical orientations to and results from our own programme of research in this area (for example, Leithwood and Stager, 1989; Leithwood and Steinbach, 1990). Taking contemporary cognitive science theory as a point of departure (Chi *et al.*, 1981; Frederiksen, 1984; Voss *et al.*, 1983) this research has investigated differences in the problem-solving processes of *expert* and *typical* principals. Gender, organizational size, administrative level and socialization processes are among the variables helping to account for those expert–typical differences which we have discovered. Among the most significant results of this research to date is a model of educational administrators' problem solving consisting of six constructs defined as follows:

- Interpretation: a principal's understanding of what is specifically the nature of the problem, often in situations where multiple problems may be identified;
- Goals: the relatively immediate purposes that the principal is attempting to achieve in response to his or her interpretation of the problem;
- Principles/values: the relatively long-term purposes, operating principles, fundamental laws, doctrines, values and assumptions guiding the principal's thinking;
- Constraints: barriers or obstacles which must be overcome if an acceptable solution to the problem is to be found;
- Solution processes: what the principal does to solve a problem in light of his or her interpretation of the problem, principles, goals to be achieved and constraints to be accommodated;
- Affect: the feelings, mood and sense of self-confidence the principal experiences when involved in problem solving.

These constructs, along with research findings about expert–typical differences related to each of them, were used as a guide for data collection and provided an initial structure for coding and data analysis.

The present study was intended to advance our own previous research on administrators' problem solving in three ways. First, principals included in our previous studies showed evidence of using primarily two of the four dominant forms of practice described above: 'expert' principals were usually programme managers (style C); those we labelled 'typical' usually demonstrated a focus on interpersonal relations (style A). The present study offered the potential to learn more about the thinking of principals who used other styles or patterns of practice, as well. Second, women have been grossly underrepresented in the samples of principals included in our studies to date (as well as in the field of administration, as a whole): the present study provided an opportunity to redress this imbalance. Finally, our previous data were collected in response to a wide variety of administrative problems, many of which could be solved in a short period of time: the present study provided data about responses to a single type of problem, one requiring an extended or open-ended time frame for solution. As Mehan (1984) suggests, such a time frame is typical of many institutional problems and may stimulate different strategies for problem solving, about which little is known.

The consequence of principals' practices

At least four dozen empirical studies, reported in the English language literature, have investigated principals' direct impact on students and teachers (Leithwood *et al.*, 1990). With respect to students, the practices of some principals are reported to have a positive impact on attitudes towards school, achievement in basic mathematics and reading skills and reduced vandalism and absenteeism. Some patterns of practice also are reported to have a positive impact on teachers' job satisfaction, use of innovative practices in the classroom, perception of principals' leadership, loyalty to the principal and readiness to accept principals' decisions. While these results are informative, the choice of these outcomes or dependent variables in most studies has been, at best, atheoretical and, at worst, arbitrary. In a study of the contribution of principals' practices to *school* improvement (in particular, the early stages of such improvement), what choice of outcomes is most warranted?

While improving student outcomes is one central, long-term purpose driving many school improvement initiatives, there is no compelling rationale for its choice in the present study for two reasons. First, school improvement efforts can be expected to consume at least three to five years (Fullan, 1982; Huberman and Miles, 1984) before being implemented well enough reasonably to expect detectable changes in student outcomes. Our study was conducted during the first year of school improvement. Second, even quite effective forms of principal practice are reported to have largely indirect effects on students (Bossert *et al.*, 1982; Heck, 1990; Leithwood and Montgomery, 1986; Pitner, 1988).

In theory, it ought to be possible to trace these effects on students through a chain of intervening variables. But as yet we do not know enough about what these intervening variables are to model a plausible chain (see Joong (1991) for one such attempt). This provides a rationale for greater attention to the identification of variables mediating the effects of principals on student growth and the use of these variables as dependent measures in studies of principals' practices. Such variables ought to have a theoretically and/or empirically demonstrable impact on student growth directly and ought to be susceptible to influence by principals.

Three sets of variables, chosen for the present study, are among those meeting these criteria, in a school improvement context. School culture – both content and form – is one such variable. Compelling evidence links this variable to the effectiveness of schools (see Little, 1982; Mortimore *et al.*, 1988) and to the success of school improvement processes; some principals also seem able to shape school cultures through their practices (Deal and Peterson, 1991; Firestone and Wilson, 1985; Hargreaves, 1990; Leithwood and Jantzi, 1990).

Teacher development – changes in their attitudes and behaviours – as well as activity designed for that purpose is a second variable meeting our criteria. Fullan (1990) and Shanker (1990) are among those currently arguing for a reconceptualization of school improvement from a narrow focus on implementing specific innovations to a broader concern with developing the capacity, if not altering the role, of teachers. These arguments are rooted in the disappointing consequences of attempting to improve schools without significantly restructuring them (Sarason, 1990). Some principals appear able to exercise a strong influence on teacher development (Leithwood *et al.*, 1991; Reid, 1991), especially their informal learning.

A final outcome variable included in our study was teachers' perceptions of the helpfulness of the principal's leadership. Such perceptions influence teachers' commitments to the collective mission of the school, a central variable, for example, in Rosenholtz's (1989) explanation of school effectiveness. Evidence suggests, in addition, that similar leadership practices will be interpreted differently by individual recipients (Yamamoto and Bass, 1990).

METHOD

Sample

Twelve schools in three districts (four schools per district) were selected for the study. Eight of these schools had volunteered to be pilot schools for implementing the new Primary Program policy. Four were chosen from a total of seven elementary schools in one district all of which were initiating activities related to the policy. Within these schools, data were collected from each of the 12 principals and all 44 primary division teachers in the 12 schools.

Aside from willingness to participate in the study, school selection criteria aimed to ensure variation in district size, rural/urban location, school size, gender of school administrators and their length of experience in either vice principal and/or principal positions. These five demographic variables served as sampling criteria because of their plausible contributions to variation in approaches to policy implementation and school improvement. For example, Walberg and Fowler's (1987) review of evidence concerning district size suggested that 'smaller districts obtain more achievement value per dollar' (p. 8). Coleman and LaRocque's (1989) evidence, also associating greater effectiveness with smaller districts, explains such effectiveness in terms of the culture fostered by superintendents. Evidence provided by Louis (1989), demonstrates quite direct effects of district location on approaches to school improvement, as well as the propensity to change; more directive, 'hands-on' forms of leadership from the superintendent seemed necessary for school improvement initiatives to succeed in rural as compared with urban districts.

School size potentially shapes approaches to school improvement. As Rosenholtz (1989) suggests, this variable may influence the ease of teacher and administrator contact; the larger the school, the fewer the opportunities for substantive interaction. A much debated variable, administrators' gender, has also been used to explain variation in approaches to change: female administrators, on average, are reported to devote greater and more direct attention than males to classroom instructional practices and to use more supportive leadership behaviours (see Shakeshaft, 1987). Finally, there is little solid evidence to suggest that length of experience as an administrator is significantly associated with variation in administrators' approaches to school improvement (see Salley *et al.*, 1978). Administrative experience was used as a sampling criterion in this study, however, because of the nature of the policy serving as the focus of school improvement efforts. This policy, as described earlier, represents a dramatic departure from instructional practices considered effective in schools a decade ago and hence the likely instructional practices of principals with lengthy administrative experience. In contrast, the policy legitimates and extends instructional practices that may have been well mastered by those recently appointed to administrative positions. As a consequence, these two groups of principals may be expected to vary considerably in the nature of the leadership they are prepared to offer in implementing the policy.

Data collection procedures

Table 3.1 summarizes procedures used to collect data and indicates which procedure provided data for each of the three sets of research questions. Information about patterns of practice used by principals for school improvement was obtained from principals through a bi-weekly journal which they kept. Both principals and teachers were also interviewed at two points in the year, autumn and spring, about the nature of school improvement processes in their schools and related leadership initiatives. These semi-structured interviews each required an average of 45 minutes for teachers and about 90 minutes for principals.

In the spring, teachers and principals responded to an 87 item, five-part, mailed questionnaire which also provided information about principals' practices. Parts 1 and 5 of the instrument included questions regarding selected aspects of respondents' background as well as overall responses to the school improvement process. Part 2 asked for responses to 13 leadership strategies identified through reviews of previous research (Craig, 1990; Trider and Leithwood, 1988) as potentially helpful for school improvement. The third part of the survey asked questions about a set of 38 factors, identified through previous research (Scott, 1990; Trider and Leithwood, 1988) as influencing school improvement.

A final set of 17 survey items, as well as the two school improvement process interviews, provided information about the outcomes of the school improvement process, a second research question.

Questions about principals' thinking and problem solving were collected using three types of process-tracing methods (Hayes and Flower, 1983) in total. Data for this study were provided by only one of these methods – a

Table 3.1   Procedures for collecting data related to the three sets of research questions

Data collection procedures	Research questions		
	Patterns of practice	Principal's thinking	Outcomes
1 Simulated problem solving and focused interview (principal)		×	
2 Stimulated recall (principal)		×	
3 Journal (principal)	×		
4 School improvement process interview #1 (teach. & princ.)	×		×
5 School improvement process interview #2 (teach. & princ.)	×		×
6 School improvement process survey (teach. & princ.)	×		×

semi-structured interview with principals about how they were solving the current school improvement problem; that is, implementing the Primary Program policy.

Data analysis

All interview data, from principals and teachers, were tape recorded, transcribed and analysed for content using codes suggested by the conceptual frameworks guiding the study. Principals' journals were content analysed in a similar manner. Responses to the survey were entered into a computer file and a series of statistical analyses were carried out to help answer relevant research questions. Analyses were carried out separately for the responses of principals and teachers. Combined responses were also analysed.

RESULTS

How do the practices used by principals to foster school improvement differ? What is the nature of the thinking or problem solving giving rise to differences in these practices? What are the consequences for school improvement of differences in such practices? This section of the chapter describes the answers provided by data from our study to each of these questions. This section also describes several demographic characteristics of the sample of 12 principals.

Principals' practices

Evidence concerning patterns of practice came from interviews with the principals which focused on their efforts to implement the Primary Program. Data from these interviews were examined initially by one researcher for similarities and differences in overall approaches to school improvement. This resulted in identification of four broad categories of approaches to school improvement. Two additional researchers were then provided with a description of these patterns and the interview transcripts. They were asked independently to assign principals to one of the four patterns. There were no discrepancies in the judgements of the three researchers.

Two of the four patterns of practice closely correspond to what was described earlier as leadership styles D (building manager focus) and A (interpersonal relationships focus). Two of the 12 principals demonstrated a building manager focus. These principals headed schools in a district which had hired primary consultants to help schools implement the Primary Program. These principals were little involved in policy implementation. While this district's decision to rely on primary consultants appears to reduce the leadership demands on principals, it is interesting to note that the other two principals in the same district did not behave like building managers; this suggested that there were many useful leadership functions to be performed in addition to those performed by the primary consultants.

One of these two principals and one principal from another district engaged in a pattern of practice focused on interpersonal relations or teacher-centred management. These principals were supportive of the school improvement effort and reasonably knowledgeable about the Primary Program. They were also intellectually engaged in the improvement process, interacting from time to time with teachers. But their involvement was neither intensive nor particularly direct.

The two other patterns of practice evident in our data were variants on, rather than direct reflections of, what was described above as student growth and programme-focused patterns of leadership. Five principals were engaged in a pattern of practice we labelled 'indirect instructional leadership'; one of these principals was from the district which had primary consultants. Principals engaged in this pattern were very knowledgeable about and supportive of the implementation effort. In addition, however, they were intensely involved in creating conditions in the school – second-order changes – which would give teachers the best chance of successfully implementing the Primary Program: for example, group meeting time, greater involvement in decision making. They developed a positive school climate and ensured opportunities for teacher collaboration, for example. They also monitored implementation progress, staying on top of it and making sure that it occurred. However, they did not become involved in modelling classroom practices.

Three principals were much involved in the classroom practices associated with the Primary Program. We labelled this pattern 'direct instructional leadership'. It involved the demonstration of new practices, in-class assistance to teachers, coaching and the like. These principals also paid close attention to the need for second-order changes in their schools.

In sum, there were significant differences in the practices used by principals for school improvement. These differences appeared to be manifestations, in a school improvement context, of three of the four patterns of practice observed also among principals in a variety of other contexts. Furthermore, the results also suggest that instructional leadership patterns of practice may take either direct or indirect forms.

Problem-solving processes

Several different types of process-tracing methods were used to collect evidence about principals' problem-solving processes. In this section, attention is limited to the results of semi-structured interviews with principals concerning processes which they were using to solve the problem of implementing the Primary Program. The six components of our problem-solving model provide the structure for reporting results in this section; within each component, similarities and differences in the thinking of principals using each of the four patterns of practice are described. The intent is to demonstrate that how one thinks about a problem helps to determine the pattern of practice.

Problem interpretation

The focus on the learning rather than a lock–step kind of sequential program that we had been doing was much more exciting for students. (direct instructional leadership – DIL)

It's not too unlike sitting down to a very, very large meal [with] a whole variety of things for you to savour... and it's not a 15 minute lunch break and so you can really sit down and relax. (indirect instructional leadership – IIL)

First of all, I don't believe it's a new primary program; it's a primary program that has existed for a long time.... That is more than obvious when you work with the teachers who have been teaching in that model and style for a good number of years....

So here we are developing brand new structures in our school system with no guidelines, with administrators who are in the growing process themselves so it's like the blind leading the blind at the present time. (teacher-centred managers – TCM)

They [the primary teachers] convinced me there really wasn't much difference to what we're already doing. (building-centred managers – BCM)

These quotations illustrate dramatically different interpretations of the problem of implementing the Primary Program.

The three direct instructional leaders (DIL) interpreted the problem as 'a
wonderful answer to the needs of all children' and they highlighted the
importance of 'teaching to the child as opposed to having the child adjust to
the curriculum'. They saw the problem as complex but manageable and they
believed that the new Primary Program was the best way to teach children.
The aspects that are problematic for them involve some of the details such as
educating parents, reporting, assessment and organization.

The five indirect instructional leaders (IIL) also viewed the innovation as a
very welcome thrust because of the benefits for children and because it finally
sanctioned 'all of the little things that we have been doing and believing all
along'. Again, it was seen as complex but manageable with the major focus
being on the professional development of teachers.

Both building-centred managers (BCM) and teacher-centred managers
(TCM) interpreted the problem very differently from the instructional leaders.
The two teacher-centred managers themselves differed in their interpretations.
One saw it as business as usual whereas the other saw it as a 'massive upheaval
in the way we operate our school system'. Yet they both viewed it primarily
as the teachers' responsibility: the first because he felt he had exceptionally
capable staff and the second because he felt he lacked enough knowledge to
lead effectively. They both saw the need to proceed slowly.

The two building-centred managers interpreted the programme as one that
teachers were very much in favour of and for which they needed the freedom
'to do what they think is a good idea'. They were accepting of the initiative
and primarily saw the problem in terms of budget and organization: keeping
things running smoothly so the teachers can do what they need to do. The
above quotation also indicates a low level of involvement in the programme.

Goals

Given such different interpretations of the school improvement problem,
different goals for problem solving are to be expected. These are reflected in
the following comments:

When I saw the six goals and objectives of the program, I thought, 'right
on; you've got it'. (DIL)

It's critical for the teachers to understand and believe in the underlying
notions of the program so that they might do a different activity but it's
only the activity that's different. (IIL)

My approach has been to try to slow people down, because they're rushing too fast into something that doesn't have clear guidelines....

How do you slow down the initiative and the drive and the snowball effect of the dedication of the teachers? (TCM)

[I want to] get off to a smooth start. (BCM)

Goals set by the direct instructional leaders, together with their staffs, focused mainly on programmes or instructional activities ('Implement all the stuff that's best for kids'). A second goal for all of them was fully to involve the parents. Other goals included building commitment and teamwork and encouraging their teachers in the school improvement process.

Goals identified by indirect instructional leaders were wide ranging. Along with a strong desire to see the six goals of the Program be achieved in their schools, these principals wanted their staffs to believe in and understand the Program. They wanted to be well informed and they wanted their teachers to be well informed. Other goals included ensuring the support of parents and productive working relationships among primary teachers.

The goals of the instructional leaders were in stark contrast to those expressed by principals using the other two patterns of practice. Teacher-centred managers had in common the goal of slowing down their teachers: one because he believed they were not ready due to lack of guidelines and materials and also because he was afraid his mostly traditional staff would feel insecure; the other worried that his teachers would 'burn out'. Other goals expressed by these two principals were to learn about the Program, keep parents informed and move towards better instruction in the school.

Building-centred managers did not espouse any goals related to children, although one knew that 'the main goal of the program is that kids should progress at their own rate'. He went on, 'I don't know how to do it, but we've got this year to find out.' Other goals were to keep parents informed, provide teachers with time to plan, and get teachers to go to workshops. An implicit goal of both of these principals seemed to be to keep teachers happy.

Values

Differences in the values guiding solutions to the school improvement problem on the part of the four groups of principals are reflected in these comments.

It makes each kid smarter. It makes each kid feel really valued, important. (DIL)

The role of the teacher is the key role in this and I need to do whatever I can to make sure that I focus on that. (IIL)

The teachers are working so hard that the second part of my concern is the stress level and the fatigue.

I want them to feel secure. (TCM)

I don't impose on them [the teachers]. All I do is approve or I might make a suggestion here or there with class lists. (BCM)

Not surprisingly, the values of the direct instructional leaders reflected their dominant concern for consequences for children. They also placed great importance on fully understanding the programme (knowledge), being able to take risks (courage) and encouraging participation and sharing. Leadership responsibility was taken very seriously. As one principal said, 'My role as enabling and empowering the teacher is very clear. That doesn't change.'

There was ample evidence that consequences for children – for example, '[the Primary Program allows you] to create an environment that enables kids to grow as opposed to an environment that tells them what they can't do' – and consequences for parents – 'we have to have the partnership of parents' – were important to indirect instructional leaders. However, these values were overshadowed by a concern for the consequences for teachers and sub-sequently for children: 'I try to have all the staff meetings with a little bit of professional development in it' is an example of the kind of thinking that guided the practices of these administrators. Knowledge, respect for others, participation, sharing and commitment were also frequently mentioned.

Concern for teachers' comfort was a value frequently mentioned by the teacher-centred managers. This was manifested in their desire to proceed slowly and with caution. One principal saw one aspect of his role as advising teachers not to throw out the 'basals with the bath water' (carefulness). The other principal said of his role, 'I didn't have much to do except slow the ship down and steer it maybe once in a while.' Responsibility as an educator and consequences for students were evident but not as ubiquitous with the instructional leaders. Knowledge, respect for others, sharing and commitment were other values mentioned.

Both building-centred managers espoused great respect for their staffs and claimed that their teachers know best. They valued order and serenity: 'I have a great staff; I've been here ten years and I've never heard a voice raised in anger. They get along very well.' Specific role responsibility was the most prevalent value, a value which manifested itself in handing responsibility to teachers.

Constraints

Principals demonstrating different patterns of practice identified quite different constraints to be overcome in solving the school improvement problem. These constraints, as the following quotations illustrate, vary in the degree to which they are under the control of the principals:

Probably the most difficult part, and it hasn't been terribly difficult, has been the parents. (DIL)

Another problem is teachers of varying ability – to pull them all along at the same rate is difficult. (IIL)

Teachers are moving too fast. (TCM)

The difficulty is really the lack of finance, the uncertainty, the options, ... the numbers, ... time, ... space. (BCM)

For direct instructional leaders, there were few constraints and these were not seen to be impenetrable barriers to success. There was, above all, the need to deal carefully with the community because as one principal said, 'parents fear that we've moved back to the loosey goosey '70s business'. Getting information to the parents effectively without wasting their time was a concern, but all three administrators had identified numerous ways to do this. While some differences in staff readiness were identified, these principals perceived this mainly as a challenge to find the best way to have everyone be comfortable and confident.

Because indirect instructional leaders viewed teachers as the most critical factor in school improvement, teachers who were not as willing and able to proceed were viewed as the biggest constraints. As one principal put it, 'I am worried about that weak link.' Other challenges were lack of clarity about specific details, time to meet, how to educate the parents, and dealing with the teachers' union.

Teacher-centred managers were most concerned about teachers making changes too quickly. One such principal was also having trouble accepting the philosophical base upon which the Primary Program was based but he thought he would accept it in time. His inability to lead, in this unfamiliar environment, coupled with the belief that most of his teachers were too entrenched in traditional ways of teaching to accept the change easily, were severe constraints. Both these principals identified as an obstacle that 'there's not much chance to sit back and reflect'.

There was in the minds of building-centred managers a lengthy list of constraints affecting the solution processes, and lack of money headed the list. Although both principals would have liked more money, they seemed to want the funds to appease their teachers' excessive – in the principal's mind – demands for substitute teachers and materials, not because they were considered essential for school improvement. Dipping into the operating budget was one way of easing the financial dilemma and one principal covered a class so the primary team could have time to plan.

Solution processes

Data provided by the interviews regarding solution processes provided insights less about principals' thinking than about the consequences of their thinking for action. Differences in these consequences are evident in these reflections:

> Usually I as principal do the strategy with the whole staff partly to let them know I'm willing to risk and partly to teach it. (DIL)

> First of all we have to become familiar with the new primary program. We have done a lot of jigsawing of the introduction to Goodlad's book, the *Year 2000* document, and the primary program binder. (IIL)

> I have somebody else who has more expertise in the primary program doing a lot of the things that I should be able to do but can't. (TCM)

> And if there's a problem I'll tell them 'Look, I'll solve the problem for you, but I'd rather you do it yourselves, and then tell me what the solution is, if that's okay, fine, that's the way it'll be.' (BCM)

The solution processes step that distinguishes direct instructional leaders from the other three groups is the fact that they modelled instructional strategies either in the classroom or at staff meetings. These administrators were already either very knowledgeable about the methods or else sure that they learned them. Other steps included hiring teachers who were willing and able to implement, educating themselves and the parents, and meeting regularly with the teachers to encourage and support.

For indirect instructional leaders, the steps involved in solving the problem were centred on making sure teachers were as knowledgeable as possible. They were diligent about providing information for their staffs and they treated their staff meetings like seminars where relevant articles were discussed. Staff meetings were carefully planned in advance. In addition to providing opportunities and encouragement, these principals made the necessary arrangements for teachers to visit other schools and to attend conferences and workshops. They often accompanied the teachers. Collaborative planning was important to them and one principal spent considerable effort on altering the school building 'to get it ready for more teacher interaction'.

Both teacher-centred managers depended on their teachers to lead the school improvement effort. One of these principals believed that his entire staff was extremely capable and already implementing 90 per cent of the Primary Program; the other felt that he had one exceptionally expert primary teacher whom he had selected to coordinate school improvement activity. About that decision he said, 'I think that's one of the smartest moves I made all year.'

Providing time for teachers to attend extra conferences and workshops and buying books were the most important steps these principals took: 'I want to gain every resource possible that I can for those teachers.' What made these administrators different from the Indirect Instructional Leadership group is their degree of involvement with staffs. The indirect instructional leaders personally made sure, for example by being at the meetings, that teachers had the knowledge, skills and materials they needed; the teacher-centred managers were more likely to provide encouragement and opportunity. Other steps taken by these principals included learning more about the Primary Program and informing the parents about its implementation in the school.

The solution processes of the two building-centred managers are best characterized as *laissez-faire*. The staffs made the decision to become pilot schools and the principals provided as much money and release time as they were able. Other steps included informing the parents, creating a new primary classroom to handle the large numbers of children, attending institutes and talking to teachers.

Mood

The following remarks demonstrate the wide range of feelings displayed by principals to being involved in implementing the Primary Program – from elation to resignation:

> I am so lucky to be here right now. All the things we've been fighting for for special needs kids are there for everyone. Isn't it wonderful? (DIL)

> Because [staff] were so positive, it enabled me to feel that we could go forward very confidently into this. (IIL)

> I really do feel blessed. They [the staff] are a dynamic bunch. (TCM)

> I feel there's no one out there to get me going and feeling good about things. I'm the one supposed to be doing it for the teachers and they're feeling even worse. (TCM)

> It's my perception that every time I turn around there's another blooming meeting going on somewhere. (BCM)

The prevailing mood among the three direct instructional leaders was unalloyed excitement and delight that the Ministry was spearheading this wonderful programme for kids. Although there was minor uneasiness about how some of the details would work themselves out, they were confident that 'the fog will lift'.

Indirect instructional leaders also were pleased about the initiative. They felt comfortable with it and were confident that 'the way I solve problems will work in this case'. Still there was some nervousness around the logistics of school improvement and one administrator was feeling a little unsure about how to provide direction to her staff, especially because of the 'union stuff'.

The two quotations, one from each principal, from the teacher-centred managers signal two obviously different emotional states. The first principal was mainly pleased – for example, 'I am excited about the teacher who has found that this is exciting for her', but he also felt uneasy with the rapid pace:

he was disappointed that his school was not selected to be a pilot school (he was not aware of the proper procedures). The second principal was mainly feeling uncomfortable and insecure, primarily because of his lack of knowledge. In addition, he was uncertain about the worth of several aspects of the Program. However, he, too, felt quite lucky to have such an exceptional primary lead teacher to help him.

The prevailing mood among the building-centred managers seemed to be resignation to the fact of Primary Program implementation. There was also some resentment about having to take money from the operating budget for this purpose and exasperation about what is considered to be exorbitant demands for release time. One of these principals was frightened at first because of the uncertainty associated with implementing the Primary Program.

In sum, the problem-solving processes of principals using four different patterns of practice to foster school improvement were described using a model of problem solving consisting of six components. Substantial differences were evident among the processes used by principals associated with each pattern. Such differences, however, were least dramatic when direct and indirect instructional leaders' processes were compared. Many of the differences in problem-solving processes flow easily from differences in principals' initial interpretation of problems.

Consequences of principals' practices

Some previous research supports the claim that different patterns of principals' practices are related to different levels of contribution to school improvement outcomes. This section explores the extent to which this claim finds support in evidence from the present study. Patterns of practice include the direct and indirect instructional leadership patterns as well as the teacher-centred and building-centred management patterns described above. These patterns are related to the three sets of outcomes discussed in the Framework section of the chapter: teachers' ratings of principals' helpfulness, school culture and teacher development. Both qualitative (interview) and quantitative (survey) data are reported for each set of pattern–outcome relationships. Table 3.2 provides an estimate of the degree of support found in our data for claims regarding a relationship between principals' patterns of practice and outcomes. Overall, the support is moderate.

Teachers' ratings of helpfulness

Qualitative data about teachers' perceptions of the helpfulness of different patterns of principals' practices were provided in response to several direct interview questions. All three direct instructional leaders, four of the five indirect instructional leaders, and both teacher-centred managers were con-

Table 3.2   Estimates of strength of relationship between patterns of principals'
practices and school improvement outcomes

Types of school improvement outcomes	Types of data	Strength of relationship: principals' patterns and outcomes
1 Perceived helpfulness of principal	• Qualitative • Quantitative	• Moderate to strong • Moderate
2 More collaborative school culture	• Qualitative • Quantitative	• Moderate • Nil
3 Teacher development: activity, attitude, behaviour	• Qualitative • Quantitative	• Moderate • Moderate

sidered to be very helpful by their staffs, as a whole. One indirect instructional leader was considered to be moderately helpful. Both building-centred managers were given low ratings. When asked what had been the single most helpful factor in implementing the Primary Program, the staffs of all three direct instructional leaders identified the principal's support, in one form or another; none of the remaining nine staffs identified their principals in this way.

Six items included on the survey instrument concerned various aspects of principals' practices. A one-way ANOVA conducted on teachers' ratings of the helpfulness of these practices identified statistically significant differences ($p < 0.05$) on ratings of four of these six items when responses were analysed by pattern. These items concerned principals' involvement in planning; principal pressure; the priority awarded by the principal to Primary Program goals; and working relationships between principal and staff. On all four of these items, building-centred managers were given lowest ratings; direct instructional leaders were always rated either first or second. Both direct and indirect instructional leaders were rated significantly higher than building-centred managers on three of the four items. Teacher-centred managers were rated significantly higher than building-centred managers on two of the four items.

In sum, these data were unambiguous about the relatively high and low degrees of helpfulness teachers awarded direct instructional leadership and building-centred manager patterns, respectively. While the relative helpfulness of the remaining two patterns of principals' practices is less clear, the data hint at different effects of the two instructional leadership patterns.

School culture

No significant relationships were evident in the survey data between patterns of principals' practices and either the form or content of school culture.

Interview data did provide evidence of moderate relationships, however. These data were primarily concerned with the form of the culture – the extent to which primary division staffs worked collaboratively or in isolation from one another. These data were content analysed using codes derived from four dimensions of collaboration identified in Judith Little's (1982) research, as follows:

- teachers engage in frequent, continuous and increasingly concrete and precise talk about teaching practices (*teacher talk*);
- teachers plan, design, research, evaluate and prepare teaching materials together (*joint planning*);
- teachers are frequently observed and provided with useful critiques of their teaching (*teacher observation*); and
- teachers teach each other the practice of teaching (*teacher teaching*).

Indications of more general collaboration in school decision making were also coded.

The majority of primary staff members in all schools reported evidence of collaboration in terms of *teacher talk* and *joint planning*. Evidence of *teacher observation* was provided by staffs working with one of the two building-centred and teacher-centred managers, two of the five indirect and two of the three direct instructional leaders. There was no evidence of *teacher teaching* in the four schools of the building- and teacher-centred managers. Such evidence was available in schools of two of the five indirect and two of the three direct instructional leaders. Neither principal engaged in building-centred management patterns appeared to encourage teacher collaboration in decision making; all others did.

In sum, interview but not survey data provided moderate support for claims regarding the relationship between patterns of principal practices and forms of school culture. Evidence suggests that teacher talk and joint planning may develop for reasons unrelated to, or in spite of, what principals do. Teacher observation and teacher teaching, dimensions of collaboration that are much more difficult to develop (Hargreaves, 1990; Leithwood and Jantzi, 1990; Little, 1982; Rosenholtz, 1989), seem more likely to arise in the context of instructional leadership patterns of principals' practices.

Teacher development

Included among this category of outcomes were direct changes in teachers' attitude and behaviours reflecting the intentions of the Primary Program. Also included were activities initiated by principals for teacher development purposes.

Information gleaned from interviews provided teachers' perceptions of the extent to which their principals initiated teacher development activities: for example, activities intended to stimulate commitment to implementing the

Primary Program and providing staff development resources. The majority of staff members working with all eight direct and indirect instructional leaders perceived these principals to have initiated such activity. This was the case with only one of the other four principals, a teacher-centred manager.

The survey contained only one teacher attitude item (high expectations for students). Nine teacher behaviour items were combined into one scale (reliability = 0.89 – Cronbach's alpha). A one-way analysis of variance showed no significant differences between teachers' ratings of the one attitude item and patterns of principals' practices. There were significant differences in the ratings awarded the nine-item teacher behaviour scale, however. Direct instructional leadership patterns were associated with significantly higher ratings than indirect instructional leadership patterns.

In sum, the results provide modest support for the claim that different patterns of principal practice are related to different types or levels of teacher development. These relationships are most evident in comparisons between instructional and non-instructional leadership patterns. But, as with some of the previous data, there is also the suggestion that direct forms of instructional leadership have an especially strong relationship with key types of teacher development (behaviour change).

Demographic characteristics

Information about four demographic variables is summarized in Table 3.3. This table shows that: all but one of the instructional leaders were female and had considerably less experience as principals than did non-instructional leaders; three of the four non-instructional leaders were from the same district, all but one of the indirect instructional leaders were from the same district and all direct instructional leaders were from the same district; school size appears unrelated to pattern of practice. What do these demographic characteristics mean? While there are several possible interpretations, the most plausible, in our view, appears to be a strong interaction effect between gender and district-level socialization and selection processes.

Table 3.3   Demographic characteristics of principals

Pattern	(N)	Gender F	M	Mean years exp. as principal	District affiliation	Mean school size (students)
DIL	(3)	3	0	1	3 = D3	300
IIL	(5)	4	1	9 (4.5)*	4 = D2/1 = DI	280
TCM	(2)	0	2	20	I = DI/I = D3	373
BCM	(2)	0	2	16	2 = DI	280

*Mean years of 9 includes one principal with 28 years experience. Removing this person reduces average years to 4.5

In our sample, there were seven female and five male administrators. All instructional leaders but one (an IIL) were female; all teacher-centred and building-centred managers were male. This lends support to the finding that female administrators, on average, devote greater and more direct attention than males to classroom instructional practices (see Shakeshaft, 1987). Gender alone, however, is not a sufficient explanation for leadership style. In addition to being female, all three direct instructional leaders were also first-year administrators. Two related interpretations are possible.

First-year principals may be more inclined to model instructional strategies in the classroom not because they are women, but because they are very familiar with the strategies and feel confident to teach them. This may well be the situation here, since the Primary Program policy encourages instructional practices that are quite different from those considered effective a decade ago and, thus, would not be as familiar to principals who had been in post for a long time.

A related explanation concerns the notion that new administrators may be in a 'transition' year and are finding a way to bridge the gap between the teacher's classroom and the principal's office. Support for this notion is provided by the fact that indirect instructional leaders were also relatively new to the role in contrast with those adopting the two other styles.

Whether it is due to reluctance to break with the past, a love of teaching, a strong belief that he/she knows how to do it best, or an awareness that teachers learn best when new strategies are modelled for them, number of years in the role may provide some of the rationale for leadership style.

The two anomalies in the sample tend to confirm the above interpretation. The one male instructional leader is from a district where all of the principals in our sample were indirect instructional leaders (possible district effect); however, he had also been a principal for a short time (seven years). One instructional leader was in a district that had no other instructional leaders and had been a principal for 28 years, but she was female.

While these data are far from conclusive, they do indicate some interesting connections and perhaps point the way to future research.

CONCLUSION

Do practices used by principals to foster school improvement differ? Our data suggest an unequivocal 'yes' in response to this question; these differences reflected at least three if not all four of the patterns of principal leadership demonstrated in previous research concerned not only with school improvement but also with other areas of school leader responsibility.

Can variations in patterns of practice be explained by differences in problem-solving processes? Such processes appear to account for much of this variation. Principals faced with the same 'objective' problem – how to implement the Primary Program – interpreted the problem in widely different ways:

as 'a wonderful opportunity to better meet students' needs' to a blur of confusing, uncomfortable demands. Much of how principals thought about the school improvement problem flowed from this interpretation; and much of this interpretation seemed to depend on how knowledgeable the principal considered him- or herself to be with respect to primary programming. Subsequent research would do well to attend, more explicitly, to the role of domain-specific knowledge in administrators' problem solving.

Do variations in principals' problem-solving processes and the practices arising, at least in part, from such processes matter? While our data could be stronger on this matter, a positive answer is clearly warranted. The study supports a hierarchical view of the impact of different patterns of thinking and practice. It also offers an answer many will be reluctant to accept: that is, even apparently quite sophisticated and knowledgeable forms of indirect instructional leadership may not accomplish as much as more direct forms – modelling effective instruction, for example.

REFERENCES

Blase, J., Dedrick, C. and Strathe, M. (1986) 'Leadership behavior of school principals in relation to teacher stress, satisfaction and performance', *Journal of Humanistic Education and Development* 24(4): 159–71.

Blumberg, A. and Greenfield, W. (1980) *The Effective Principal: Perspectives on School Leadership*, Boston: Allyn & Bacon.

Bossert, S., Dwyer, D., Rowan, B. and Lee, G. (1982) 'The instructional management role of the principal', *Educational Administration Quarterly* 18(3): 34–64.

Brady, L. (1985) 'The supportiveness of the principal in schoolbased curriculum development', *Journal of Curriculum Studies* 17(1): 95–7.

Chi, M.T.H., Feltovich, P.J. and Glaser, R. (1981) 'Categorization and representation of physics problems by experts and novices', *Cognitive Science* 5: 121–52.

Coleman, P. and LaRocque, L. (1989) 'Quality control: School accountability and district ethos', in M. Holmes, K. Leithwood and D. Musella (eds) *Educational Policy for Effective Schools*, New York: Teachers College Record.

Craig, A.J. (1990) 'Principals as entrepreneurs: An examination of the management of instructional and curriculum implementation in secondary schools', Unpublished Doctoral Dissertation, Toronto, OISE.

Deal, T. and Peterson, K. (1991, January) 'Instrumental and expressive aspects of school improvement', Paper presented at the Annual Meeting of the International Congress on School Effectiveness and School Improvement, Cardiff, Wales.

Firestone, W.A. and Wilson, B.L. (1985) 'Using bureaucratic and cultural linkages to improve instruction: The principal's contribution', *Educational Administration Quarterly* 21(2): 7–30.

Frederiksen, N. (1984) 'Implications of cognitive theory for instruction in problem solving', *Review of Educational Research* 54(3): 363–407.

Fullan, M. (1982) *The Meaning of Educational Change*, New York: Teachers College Press.

—— (1990) 'Staff development, innovation, and institutional development', in B. Joyce (ed.) *Changing School Culture through Staff Development* (pp. 3–25), Alexandria, VA: Association for Supervision and Curriculum Development.

Hall, G., Rutherford, W.L., Hord, S.M. and Huling, L.L. (1984) 'Effects of three principal styles on school improvement', *Educational Leadership* 41(5): 22–31.

Hargreaves, A. (1990, April) 'Individualism and individuality: Reinterpreting the teacher culture', Paper presented at the Annual Meeting of the American Educational Research Association, Boston.

Hayes, J.R. and Flower, L.S. (1983) 'Uncovering cognitive processes in writing. An introduction to protocol analysis', in P. Mosenthal, L. Tamor and S.A. Walmsley (eds) *Research on Writing: Principals and Methods*, New York: Longman.

Heck, R. (1990) 'Principal instructional leadership and the identification of high- and low-achieving schools: The application of discriminant techniques', *Administrator's Notebook: The University of Chicago* 34(7).

Heck, R., Larsen, T. and Marcoulides, G. (1990, April) 'Principal leadership and school achievement: Validation of a causal model', Paper presented at the Annual Meeting of the American Educational Research Association, Boston.

Hoy, W.K. and Brown, B.L. (1986, April) 'Leadership of principals, personal characteristics of teachers and the professional zone of acceptance of elementary teachers', Paper presented at the Annual Meeting of the American Education Research Association, San Francisco.

Huberman, M. and Miles, M. (1984) *Innovation Up Close*, New York: Plenum Press.

Joong, P. (1991) 'An investigation into the relationship between principals' practices, selected school characteristics and student retention', Unpublished Doctoral Dissertation, Toronto, OISE.

Leithwood, K. and Jantzi, D. (1990) 'Transformational leadership: How principals can help reform school cultures', *School Effectiveness and School Improvement* 1(4): 249–80.

Leithwood, K. and Montgomery, D. (1982) 'The role of the elementary school principal in program improvement', *Review of Educational Research* 52(3): 309–39.

—— (1986) *Improving Principal Effectiveness: The Principal Profile*, Toronto: OISE Press.

Leithwood, K. and Stager, H. (1989) 'Expertise in principals' problem solving', *Educational Administration Quarterly* 25(2): 126–61.

Leithwood, K. and Steinbach, R. (1990) 'Characteristics of effective secondary school principals' problem solving', *Journal of Educational Administration and Foundations* 5(1): 24–42.

Leithwood, K., Begley, P. and Cousins, B. (1990) 'The nature, causes, and consequences of principals' practices: An agenda for future research', *Journal of Educational Administration* 28(4): 5–31.

Leithwood, K., Jantzi, D. and Dart, B. (1991, January) 'Toward a multi-level conception of policy implementation processes based on commitment strategies', Paper presented at the Fourth International Congress on School Effectiveness, Cardiff, Wales.

Little, J. (1982) 'Norms of collegiality and experimentation: Workplace conditions of school success', *American Educational Research Journal* 19(3): 325–40.

Louis, K.S. (1989) 'The role of the school district in school improvement', in M. Holmes, K. Leithwood and D. Musella (eds) *Educational Policy for Effective Schools*, New York: Teachers College Press.

Mehan, H. (1984) 'Institutional decision-making', in B. Rogoff and J. Lave (eds) *Everyday Cognition: Its Development in Social Context*, Cambridge, MA: Harvard University Press.

Mortimore, P., Sammons, P., Stoll, L., Lewis, D. and Ecob, R. (1988) *School Matters: The Junior Years*, London: Open Books.

Pitner, N. (1988) 'The study of administrator effects and effectiveness', in N.J. Boyan (ed.) *Handbook of Research on Educational Administration* (pp. 99–122), New York: Longman.

Primary Program. Foundation Document (1990) Victoria, BC: British Columbia Ministry of Education.

Reid, E.J. (1991) 'The elementary school principal as facilitator of adult learning', Unpublished Doctoral Dissertation, Toronto, OISE.

Rosenholtz, S. (1989) *Teachers' Workplace*, New York: Longman.

Salley, C., McPherson, R.B. and Baehr, M.E. (1978) 'What principals do: A preliminary occupational analysis', in D.A. Erickson and T.L. Reller (eds) *The Principal in Metropolitan Schools*, Berkeley, CA: McCutchan.

Sarason, S.B. (1990) *The Predictable Failure of Educational Reform*, San Francisco: Jossey Bass.

Schwenk, C.R. (1988) 'The cognitive perspective on strategic decision-making', *Journal of Management Studies* 25(1): 41–56.

Scott, G. (1990) 'The change process in a teacher education institution', Unpublished Dissertation, Toronto, OISE.

Shakeshaft, C. (1987) *Women in Educational Administration*, Beverly Hills, CA: Sage.

Shanker, A. (1990) 'Staff development and the restructured school', in B. Joyce (ed.) *Changing School Culture through Staff Development* (pp. 91–103), Alexandria, VA: Association for Supervision and Curriculum Development.

Stevens, W. and Marsh, L.D.D. (1987, April) 'The role of vision in the life of elementary school principals', Paper presented at the Annual Meeting of the American Educational Research Association, Washington, DC.

Trider, D. and Leithwood, K. (1988) 'Influences on principals' practices', *Curriculum Inquiry* 18(2): 289–312.

Voss, J.F., Greene, T.R., Post, T.A. and Penner, B.C. (1983) 'Problem-solving skill in the social sciences', in G.H. Bower (ed.) *The Psychology of Learning and Motivation* (pp. 165–213), New York: Academic Press.

Walberg, H.J. and Fowler, W.J. (1987) 'Expenditure and size efficiencies of public school districts', *Educational Researcher* 16(7): 5–15.

Watson, D.J. (1989) 'Defining and describing whole language', *The Elementary School Journal* 90(2): 129–41.

Yamamoto, F.J. and Bass, B.M. (1990) 'Transformational leadership and multiple levels of analysis', *Human Relations* 43(10): 275–95.

Year 2000 (1989) *A Curriculum and Assessment Framework for the Future*, Victoria, BC: British Columbia Ministry of Education.

Chapter 4

Restructuring schools
Lessons from school leaders

Shirley Hord and Cyril Poster

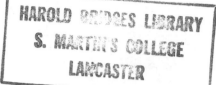
Organizations are built on the unification of people around values.
(Greenfield, 1986)

In the past decade the professional and public press alike have given global attention to the role of school leaders. The significance of this leadership position is now almost universally recognized. Even those school management systems which in the past operated without a formally appointed school director or leader, as in the Canton of Zurich, Switzerland, for example (Topping, 1985), now appear to see the need for a central figure to manage daily routines, and to guide and assist staff in change.

It is no surprise, then, that during the past ten years a growing knowledge base has developed that reports at the international level about the performance and roles of school leaders in the process of school reform and improvement. The work of the International School Improvement Project (ISIP), supported by the Organization for Economic Cooperation and Development (OECD) with its headquarters in Paris, has contributed significantly to this knowledge base (Blum and Butler, 1989; Hopes, 1986; Stego *et al.*, 1987). In the first two of these three ISIP volumes, case studies from Australia, Canada, England and Wales, France, Italy, Japan, The Netherlands, Sweden, Switzerland and the United States reveal the strategies and procedures used by school leaders to bring about school improvement. The third book contains a review of 14 programmes from ten countries that provide professional development for school leaders' efforts towards school improvement and reform.

In what types of reform might leaders in schools be involved? Raywid (1990) identified three waves of educational reform. The first, labelled pseudo-reforms, called attention to needs, mandated cosmetic approaches, and seldom touched classroom practice. The second wave shifted to calls for change focused on achievement of basic skills, and occasionally on higher-order skills, and were categorized as incremental reform. However, many educationists concluded that truly important change would require fundamental rearrangements by which schools operate: restructuring, the third category. Restructuring has been further defined by Corbett (1990) as changes in roles, rules, relationships and results. This chapter addresses Raywid's third category, describes changes in two schools' roles, rules and relationships, and offers case studies that demonstrate how the work initiated by ISIP is taking hold.

The restructuring accounts described in this chapter concern two primary schools located on either side of the Atlantic: Dudley in the West Midlands of England, and New Mexico in the south west of the United States. The British school is led by a woman who has had a wide and varied career in education, the American school by a man who had a marketing career in the private sector before he found greater satisfaction in guiding the schooling of young children. In both cases, the principals made fundamental rearrangements in the manner in which their schools operated.

In each of these case studies a brief description of the school's context is followed by an account of the strategies and events used by the leaders with their staff in the restructuring efforts. The studies are based mainly on the self-report of the leaders and their responses to questions framed for eliciting their stories. Additional sources were minutes of meetings and other written documents, staff responses in tape-recorded interviews and questionnaires, data collected on the change process utilizing procedures from the Concerns Based Adoption Model (Hall *et al.*, 1973; Hord, 1987), reports of LEA and district office visitations and reports by the authors as they observed, consulted and conducted training and professional development sessions in the schools. After the accounts from England and the United States, there follows an analysis of similarities and differences in the two leaders' methods, and of their fit with a scheme developed by Rutherford (1985) summarizing the work of effective principals. In his five-factor framework, Rutherford characterizes effective principals as:

- having clear visions and goals for their schools;
- being able to articulate and translate the vision for all school constituents;
- providing a supportive environment that enhances teaching and learning;
- monitoring classroom and school practices;
- actively intervening to reinforce positive features of the work of teachers and students but also taking corrective action to target problems.

RESTRUCTURING AT KATE'S HILL

There are in England and Wales about a hundred local education authorities (LEAs) ranging in size from the Isle of Wight with a population of 120,000 and some 50 schools, to Essex with a population of 1.5 million and over 700 schools. Each LEA's education budget is currently funded in part from a central government grant and in part from local taxation.

The context

Half of these LEAs are counties, rural areas that usually contain at least one major city, the other half are metropolitan boroughs. Dudley is one of the latter, relatively small, serving a population of 300,000. The borough is, in socio-economic terms, very diverse. It is a manufacturing area: high quality crystal glass is one of its main contributions to the export market. The outlying parts are very desirable residential areas for the industrial and commercial conurbation of the West Midlands, in particular for Britain's second city, Birmingham.

Kate's Hill Primary School is, however, not in one of these more salubrious areas. Only 27 per cent of the pupils of this primary (5–11) school are white. Of the rest, 7 per cent are Afro-Caribbean or of mixed Afro-Caribbean parentage. The rest are Asian, with over 55 per cent of the pupils on roll coming from Pakistani immigrant families.

Although there is considerable unemployment in the area, the houses are generally in a reasonable state of repair, though there is some overcrowding. White families live mainly in rented property owned by the metropolitan borough council. Most Asian families, on the other hand, have bought houses, often initially in a poor state of repair, and have done much to improve them. Asians are very caring of their children and visitors to the school are struck by the blaze of colour, of girls in particular, in sari or salwar and kamiz. Four in five of the Asian children are Muslim, the rest mainly Hindu. The multi-ethnic composition of the school and the community has very profound implications for the way in which the school addresses the issues of its role and function, as will later become evident.

The school roll remains constant at 380, despite a governmental policy of open enrolment which might well have seen a drift of pupils to schools in the more leafy suburbs of Dudley. There is, additionally, a 60 place nursery unit for children aged 3 to 5, integral with the school accommodation and within the management control of the headteacher. Thirty per cent of the children who attend morning or afternoon are Asian and there are just over 100 children attending this nursery unit part time, with a few special cases attending full time.

The headteacher was appointed in 1986. Her predecessor, who had been in the post for ten years, made *ex cathedra* decisions in conjunction with the deputy head only, had little communication with the rest of the staff, encouraged no discussion, and rarely sought opinions. The management structure was nominal, his teachers having no responsibility to or for each other. There were no assigned middle management roles, and staff who received enhanced salaries for curriculum responsibility were in fact responsible not for areas of the curriculum, but only for the organization and provision of the material resources for teaching. Schemes of work were inflexible and staff were required to implement them rigidly. Content and methodology were never reviewed and consequently much of what was written down was out of date. There was no attempt to implement staff development.

The change process: first steps

The arrival of the new headteacher coincided with the allocation of some funding for building improvements. She had observed that money had previously been spent in carving up the purpose-built open-plan school into little boxes. Her observations when in post further convinced her that the only way rapidly to develop a sense of collegiality among the staff was to create areas of group responsibility in which communication might take place. The increased professional development and more effective instruction for students that could occur from staff interaction and collegiality formed the rationale for her restructuring actions. She proposed that the building boxes be opened up into year-group areas and that responsibility for the management of these be given to a team of middle managers. The team included, but was by no means confined to, those who were in receipt of salaries above the basic scale. This innovation, which was both structural and organizational, provided her with the opportunity to initiate discussion on the nature and scope of these new responsibilities.

Even before these changes could take effect, the headteacher had held a series of staff meetings to brainstorm curriculum development within the school. It is interesting to observe from the record of one of these meetings that the word children heads the page, with subheadings of ethos and community. Analysis of the curriculum includes assessment, content, resources and methodology. The subsequent agreed minute of the meeting begins:

> It should be the aim of the school to create a caring, happy, lively and stimulating atmosphere, encouraging self-discipline, self-confidence and a desire to learn, and inculcating the feeling that we are part of the community within society.

Not all was immediate sweetness and light. For example, the previous headteacher's policy that parents might not appear on the school premises without observing very formal procedures was changed to one of open access. While in principle this was welcomed by staff, inevitably in its early days it imposed stress on those teachers as yet ill-equipped to respond to this new style. Staff saw their classrooms as their exclusive territory and felt vulnerable and threatened when visiting parents, or even their colleagues, observed what was happening in their classrooms. Gradually it became clear to staff that parents who were kept in ignorance of what was actually happening in the learning process would remedy the gaps in their knowledge with pure invention.

Change in teacher attitudes was not achieved overnight, but there is now open access for parents into the school. Evidence of this new openness can be observed in the school entrance where the school secretary has been relocated in order to welcome parents and other visitors as they enter, notices in multiple ethnic languages welcome visitors and give helpful directions, and an exhibition of photographs helps visitors to identify teachers and ancillaries. Regular newsletters in the community's main ethnic languages communicate with parents about school events and contain other relevant information. An office has been created to provide a comfortable, private setting for parent conferences. Any parents who question what is happening within the classroom are invited to work alongside the teacher and their children, to witness at first hand and make informed judgements.

Needless to say, it also took time for the staff to learn to communicate with each other and to appreciate that their contribution to the overall management of the school was being valued. The headteacher, ever an opportunist, used a day when the school had to be closed because of inclement weather to initiate a series of staff development interviews with every member of staff. The main purpose of the interviews was to give all teachers the opportunity to say how they saw their careers developing and to indicate the kind of in-service training and other support they might need. During these interviews, however, they revealed a host of concerns about management, in which problems of communication featured prominently. The headteacher brought all these issues into a staff meeting for open discussion, so that their resolution was seen, not as a task for her as leader, but for all the staff corporately, including her. It was through tactics such as this that the concept of collegiate management was introduced and accepted.

The GRASP innovation and Kate's Hill

In 1986 the Comino Foundation, in collaboration with the government Department of Trade and Industry (DTI) as it is now called, invited Dudley LEA to pilot an innovative process called Getting Results and Solving Problems (GRASP). The GRASP approach to problem solving is to ask the significant questions, 'What result do I want? And why?' At the same time, opportunities and constraints, and the criteria on which action decisions will be based, must be identified in advance.

The second stage is to generate all the possible ways of achieving the purpose. When the full range of possible ways forward is identified, then the criteria are used to select the best route to the desired end. Thinking and planning have provided the means to enter the action phase with an expectation of success.

However thorough the preparations, the action may fall short of the desired achievement. Monitoring progress is therefore essential so that the plan can be brought back on course. Finally, having completed the task, it is essential to review and assess. Has the desired end result been achieved? Even if it has, is the goal still valid for repeat activities, or have circumstances now changed and brought about the need for a reassessment of the purpose? Does hindsight now

suggest better ways, and therefore indicate previously unconsidered ways
forward for the next occasion? Has this achievement opened doors to new
possibilities? These stages and steps comprise the GRASP process.

GRASP is a process that involves everyone – students in a class, teachers in
a teaching team, trainers of teachers – so that there is a homogeneity of
approach at all levels. Many of the teacher practitioners of the GRASP process
use it not only in the classroom and in their teaching preparation but also for
decision making in their daily lives. The holism of the approach is, at one and
the same time, its most attractive and most challenging feature.

The headteacher had been involved, in the period immediately preceding
her assumption of her new post, in an intensive exploration of the use of
problem-solving techniques within the classroom. Because of this, she was
invited to contribute to the preparation by the LEA of an application for
funding Dudley as a GRASP pilot site. The proposal was funded and Kate's
Hill was selected as one of the 12 pilot schools for the GRASP project, to be
involved in one of the four consortia each having one secondary and two
primary schools. Among the introductory learning activities for the project
was a two-day residential workshop in team building conducted for each
consortium by the British co-author of this chapter. The main thrust was the
development of collegiality within staff teams underpinned by trust, good
planning and effective delegation. The headteacher perceived that the problem-solving techniques of GRASP provided a significant tool to this end and
she introduced the GRASP methodology into the management of the school.
She took full advantage, both for herself and for her staff, of a wide range of
facilitating workshops available through the funding of the GRASP project.

Managing curriculum change

In no school were the outcomes of using implementation strategies and
assessing their results more effectively debated and absorbed than in Kate's
Hill. The late 1980s was a time of radical change nationally in the primary
school curriculum. The Kate's Hill staff had, in their new experience of
learning to work collegially, reached a stage in which communication, both
vertical and lateral, was much improved and in which assistant staff had learned
that their contribution to the overall management of the school was being
valued. Nevertheless, as with any major restructuring change, there were times
when some looked back with nostalgia to the less challenging times when they
had been told what to do.

It is a basic premise that there can be no effective student learning without
organization and discipline in the school and classroom. Under the previous
headteacher, discipline had been the responsibility of the deputy head, and
those who taught in the school in those days recall the files of children outside
the deputy head's door awaiting punishment. Now, although staff could be
assured of support in cases of extreme difficulty, the school's current head-

teacher had made clear the expectation that, since much ill discipline arises from poorly planned and uninspiring lessons, it was vital that teachers looked critically at their own methodologies and relationships with their classes before seeking support. Nevertheless, while reason told them that this was the only profitable way forward, some in their less reasonable moments chose to see discipline as the task of those who were paid to run the school.

Yet new demands were about to be made on all schools that made concerns about disciplinary procedures pale into insignificance. For the first time in the history of the educational system of the British Isles, central government was introducing a national curriculum with extensive testing and record keeping. It was therefore vital that the organizational management of Kate's Hill was reviewed in the light of coping with rapid curriculum development. Applying the GRASP problem-solving approaches to this new situation, there evolved the concept of curriculum teams rather than curriculum leaders: more restructuring of roles and relationships. Working in teams rather than as individuals would, it was decided through a series of brainstorming sessions, lead to:

- the pooling of knowledge and expertise;
- the involvement of all staff and the consequent promotion of staff development;
- the reflection, in guidelines written by groups rather than individuals, of the ideas and knowledge of the staff as a whole;
- the ownership and extended use of the guidelines as a consequence of involvement in their creation;
- the promotion of cross-phase thinking since the composition of each group was structured to reflect the full age range of the school.

The importance of achieving in management what they were beginning to achieve with students was now becoming evident to all staff. The whole school was rapidly becoming more purposeful. Comments from a staff questionnaire survey are revealing:

- We must practise what we preach.
- How can we ask students to do what we do not do ourselves?
- How can they be taught to value something if we think it has no purpose?
- If staff are not committed, you cannot achieve with children.
- The more areas of operation in which GRASP can be applied, the more the processes will be internalized and will become an intrinsic part of the management of staff, of children, of learning.
- If you achieve the effective use of GRASP in staff meetings, workshops and so on, the more likely are the processes to transfer to the classroom.

GRASP and collegial management

Since collegial management has been in the vocabulary of management literature for some time – though not always, the writers suspect, with a full understanding of its application to school management – there is a need to test out the premise that the GRASP decision-making process brings to it something of unique value. Collegiality is a term that describes a managerial style. It is not in itself a means of reaching a desired end. To quote a member of the Kate's Hill staff:

> GRASP provides the process and methodology for achieving corporate or collegial management. You are not comparing two similars: collegial management is a system, GRASP is a tool to help you achieve the aims of that system.

It has to be said that collegiality has at times been a cloak for the pseudo involvement of subordinates in decision making. It may rely too heavily on a nebulous goodwill which, in circumstances of stress or disaffection, will disappear like the morning mist. There was an occasion in the development of collegial management in Kate's Hill School when the headteacher promoted the idea of a more involved community role for the school, to be undertaken by the school staff. She was taken aback when one of her best teachers, a Sikh who was more concerned than most to involve those who had emigrated from her own subcontinent, openly challenged the proposal.

The headteacher wisely avoided confrontation and stepped back to consider whether her approach to the issue had been sound. She realized that she had been relying on the power of her role, however well disguised; and that she had bypassed the decision-making processes that were being used in the classroom and by her teaching teams. She had assumed that agreement to one set of action steps carried with it agreement to a totally different set, simply because the long-term aim of school and community cooperation underpinned both. She returned to the issue after an interval and, this time using the GRASP paradigm, won full support from the whole staff for what was to prove a considerable undertaking. It is interesting to note that the 1990 development review carried out by a team of LEA advisers with responsibility for the school included the statement:

> Staff have a shared vision of a curriculum and ethos in which partnership with the community is the major theme.

The Just School Project

While the introduction of GRASP into a number of schools in Dudley LEA may properly be called a project, it is necessary to realize that GRASP itself is a tool. It may therefore be used in deciding whether or not to engage in other projects and programmes. GRASP methodology has enabled Kate's Hill School to be eclectic in the selection and use of educational materials and processes because there is a clearly defined sense of purpose within the institution and the ability to innovate without destroying the infrastructure.

The Just School Project is a case in point, one that was to lead to a considerable restructuring, not on this occasion of the school's management, but of the relationships among staff, pupils and home. It may be helpful to an international readership at this point to comment briefly on immigrant family life in the UK. Despite having been in the UK for upwards of 40 years, both Muslims and Hindus tend to continue to live in enclaves within the cities and to perpetuate family structures that they brought with them from their original homelands. Theirs is a male-dominated society, for Muslim women in particular, since many continue to observe some degree of purdah, often have only a rudimentary command of English, and rarely have interests outside the home and their children. Hindus, particularly those in commerce and the professions who were expelled from Kenya and Uganda as a consequence of the Africanization of these countries, assimilate more easily but still retain a strong cultural and religious identity. In both cases, though more particularly in the Muslim community, it is the father who traditionally has dealings with the school. However, because he works long hours, it is likely that home–school contact will in many schools be tenuous.

The children are caught between two cultures. Normally extremely obedient, law abiding and respectful, some will be influenced by the white peer group to behaviours that are totally unacceptable in school and that confuse and distress their families. Despite the time and effort spent by Kate's Hill teachers on developing relations with the parents and the school's community, petty thieving, playground bullying, misbehaviour in the school toilets and during the school assembly were on the increase. There was a growing tendency for the parents to blame the school and the school to blame the home.

What to do? In both the UK and the USA it has become evident that explicit curriculum courses in moral education, though effective in promoting moral learning, do not necessarily lead to changes in behaviour. During the 1980s, the work of Kohlberg on the development of a school–community approach to moral education attracted the attention of the School Council's Moral Education Project; and, in the latter part of the decade, what was now becoming known as the Just Community approach (Power, 1988) was studied at first hand by a team from Leicester University. The increasing body of research on school effectiveness on both sides of the Atlantic and in Australia (Rutter et al., 1979; Goodlad, 1984; Sizer, 1986; Beare et al., 1989) suggests that, if schools become concerned with the moral dimension, their effectiveness as learning institutions is also enhanced.

In 1989 the headteacher of Kate's Hill was nominated to attend a seminar in Oxford sponsored by the Social Morality Council, which explored the possibilities of devising and implementing a research and development project to introduce the Just School concept into a pilot group of schools. She recognized that the aims and methodology of the project meshed well with the

GRASP process. Involvement would not mean joining another bandwagon, but rather providing solutions to existing problems.

It was no part of the headteacher's newly restructured management processes to take decisions *ex cathedra*. She presented the outcomes of the seminar to the staff and sought their views. By this time Kate's Hill teachers had become used to the techniques of brainstorming and visually displaying their ideas. Their discussion pointed to the potential coherence between the Just School and the GRASP projects. Involvement in the moral education programme was not merely desirable, it was essential if the caring school was to extend its influence over individual and group behaviour, both within the school and in the community. The process of adopting the Just School Project is an example of restructuring that is promoting change in all four Rs identified by Corbett (1990): roles, rules, relationships and results. It is achieving this by involving staff and pupils in new decision-making roles and relationships, and in redrawing rules for school governance to include parents.

Children are powerful intermediaries and their role can be positive or negative to the relationship between home and school. They have the ability, on the one hand, to suppress or distort information and, on the other hand, to bond home and school. The groundwork for this bonding had already been established. The open school policy was obviously a major step forward. The school also had the full-time services of a home–school liaison assistant, a Muslim woman whose ability to speak with parents in their mother tongue had greatly enhanced communication. Mothers now regularly came to activities in a mobile classroom that had been installed alongside the nursery unit. Within the school, they were contributing to multi-faith festivals and ceremonies, such as Diwali and Id, and to demonstrating traditional costume and cooking from their cultures.

Now, something of profound significance was being asked of parents. They had not always been open about their child's behaviour: Asian parents feel a great sense of shame if their children misbehave and may well seek to avoid the acceptance of any responsibility for that misbehaviour, even to the extent of denying that it took place, whatever the evidence. They were now being asked to become directly involved in behaviour modification contracts, in discussion and counselling, in trusting the school and earning the trust of the school. They were required also to think beyond the behaviour of their own child and into the behaviour of the peer group. This, in a multicultural neighbourhood, was a very significant step. There now had to be a recognition of the differences in behavioural norms both within a culture and across cultures, a mutual acceptance of, for example, the Asian extended family at one extreme, and the white, Afro-Caribbean, or mixed race single-parent family at the other. This required of the school's neighbourhood community a radical reappraisal of relationships. In this kind of process the school cannot control; it can only act as a catalyst.

The LEA was not slow to recognize the school's efforts and their results. The Development Review report, referred to earlier, includes the statement:

> The school has pioneered home–school contracts, discussed and agreed at parent interviews. These are an example of very good practice and have been a major factor in establishing good relationships with parents. Attendance at interviews was almost 100 per cent.

In 1991 there was to be further, more tangible, recognition of the school. It was to receive one of the prestigious Jerrold awards for achievement in education, which carried with it a gift of £5,000 to be used for the benefit of the school and community.

Support for the school

School improvement is enhanced by, and may be dependent on, support from the LEA or district level. Kate's Hill has been fortunate in operating in an LEA which, despite being bombarded by legislative change and starved of physical, material and manpower resources, continues to maintain a caring and effective role.

The contribution of the officials and elected lay members of Dudley LEA to the restructuring process at Kate's Hill and other schools for which it is responsible, and to the effective schools movement in general, can be summed up as follows. Management, it maintains, is getting things done with and through people. To achieve this, clear communication, both vertical and lateral, is essential. At all levels of service it is vital that postholders have confidence in their own management capacity and in that of their superiors. There must be a strong belief in the unity of the team and in supporting shared values, in the evolution of which each has played a part.

The British co-author of this chapter was invited to act as discussant to a Dudley LEA day conference for its officers and advisers held in July 1991. He was able to report that, despite many externally imposed difficulties, the LEA 'had lost none of its sense of purpose and vision' (Poster, 1991). There is clear observational evidence that school restructuring thrives in such a climate.

RESTRUCTURING AT INDIAN HILLS

In the United States there has been a decades-long campaign to persuade and prepare school principals to be instructional leaders, supporting and guiding their schools towards increased instructional effectiveness. More recently, school change and improvement discussions have focused on restructured roles and relationships among principals and staff in making decisions and providing leadership to improve learning for students.

The story of Indian Hills is an example of a school principal developing the role of instructional leader, and simultaneously changing his own views and values as he struggled to accommodate the participation of teachers as instructional decision makers and leaders with him. In the description that follows, short quotations, taken from taped interviews with the principal and staff, are included to convey the feeling and perspective of those who lived this story for several years in the everyday life of their school.

The principal's path to Indian Hills Elementary School crossed several career areas. After graduating with a bachelor's degree in psychology with a minor in business, he served six years as a naval officer. The subsequent eight years were in the private sector in sales and marketing with a multinational, located in southern California. In a mid-life move, he switched to education and relocated in Gallup, New Mexico, where he taught as a relief teacher for a year, as a pilot test to ascertain if he really wanted to be in education. This experience proved positive, so he travelled regularly 140 miles to Albuquerque to obtain educational credentials and a Masters' degree in educational administration. He taught elementary grades 3, 5 and 6 for four years before moving to central office to manage the district's Chapter 1 programme for children in need of additional academic attention. During four years in administering this position, he counselled 3500 families in efforts to support students to remain in school. These counselling activities resulted in his creation of the Hearing Authority, a due process procedure for families of students in danger of school expulsion. In 1985, he was invited to become principal of Indian Hills.

Context of Indian Hills

The Gallup–McKinley County School District (5000 square miles in size) is a remarkable system of 29 schools that includes much of the Navajo Indian Reservation to the north and borders the Zuni Reservation on the south. There are 18 elementary, five middle and six high schools spread over an area larger than the state of New Jersey. About 75 per cent of the district's children qualify for free or reduced cost lunches. The source of family income is predominantly from Indian arts and crafts, tourism, mining and service-related business. While most of the district is rural, Indian Hills snuggles against the eastern edge of Gallup, a city whose population is about 20,000: 50 per cent Native American, 25 per cent Hispanic and 25 per cent Anglo.

In the midst of this high desert setting is Indian Hills Elementary School, with 420 students: 64 per cent Native American, 17 per cent Hispanic and 19 per cent Anglo. Serving these children in grades K–5 is a team of 18 classroom teachers, three kindergarten paraprofessionals, bilingual and Chapter 1 programme staff, and one building administrator. In the immediate vicinity of the school are middle-class and lower-middle-class homes. Students who are bused in from the rural areas live in humble circumstances with only wood-fire heating and no plumbing.

In the beginning

When he first came to Indian Hills six years ago, the principal gave immediate attention to improving facilities and increasing the building's appeal for staff, students and parents and had the 'school painted and spruced up'. He added Navajo and Zuni designs as decorative touches. As this occurred, teachers were heard to wonder: 'Will he allow us to mount students' work on his fresh paint?' They were reassured to learn that he had no objection!

The previous principal had been in the position for many years at Indian Hills. When the new principal accepted the central office's invitation to serve as Indian Hills administrator, the staff were a group of traditional, self-directed individuals, selecting texts and materials, doing their own ordering, determining on which academic discipline to focus and how much time to spend, and exercising power in various ways. Because the school was not in compliance with some of the standards set by the state department of education, the principal 'took over' these unattended items: organizing material orders, managing discipline incidents, enforcing state-level requirements for teaching of various subjects so as to ensure that all students had access to all relevant curricula, and realigning staff assignments in compliance with state standards.

Some teachers were pleased that he was moving ahead, supporting them with such administrative actions, taking hold and providing direction. Others were not so happy; they had had freedom of choice and no pressure for change. They could do whatever they considered appropriate with no accountability procedures.

Because he was busy with administrative logistics, the principal did not immediately concern himself with the school's educational operations; but when he accomplished the necessary basic management functions, he began to turn attention to what was needed for the improvement of the instructional programme. He understood that teachers should be involved and have a major role in any improvement, but he had only just weaned the staff from a situation of 'everyone do your own thing' to a centrally controlled, functioning orderly system. He had done this at the price of some pain, having come to the school from central office, which was regarded by some staff as adversarial rather than supportive. Now, at least, some staff members were generally satisfied that he was doing his appropriate administrative job.

The principal's struggle

Sometimes the principal's role in running a school is in conflict with the teacher's perceived role in educating children. Principals, for example, who value and insist on order and quiet in all classrooms produce frustration in teachers trying to use interactive committee work with students. Principals who are conscientious and responsible in fulfilling their role as administrator and as instructional leader, realize that these two roles, administering and teaching, will be personally defined by those administrators and teachers in the role. The roles must work well together, but must also be distinguished in terms of their ultimate responsibilities. Thus, it is important to make clear who makes decisions about what:

• Is this an administrative decision?
• Is this a professional classroom decision?
• How does it affect children?
• How does it affect teachers?
• How does it affect the school as a whole?

Lack of understanding and agreement about who makes which decisions can cause role ambiguity and decision-making friction that impact on planning for school-wide improvement.

Nearing the end of his first year at Indian Hills, the principal noted that teachers were each working on their own programmes, accustomed to thinking only about their own classroom interests. Breaking old norms and asking them to make collegial decisions that would affect the whole school would surely lead to conflict. Somehow, attitudes, responsibilities and roles – even the principal's – had to change. Part of the dilemma was the principal's role as perceived by his own supervisor and the consensus that they had developed about what his appropriate role would be in the school. Originally, he had been directed to do whatever was necessary to 'clean up' the school which implied an authoritative posture. One of the principal's actions at this time was to engage in dialogue with his central office supervisors to gain their reactions about using shared decision-making processes with his teachers, since this would surely result in more input from the school level to central office. How would this influence the central office's view of the school and what could happen at the school level?

At two different organizational levels and relationships – with teachers and with central office – the principal would have a struggle letting go of his control and defined responsibilities. For any middle-level administrator this is potentially a frightening task. He would have to listen to teachers' input, have confidence in their responsibility and professional judgement in making decisions about instructional improvement, and support them in the activities they chose to undertake in their part of the school world. Somehow everyone would need to be realistic about 'what part of the world each had' and how these interfaced to produce a successfully functioning, holistic organization serving children.

How it started

At this time, opportunity for support came in the form of an inquiry from the New Mexico State Department of Education, which had been contacted by the Southwest Educational Development Laboratory (SEDL) in Austin,

Texas. SEDL proposed to identify one school in each of the five states it served for the purpose of conducting a developmental school improvement programme, with the aim of discovering to what extent instruction could be improved without additional school funding.

In New Mexico, the state department showed an interest in the Gallup–McKinley County School District because of a forward-thinking superintendent. Local principals became involved when the superintendent informed them of the opportunity to be a part of an improvement process. Convinced that SEDL's external assistance could be a resource for the goals that he was considering, the Indian Hills principal submitted a proposal to the district's Assistant Superintendent for Elementary Instruction and was soon accepted for participation in a project about which little was articulated except that it was an opportunity to support and fulfil his newly emerging vision.

The principal had a direction in his mind for the school and what its improvement mission would be. He presented his ideas to staff about increasing students' writing skills; teachers reported that it was important for the principal to have a plan to start with. Several of the staff were enthused immediately; however, the principal recognized the importance of broad staff involvement in planning, and listened to the ideas of enthusiasts and cynics alike. Over time, as more teachers became enthusiastic, the plan evolved into a broadly encompassing series of school changes and restructuring of decision-making roles based on input from school and SEDL staff. Although it was hard for the principal and the teachers who were engaged early in the effort to accept the fact that all teachers were not committed, they learned not to spend too much time worrying about those who did not see the vision right away.

With SEDL's support, the principal requested a consultant to introduce the staff to a research-based process for planning for change. The consultant's influence would be used to help staff consider how to reshape schooling at Indian Hills. As it turned out, change for Indian Hills meant:

- realizing that there may be a better way;
- analysing the present condition;
- doing a needs assessment based on test scores and other data such as student and teacher absentees, discipline incidents and parent involvement;
- deciding on a course of action best suited for the staff and children of this particular school;
- developing an action plan.

No one told the staff what to do. SEDL staff supported but did not intrude as the school staff independently worked out a course of action. The work was not easy but something important happened: teachers at Indian Hills began to believe in themselves.

The change process: focus on students

At the end of his first year at Indian Hills, the principal had gone beyond the school's data to solicit input for improvement planning: he visited the Personnel Director of Sandia National Laboratory, a nearby scientific technology facility, to enquire what skill deficiencies there were in applicants for posts there. Verbal and written communication skills were identified by the personnel officer. Competency in critical thinking was another area identified by the district's superintendent as important to look into for student learning. To the staff, writing and thinking seemed to be linked processes. Based on the school achievement data, external assessments, perceptions of the school from the community, and some of the teachers' judgements, the faculty determined that critical thinking and writing would be their focus for study, review and consideration for improvement plans. The plans would be developed during the second semester of the principal's second year.

At this point the principal, who, in his own words, 'exercised a lot more autonomy than I do now', formed four task forces or teams of staff to be responsible for planning: one to study critical thinking, another writing, the third to focus on computer education, and the fourth to act as the Internal Affairs Committee, a support group. Knowing that teachers were critical to make everything work, the principal assigned to each team a strong teacher, one who had expressed interest in leadership, and invited staff to sign up for the team of their choice. His plan was then to facilitate, encourage and motivate the teacher teams. To support the teams, the principal actively sought participation inside and outside the school to achieve the goal of improved student performance in writing and critical thinking as well as computer processes. Teachers who were 'into computers' signed up for that team. The critical thinking group began to explore this new area for student learning, at so early a stage in its development that few people were identifying what this meant in a school. Later in their efforts, Indian Hills School became involved in a nationwide effort that developed, piloted and revised materials for national dissemination.

The change process: focus on the staff

At the beginning of the third year, the Internal Affairs Committee was asked to survey the entire staff about workshops they wanted and schedules they preferred for the school year; for instance, when to have Open House for parents. The committee summarized the information and made a recommendation for the principal's decision. This effort at broadening decision making, according to teachers, was not satisfactory: there was a distinct gap between administration and staff. Communication between these two entities 'must come closer together', the teachers concluded. Thereupon was born the Shared Decision-Making Committee, designed by principal and teachers alike.

This committee was comprised of an elected teacher representative from each grade level, special education, library services, the counsellor, secretarial staff, and teacher aides. The role of committee members was to solicit concerns and ideas from their constituents, share these with the committee in its weekly meetings, return to constituents with information and obtain their views for making decisions. Thus, a systematic, representative approach to school decision making was developed. More people were satisfied with this process because, while they did not have to go to so many large group meetings, they had nevertheless input into decisions, and the lines of communication were kept open. Some staff were heard to complain, 'Now it's the committee making all the decisions', an accusation immediately countered by a suggestion that any member might drop in on the meetings and participate at any time. The committee is still considering this suggestion.

During the principal's fourth year, the Indian Hills staff observed the decision-making committee receiving their input and making decisions, with the principal seldom, if ever, overriding a decision. He allowed them to be risk takers. 'They didn't have to feel afraid or be intimidated; he allowed them to have the possibility to fail, or not be successful.' The committee became the model for the rest of the staff. Staff now say what they are thinking whether others are likely to agree or not, very different from the situation several years ago. Indian Hills' model of shared decision making has spread district-wide. Central office has suggested that school improvement planning teams become a feature of every school. The role of the teams is to take responsibility to help their schools develop a goal and mission statement and improvement objectives for the year.

As the decision-making process was being further restructured during the principal's fourth year, some teachers expressed their desire for a stronger and more authoritative role and responsibility for the school's operations. They pushed for the teaching staff to 'take charge of everything'. Taking charge included, for instance, scheduling classes and meetings; convening the staff; and managing and allocating the school's budgetary resources to teachers. These ideas were promoted by a small but vocal group of teachers. The principal let this experiment take place and play itself out. The principal conceded areas of authority and action to the staff: those of identifying and obtaining resources for all the committees, providing staff development for everyone, managing adjustments to the schedules and calendar, and monitoring to ascertain who needed what or had problems in need of resolution. 'I didn't fight them. I was still there to help. I worked on moving individuals during this time rather than working across the whole school.' While ideally several persons are needed to guide and support change efforts across a school, there needs to be one person responsible for everything working. Typically, when 'everyone is in charge, no one is in charge'. Thus it was at Indian Hills. 'I regretted losing most of a school year in our schoolwide effort, but in some individual classrooms, good things were happening.'

During this period it appeared that no school-wide progress was being accomplished. Teachers complained they were not getting the resources they needed, and staff development was non-existent. No decisions were made to organize meetings or to pull the committees together for development and action. The principal, therefore, called a meeting to make an opportunity for teachers to review and assess progress on what it was they had planned for and wanted to have happen. 'It didn't work out; we didn't take responsibility to do what we said we would', they concluded after agreeing they had been given the opportunity. Their new decision was to work for a balance of power in decision making, delineating the decisions that needed to be made by a single person, the principal, and those to be made by the entire staff. The principal's early vision of academic improvement processes and evolutionary restructuring of decision-making procedures was very much in alignment with the desires of the staff generally. It took time, experimentation and continuous assessment of the efforts to arrive at arrangements satisfactory to all.

The change process: resources

Beginning with the establishment of the four committees during the second year and continuing thereafter, the principal consistently supported the staff's change of practice and instructional improvement. He encouraged all staff to seek information and assistance from all possible sources. Furthermore, 'he actively sought resources for teachers to do explorations, to access information, and to have inservice and training'. For the staff development the teachers thought they needed, the principal managed to get the resources, sometimes by devious means! He supported teachers who wanted to explore the IBM Writing to Read Program, which uses computers to develop writing and reading skills, arranging for them to travel to Red Mesa, one of the Navajo reservation schools, to study the IBM laboratory operation first hand for a full day in order to make recommendations about use of the programme at Indian Hills. Subsequently, the principal and the leader of the Computer Committee interacted, developed a proposal for a grant to subsidize the programme, and were successful in acquiring resources for this effort.

This principal believed that the school leader should always have a vision of 'what we, as staff, should be learning that is a year in advance of what we're doing now'. It takes that long 'to plan for a new program, gain support, and work out the kinks'. As a result of such long-range planning and looking to the future, he took three teachers on a 700 mile trip to explore literature-based reading in action, in a setting where it was working. The teachers lived in the classrooms for several days and returned home to recommend the programme to the faculty. Through further arrangements by the principal, Indian Hills became a pilot school for the programme. Two additional teachers were provided with materials and special training in the programme, expanding the base of a core group to carry this change across the school.

Reflections and results

Indian Hills now operates in a different way from six years previously. Teachers interact, work collegially, share and contribute to each other's work. They look for information that committees other than their own might utilize. They serve breakfast to each other in honour of various staff birthdays and other occasions. There is overall involvement in planning, decision making, celebrating and influencing what goes on in the school; a dramatic change in roles and relationships. Such a role change was exemplified by teachers at several grade levels participating for the first time in hiring new members to fill vacancies in their team.

These changes have been accepted, practices routinized, and an attitude adopted of 'We want to be as good as we can be. We have an atmosphere of teachers as learners and we feel good as professionals.' 'It's not a job', they say, it is 'our profession'. They are invested in their profession and in their role as decision makers and teachers. When funding last year became available to send one staff member to the National Association for Supervision and Curriculum Development's annual convention, teachers were invited to express interest and develop a statement of how their attendance would benefit their classroom. Based on this input, the Shared Decision-Making Committee selected a teacher to represent the faculty at the convention.

Their new professionalism focuses on teachers as learners, linked to improve student outcomes and to result in school-wide improvement. This attitude has come about through a lot of hard work to get better and through liking the idea of being better – this serves as a continuing motivation. The staff room talk centres on instructional strategies and not on salary levels.

A recent survey of staff to assess areas of strength and those in need of attention revealed the highest positive scores on staff morale and the staff's belief in their own capacity to change and do anything they decide to do: their strong sense of efficacy. The staff and principal have been through a lot and out of it has come trust, the basic element for working together.

Several staff expressed the importance of having access to a strong outside person, one who can add to the vision, help launch the initial effort, continue to push for implementing the school's improvement plan, and support and encourage individuals to change. This external person is particularly needed by the administrator, as a person in whom to confide, with whom to debrief, and from whom to expect encouragement and the push to continue self-change. The Indian Hills principal, teachers say, has changed a lot from 'This is where I want to go; this is what we're going to do', to real involvement of the entire staff in shared decision making.

He is still growing and changing. This year he considered making the new study groups' participation mandatory for all staff, but teachers convinced him it should be voluntary. On the other hand, in the past he has put great emphasis on standardized test scores. This year, in the light of the new reading programme that does not necessarily coincide with what is tested on standardized tests, he told them that the programme was more important than whether it tested well. He is willing to trust teachers and risk the programme's testability.

The account of Indian Hills is a three-tiered story: of school improvement to benefit students; of restructuring relationships and roles of staff in making decisions about how to plan and conduct school improvement; and of the principal's personal change that allowed restructuring to happen. Teachers advise that the principal's next goal should focus on being more visible and accessible to students. Since the changed discipline strategy is effective with children, he now has to see few children. Therefore, teachers say, he needs to be communicating with them in other ways. When the SEDL consultant asked the staff if there were plans to involve students in classroom-level shared decision making, moving this structure down to the child level, there was a long pause. Perhaps the next chapter in Indian Hills' story will focus on restructuring decision making within classrooms, with children.

COMPARING SCHOOL LEADERS' STRATEGIES

Before examining the strategies used by the two school leaders to restructure their schools, it may be helpful to review the contextual factors present.

Contextual similarities

There is a modest Anglo student population in both: 27 per cent in Kate's Hill and 19 per cent in Indian Hills. Other ethnic groups make up the balance: a combined 73 per cent of Caribbean, Pakistani and other Asians at Kate's Hill; 81 per cent of Hispanic and Native American students at Indian Hills. Indian Hills with 420 pupils, K–5, is similar in enrolment to Kate's Hill with 380 pupils aged 5–11 and 100 part-time nursery school pupils aged 3–5, the early age nursery pupils adding a unique dimension at Kate's Hill.

Other demographic data in the two settings appear to differ, with Kate's Hill situated in an inner city urban setting of unemployment and some overcrowded housing. Indian Hills is located in a small town of 20,000, in a school community of middle socio-economic status, but with low socio-economic status pupils bused in from rural areas.

STRATEGIES AND CROSS-NATIONAL SIMILARITIES

Not only do the size and nature of minority student distributions in the two school settings appear similar, but the two leaders share many of the same strategies. In the summaries that appear below, each leader's actions are enumerated, followed by a brief discussion.

Kate's Hill

The headteacher:

1 Took advantage of money for building improvements to remodel the teaching areas to be more open and support year-group areas and collegiality of staff, and to assign managerial responsibility to teachers with above basic-scale salaries through open discussion with staff.
2 Conducted staff meetings to brainstorm curriculum development in the school, resulting in a mission statement/statement of aim for the school.
3 Initiated parent visitation policy for parents' open access in the school.
4 Took advantage of inclement weather day (with students absent) to interview all staff members to learn how they saw their career development and what kind of training and support they needed.
5 Brought management and communication issues to staff meetings for open discussion for staff to solve cooperatively, introducing collegiate management.
6 Developed proposal/application for funding as pilot site for innovative project.
7 Accepted support and assistance of external consultant and utilized fully workshop opportunities that were provided.
8 Put discipline into classroom teachers' domain and related it to teachers' instructional methodologies and relationship with classes.
9 Brainstormed with staff, using GRASP innovation approaches, how to cope with rapid curriculum development, whereby curriculum teams, rather than leaders, developed.
10 Bypassed GRASP decision-making processes (using the power of her status), in promoting community involvement role, realized her error when challenged by a teacher, stepped back from confrontation, and revisited it after an interval using the GRASP decision-making paradigm.
11 Attended a seminar to explore adopting a moral education programme that restructures relationships of staff, pupils, home; took the opportunity to staff who analysed its features, its fit with their school, and who decided to implement.

Indian Hills

The principal:

1 Submitted a winning proposal to become the school in the state selected for a developmental project on school improvement.
2 Accepted colleagueship from an educational research and development agency to support the school's change efforts.
3 Requested a consultant to introduce staff to a research-based process for planning change, an effort whose purpose was to break normative thinking

and current paradigms, and to initiate planning to reshape schooling at this site.

4 Guided a needs assessment process towards identification of four instructional areas for study and review.

5 Turned the study of issues and academic areas of concern over to staff committees that were given total autonomy, and that involved all professionals and paraprofessionals.

6 Supported, assisted, encouraged and provided resources for the four committees' work, providing subject area specialists, for example.

7 Wrote proposals for additional funding to gain IBM Writing to Read Program, a computerized approach to language development.

8 Acceded to staff leaders' interest to have for themselves a larger voice and ownership of the entire change process, by stepping back to see how this would work.

9 Allowed this experiment to play out until, subsequently, teachers requested the principal's more direct involvement again.

In order to identify patterns of common actions, strategies used by both leaders to restructure their schools are set out in Table 4.1.

Table 4.1 Restructuring activities

Kate's Hill Headteacher's actions	Strategies	Indian Hills Principal's actions
#2, 5, 9, 11	Brainstormed with staff or gave staff licence to solve problems and make decisions	#5
#6	Developed proposals for funding	#1, 7
#7	Accepted or invited external assister help	#2, 3
#10	Stepped back from confrontation	#8, 9
[7 of 11 reported actions]		[7 of 9 reported actions]

Both leaders employed four strategies in their restructuring efforts: collegial problem solving and decision making; generation of funding; external assistance; and confrontation avoidance. A majority of the actions of the Kate's Hill headteacher fell in the category of what she called collegiate management, with one action in each of the remaining three categories. The principal of Indian Hills, on the other hand, took actions evenly balanced across the four categories.

Both leaders were emphasising the 'breaking of old norms and narrow paradigms' (Indian Hills) and the 'breaking open the little boxes of the school facility' that constrained teacher interaction (Kate's Hill). Both leaders had arrived at schools whose prior administrators had been in the post for a considerable time. At the entry point of the new heads, work conditions at Kate's Hill were characterized as inflexible and rigid, whereas staff at Indian Hills were traditional and self-directed. Nothing from either site hints at teacher interaction: sharing, learning and growing. The sites seem to have been protected from, or oblivious to, any input that might have stimulated broader dialogue and thinking.

When these leaders came to their new sites and their current assignments, they brought with them new ideas of leadership and how they might interact with staff. These new visions focused on changes in administrator–teacher roles and relationships so that the total staff collectively might go about the job of establishing rules and procedures for their schools. Thus, a significant set of activities used by the two leaders was in setting the staff free of old norms to engage them more actively in the operations of the school. In this area, much of the restructuring work at Kate's Hill focused on activities that were both indirect (using structural improvement to open the school staff's access to each other, action #1) and direct (leading staff in brainstorming solutions to the school's problems, #2, 5, 9, 11). The principal of Indian Hills also used opportunities for indirect actions (using an external agency to stimulate thinking for change, #2) and a more direct approach (organizing staff in committees, with a teacher leader and conveying complete autonomy to the committees to study issues and design solutions, #5).

Like many other successful school leaders, these two invested their time and energy in proposal development in order to gain additional funding (Indian Hills, #7; Kate's Hill, #6) and to gain from programmatic involvement with other agencies (Indian Hills, #1). Similarly, though without the requirements for a formally developed proposal, Kate's Hill became involved in a new programme through invitation (action #11).

Cohen (1987) maintains that it is difficult for many schools to bring about change without the aid of an external force. One might speculate that in Kate's Hill and Indian Hills schools a new force or source of stimulation for the school arrived with the new headteacher and principal who soon became internal to the system. Both these leaders, however, recognized the usefulness of additional external assistance for their efforts, and invited and accepted such support structures (action #7 Kate's Hill; #2, 3 Indian Hills).

Finally, both leaders were sensitive to the consequence of their actions and recognized when to withdraw from action (Kate's Hill, #10; Indian Hills, #8, 9).

In addition to taking account of these activities that the two leaders shared (Table 4.1) and the several that were undertaken singly by them (referred to in the lists of each principal's strategies), and reading between the lines of their stories, it is possible to articulate a number of lessons to be learned from these school leaders.

Lessons learned

By synthesizing across the accounts of the two school leaders, several lessons can be drawn that remind us of Rutherford's five effective principal factors: visioning, translating the vision, providing a supportive environment, monitoring, and intervening both to reinforce and to take corrective action (Rutherford, 1985).

First, these leaders had a new vision of the structure of their schools towards which they were moving, even though they may not have had well worked out or explicit details of the new openness and interactiveness they sought for the entire school staff. To change to more collegial roles and relationships, their vision included the involvement of teachers drawing in the details. They believed that the school would function in a more effective way if they could break up the boxes of rigidity and inflexibility, and the old norms of traditional practice and self-direction by each individual teacher. The leaders took advantage of opportunities, to which the less change-oriented school administrator might pay little attention, in order to expand and enhance their vision and their repertoire of programmes and practices that might become part of the vision.

These leaders recognized that changing existing behaviours and beliefs to realize the vision required a great deal of time. Designing new arrangements to create new roles and relationships, even when collegially including all staff, requires time for staff consideration of the new ways, their personal acceptance of them, and integration of the new structures into daily routine and practice.

Because they knew not to expect results immediately, the leaders allowed time, knowing they must re-teach staff and allow them to re-experience new activities. This is exemplified by the leaders engaging the staff consistently over time in brainstorming, decision making and problem solving. The leaders did not assume that one experience with a new organizational structure would lead to completion of the vision.

Helping the staff to understand and move towards the vision was reinforced through the leaders' actions and articulation of the new vision, and through articulating the expectation that the staff would contribute their visions and goals. Their participation was, in fact, part of the vision. Expanding and refining the vision through collegiality and consensus building was what the vision was about.

Bringing about change requires a supportive environment including both human and material resources. The leaders developed proposals to secure additional resources for staff development, training and technical assistance, and for necessary equipment and programmatic specifications. They were sensitive to individual staff, considering their expertise, needs and particular career desires. Multicultural diversity of the school staff and the school community was another important element the leaders considered in providing a climate and environment conducive to change.

Monitoring progress towards the new model being envisioned and making mid-course adjustments were additional lessons to be gleaned from these leaders. When it was necessary to take a fall-back position as a result of observing and collecting data relative to the restructuring efforts, patience was demanded of the school leaders. Finding their own appropriate roles of power and authority, juxtaposed with staff autonomy and shared decision making, required these leaders consistently to monitor themselves and the staff as they searched for, experimented with and grew towards new relationships and restructured arrangements. This was a complex undertaking that involved their consideration of individual staff needs, the organization's needs to function well, and also their own personal needs of fulfilment as the organizational leader.

Not surprisingly, the lessons from these two effective leaders parallel neatly the behaviours identified by Rutherford of effective principals in general. However, these two principals, working on school restructuring efforts, significantly accommodated the time dimension necessary for the staff to become mobilized in a new governance and decision-making structure for their schools. Enabling staff to develop and implement such new roles and relationships requires not only time, but training and re-teaching for mastery of new and complex behaviours. Time and training appear to be particularly demanding to support the process of redesigning problem identification, solution generation, and solution selection in the shared decision-making models to which these school leaders and their staff aspired.

Careful monitoring by leaders who are implementing school change provides the opportunity for assessing staff needs for additional time and training. However, too frequently these needs are missed or glossed over by leaders impatient to move on. The leaders in these stories exercised patience, provided time, and arranged additional experiences for the staff in order to realize the vision and goals. These T-lessons – change requires Time; change requires Training – are significant axioms contributing to our understanding of leaders' roles in restructuring.

The lessons delineated above were derived from the demanding series of functions and roles that these leaders played in their school restructuring. As both accounts have indicated, these roles can most successfully be played out in schools located in local education authorities or districts, the staffs of which themselves demonstrate the same set of behaviours: goal setting, support, monitoring, adjusting. Higher-level education authorities in both countries are beginning to consider the desirability for demonstrating these functions at the state and national levels. It is no surprise that these same functions have been identified as those typically important in successful change processes.

These lessons, however, should not be construed as standard recipes or step-by-step procedures for restructuring. Each school's effort is essentially idiosyncratic and will require its own unique set of leader support and guidance. These two leaders' stories reveal not only their specific behaviours in a particular setting, but also the dilemmas encountered and personal investments made in rearranging operational structures in their schools. That leaders themselves change and grow is not surprising. That we have the opportunity to learn from the personal growth experiences of these leaders while their schools are restructuring is not so common.

Acknowledgements

This chapter owes much to the presentation made by the authors to the 1991 AERA conference in Chicago, and to the principals of the two schools which feature as case studies. The authors acknowledge the contribution of Pearl White, headteacher of Kate's Hill, Dudley, and Martin Stowe, principal of Indian Hills, New Mexico, and their teachers.

REFERENCES

Beare, H., Caldwell, B.J. and Millikan, R.H. (1989) *Creating an Excellent School: Some New Management Techniques*, London: Routledge.

Blum, R.E. and Butler, J.A. (eds) (1989) *School Leader Development for School Improvement*, Leuven: ACCO.

Cohen, M. (1987) 'Improving school effectiveness: Lessons from research', in V. Richardson-Koehler (ed.) *Educator's Handbook: A Research Perspective*, New York: Longman.

Corbett, H.D. (1990) *On the Meaning of Restructuring*, Philadelphia: Research for Better Schools.

Goodlad, J.I. (1984) *A Place Called School*, New York: McGraw-Hill.

Greenfield, T.B. (1986) 'Leaders and schools: Wilfulness and nonnatural order in organizations', in T.J. Sergiovanni and J.E. Corbally (eds) *Leadership and Organizational Culture: New Perspectives on Administrative Theory and Practice*, Urbana and Chicago: University of Chicago Press.

Hall, G.E., Wallace, R.C. and Dossett, W.A. (1973) *A Developmental Conceptualization of the Adoption Process within Educational Institutions*, Austin, TX: Research and Development Center for Teacher Education, The University of Texas.

Hopes, C. (1986) *The School Leader and School Improvement: Case Studies from Ten OECD Countries*, Leuven: ACCO.

Hord, S.M. (1987) *Evaluating Educational Innovations*, London: Croom Helm.

Poster, C. (1991) *Education: The current issues*, A report on the Dudley LEA day conference, 9 July 1991, mimeo, Dudley: Dudley LEA.

Power, C. (1988) 'The Just Community approach to moral education', *Journal of Moral Education* 17(3): 195.

Raywid, M.A. (1990) 'The evolving effort to improve schools: Pseudo-reform, incremental reform, and restructuring', *Phi Delta Kappan* 72(2): 139–43.

Rutherford, W.L. (1985) 'School principals as effective leaders', *Phi Delta Kappan* 69(1): 31–4.

Rutter, M., Maughan, M., Mortimore, P. and Ouston, J. (1979) *Fifteen Thousand Hours: Secondary Schools and their Effects on Children*, London: Open Books.

Sizer, T.R. (1986) 'Rebuilding: First steps by the coalition of essential schools', *Phi Delta Kappan* 68(1): 38–42.

Stego, N.E., Gielen, K., Glatter, R. and Hord, S.M. (1987) *The Role of School Leaders in School Improvement*, Leuven: ACCO.

Topping, G. (1985) 'The role of the community: The Swiss example', *Education*, February.

Chapter 5

A values perspective on school-based management

Glenda Campbell-Evans

Schools as we know them have some attributes and characteristics in common. We can make statements about schools as a group, the expectations we hold for them and for the work with which they are charged. There are also distinctive features of schools; aspects which in some way make a particular school distinguishable, unique and identifiable from others. A particular combination of classroom factors and school-wide factors defines each school. Part of the difference between schools can be accounted for by the nature and expectations of their student and community populations, through school programmes and procedures, staff priorities and concerns, and their direction or focus. The levels of collegiality, empowerment, and staff and parental involvement in decision making also play a role. Two bodies of research literature, *school effectiveness* and *school-based management*, explore and describe these differences.

EFFECTIVE SCHOOLS' RESEARCH

School effectiveness research has focused on the differences between schools in an attempt to uncover the key elements of effective practice. This body of research seeks in general to unlock the secrets of effectiveness in terms of what difference teachers and administrators can make to students' experience of, and success in, school. The concept of effectiveness itself, when applied to schools, begs clarification. Much of the early school effectiveness research was conducted in American schools in low socio-economic areas and effectiveness was defined in terms of standardized tests scores. This narrow focus drew criticism as it raised the issues of effectiveness for whom, by whose standards and on whose terms? How does one define effectiveness? Is it the same to all, for all? What influences our response?

In Holmes and Wynne's (1989, p. 256) view, 'The school effectiveness research assumes that primacy is to be given to academic work, or perhaps in a few cases to academic work and character development.' They suggest that 'one possible explanation of the effective schools' research is that effective schools are those where the principal and teachers subscribe to the value of the criteria attested to be effective schools' research' (p. 256). Those criteria common across a number of studies include: high expectations, a focus on learning, effective use of time, professional development for staff, safe and orderly environment, use of consistent discipline, regular monitoring of achievement, rewards for performance, involvement of the community and strong leadership. These factors are generally reported in the literature as key elements of effectiveness. What influences the extent to which individuals accept or reject these are key elements of school effectiveness. Their judgements will be based on the aggregate of their knowledge, skills, values and experiences of schools.

SCHOOL-BASED MANAGEMENT

Developing from the effective schools' research, the concept of school-based management has attracted interest and application in varying degrees throughout the Western world. Currently, there is limited empirical evidence to indicate whether or not the approach has suitability or efficacy. The existing literature does, however, warrant attention. Writers such as Purkey and Smith (1983) suggest that it is through the adoption of self-management approaches and techniques that the characteristics of effective schools can be developed and promoted. Tied to the trend of decentralization, school-based management refers to the management of physical and human resources at the school rather than at a system or centralized level. Caldwell and Spinks (1988) define a self-managing school as one, 'for which there has been significant and consistent decentralization to the school level of authority to make decisions related to the allocation of resources' (p. 5). Here, types of resources include knowledge, technology, power, material, people, time and finance.

School-based management demands greater participation by staff and parents in the policy- and decision-making processes of the school. By definition, decisions are made collectively and collegially by relevant stakeholders, not individually by the principal and/or deputy principal of the school. Within the context of self-managing schools, opportunities exist for increased professionalism for staff and for parent–staff partnerships in the education of students. The development of school-based decision-making groups and processes of school development planning in Western Australia are examples of moves towards greater decentralization and the self-determining schools called for in the Ministry of Education's *Better Schools* (1987) report.

Concern with the quality of the teaching–learning process, increasing devolution of responsibility and accountability to the school level, a more diverse client base, and ever-increasing pressure on schools to educate and prepare students for the world and jobs of tomorrow dominate the attention of educators in many countries around the world. Professionals cannot escape the contradictions evident in the public's expectations for schooling. Contradictions such as public despair with education systems, but parental support for the teachers of their children; pressure for cost effectiveness and efficiency at a government level, but indignation at the closure of the local school; and cries from some employer groups for specific job-related skills, but demands for generic thinking and living skills from others, are common. Such contradictions exemplify the diversity of the value positions of stakeholders. One challenge of school-based management is for principals to identify and negotiate the common ground which lies between disparate views.

Changes in educational thought and practice are necessary to cope with the circumstances described. The effective schools' and self-managed schools' research provides a context for discussion about the options and directions available to those responsible for the management of schools. While the primary concern of the classroom teacher continues to focus on the teaching and learning process, the school principal must expend energy and attention on school-level issues which have consequences for classroom and school-level practice.

This chapter addresses some of these issues surrounding the principals' role in school-based management and school effectiveness. Specifically, it will do so from a value orientation, that is from a view which proposes that recognition of the importance of the role and influence of values is useful in exploring the world of schools and the administration of them. Traditional approaches to school administration vary in their emphasis on aspects of leadership, vision, participation and culture. The level of importance and meaning attached to each element differs considerably from one perspective to another. For example, leadership can be viewed as the responsibility to: ensure smooth operation of school procedures in order to allow teachers to teach; cater for positive human relations among and between students, staff and parents; be directly and actively involved in the teaching and learning process. These different orientations illustrate the variety possible within the manifestation of leadership. In addition, leadership itself may be attributed greater or lesser significance in relation to other elements such as vision, participation and culture. Consequently, in one school, leadership-related issues may be the dominant force, while in another, issues of culture may typify practice.

It is proposed that the discussions which surround each approach can be enlightened when placed in a value framework. How does a value orientation to the role of principal manifest itself in the experience of school? Although often presented and discussed in isolation, the critical elements of school leadership and school effectiveness are interactive and interrelated. It may be helpful to conceptualize the separate parts as fitting together in a way which sees values reflected through personal and public means.

Values are, first, private and personal. They provide a structure for individual choice between alternatives. Values are displayed, exhibited and revealed through words and actions. What we say and do reflects our value position. The style of leadership, the emphasis in the school vision, priorities and purposes, the culture which is supported, developed and encouraged are all reflections of values. A vision or mission statement is a public statement of those values. It may be the leader's personal vision or it may be shared by some or all of the members of the organization. The style and priorities of the leadership will influence the extent to which the values espoused in the vision statement are shared. Then, it is through the school culture that the values are transmitted and practised. The culture is the manifestation of publicly stated personal values which have come to be shared and endorsed by others within the organization.

FACTS AND VALUES

Facts and values both influence school life. Facts are the 'is' component of experience. In the context of school improvement, the concrete, identifiable elements of effectiveness – test scores, enrolment figures, retention rates, curriculum documents – represent the facts. Facts provide an information pool which can be drawn upon when an individual is faced with making a choice between alternatives. In the course of the school day, a principal makes numerous decisions, frequently choosing between alternatives. Decisions ranging from the trivial to the significant, from the involvement of one to many, from the immediate to the long range, from the planned to the unexpected, are virtually continuous in the school setting. For principals, the process of decision making is an integral and central part of their daily activity. This process is aided by reliable and available information – facts of the matter. It is these more routine, *information-rich* situations that Schon (1983) refers to as *high ground* tasks. When school leaders are clear about the facts, the goals and possible obstacles and procedures for overcoming those obstacles, they are on the *high ground*.

Every school has its own high ground. In some cases the high ground will be self-constructed; in others, it will be imposed. Educators create high ground through the development of policy, rules, regulations and established practice. The high ground tasks of bus scheduling, timetabling, ordering equipment and supplies, inducting relief teachers into school routines, meeting procedures, and information systems are conducted according to a system or routine which reduces the need for judgement in each instance. Educators also create high ground by articulating goals and directions. This provides a framework and boundaries for decision making in respect to the stated goal by limiting viable options. The development of a goal statement is generally a demanding process but the product provides structure for later decisions. These subsequent decisions are made on the high ground.

Principals may be alone on the high ground, or they may be in the company of others. The nature of self-managing schools requires increased levels of staff and parental involvement in decision making so it is no longer enough for the leader alone to be clear about the facts, the goals and the possible obstacles. For collaborative decision making to occur, information must be shared. This has implications for communication patterns in the school and for the skills required by the school leaders. In addition to the skills of gathering information, generating alternatives, and making a choice of one from many, the principal of a self-managing school must also be skilled in providing and clarifying facts for others, mediating between different interpretations and preferences, and negotiating a consensus. Old individual practices must give way to new group processes.

Choices still need to be made between the *factual* alternatives generated in a decision-making situation. What guides this action? Facts and possible alternatives are interpreted through one's system of values; the 'ought' component. For Rokeach (1973) a value system is 'a learned organization of principles and rules to help one choose between alternatives' (p. 14). Through a sense of the 'ought', the facts of the matter are screened and evaluated. The individual selects appropriate action based upon the fit of facts to values. Kluckhohn's (1951, p. 395) definition of values specifies that 'A value is a conception, explicit or implicit, distinctive of an individual or characteristic of a group, of the desirable which influences the selection from available modes, means, and ends of action.' Kluckhohn specifies *desirable, conception* and *selection* as the three focus words in the definition. The concept of the *desirable* operates at an affective level. Here, one refers to what one and/or others ought to want. The term is used to highlight the notion that values always have an affective dimension. Use of *conception* in the definition emphasises the cognitive element of value. Value is identified as a logical construct. Kluckhohn, therefore, recognizes and incorporates reason and feeling into his treatment of values. *Selection* is used as a neutral synonym for choice.

From this conception of the desirable emerges a code or standard of behaviour. This standard reflects a *fit* between facts and values. Values are expressed through action and through one's judgement of the actions of others. They are linked to needs and this link influences the conception of appropriate action which is adopted. Values guide the evaluation of objectives and actions and determine a judgement of right or good. Values shape an ongoing, persistent standard or code for action which exists over time. Individuals distinguish between good and bad, right and wrong, based on their value system.

The influence of facts and of values operates simultaneously in our world and does so in an interactive fashion. Facts and values influence each other and consequently are changed by the influence. Values are, in part, shaped by facts and subsequently shape facts through interpretation; each is a derivative of the other. When there are facts to inform decisions, they are considered through a value filter. The balance of facts and values in a decision-making situation is dependent upon a number of factors including: sensitivity and importance of the issue, available information and time, precedents, diversity of stakeholder views, experience, attitude and skill of decision makers. As the situation slides away from the high ground, values have a more pronounced role in the decision-making process.

Schools, however, rarely function in routine, consistent ways. Rather, the nature of schools may best be described as ambiguous, uncertain and changing. If we accept this interpretation of schools as organizations in which behaviour is non-rational, then we understand that facts, clear alternatives and 'best' alternatives are not the norm. Patterson *et al.* (1986) propose an image of non-rationality which focuses around the five key elements of goals, power, decision making, external environment, and teaching. They outline the difference between a rational perspective and a non-rational one for each element. For decision making, for example, they propose that from a rational point of view, 'the decision making process makes sure that all feasible options are considered' (p. 40). The non-rational viewpoint emphasises that the decision-making process 'usually ends up with a limited number of options to consider, constrained by factors such as politics, economics and finances' (p. 40) and the facts available for each.

System initiatives may be interpreted in very different ways depending upon the thinking of the individual or staff in terms of rational and non-rational perspectives. School planning, for example, if seen as a prescriptive exercise could be interpreted as a system-level attempt to impose rational processes and procedures on to schools. Alternatively, school personnel could perceive the policy as a guide to planning and practice which is adaptable to the needs and priorities of each school community. It is reasonable to describe differences in the level of adoption of the policy in terms of what clients theorize regarding the system's intent. The same system initiative could be interpreted as system support by one school community and system interference by another. The point may vary according to the degree of real or perceived rationality.

If we accept that a non-rational view may be more applicable to the reality of school life than traditional explanations of schools as organizations, then clear, precise and relevant facts may well not be available or be recognized by principals in the course of their decision-making and leadership behaviours. When leaders have only a vague understanding of the situation, have access to limited or inadequate information, do not know what a better situation would look like, they are in what Schon (1983) refers to as the *swamp*.

The distinction between the *high ground* and the *swamp* is not definitive. It is not possible to categorize situations as one or the other. One school's swamp will be another's high ground. The difference lies in the different knowledge, skills, attitudes and experiences of significant players. Different schools, on different issues, will be more willing or more able to move towards high ground as a result of their composite relevant knowledge, skills, attitudes and experiences. School communities can *reclaim the swamp* through a concerted effort of data collection, value articulation, recognition and consolidation of diverse views. By synthesising the facts, values and experiences of the community, high ground is created. School development plans serve as an example. Once members of the school community engage in the process of school development planning and produce the plan, they create high ground for themselves. Since the document represents agreement within the school community on priorities, goals and directions, it serves as a blueprint for decision making. The blueprint helps provide the answer to many of the queries that arise daily. The 'once swampy issue' of allocating monies, for example, becomes a high ground task once the development plan specifies school priorities and directions. The plan contributes towards providing the answers to spending questions.

In the 1990s, schools are collecting and tabulating more information than ever before in a bid to be accountable for student outcomes. Principals may be *in the swamp* over issues of information quantity or quality. In the case of quantity, a principal may not have collected enough information; information that may be readily available and accessible. The situation could also be 'unduly swampy' due to the quality of information; that is, the principal has not accessed information which could inform the decision. With more, and relevant, information a principal could be placed on the high ground. The distinction between *high ground* or routine problems, and *swampy* or ill-structured situations is one of degree, not kind, and the swampier the task, the more dominant the role of values.

Greenfield (1986) believes that administrators are essentially value carriers in organizations; they are both arbiters of values and representatives of them. Consequently, he identifies values as the seminal aspect of administration. The dual nature of the role has potential implications for cases of value conflict. Principals may find themselves in situations where there is a mismatch between their personal value position and that of the system or the group. What are the consequences of values conflict for school-based management? Are these the swampy problems? Consider the principal who believes in educating the whole child by attending to emotional, physical, affective and academic development. System-level or community pressure is put on the school to improve upon student academic achievement in relation to neighbouring schools. Does the principal abandon personal value preferences and 'teach to the test' to satisfy parents or meet system requirements? Any number of value conflicts may emerge between individuals or groups of staff, within the overall school community and/or between the school and system levels. Skills of negotiation and compromise are called into play, essential skills for a principal working in a self-managing school.

Values are an integral part of everyday life and due to the public nature of schooling, they have a significant role to play in education. Values underpin all thoughts and actions in school. School staff and children make hundreds of value choices daily. Which alternative is right, good, best? Choices concerning the most effective ways of operating, or directions for improvement projects, are shaped by the facts and the values of the individuals who contribute to life in the organization. In discussing the administration of schools, Holmes (1985) states that 'contemporary administrators try to develop a value-free approach to decision making. They are unsuccessful because all important decisions are made within a framework of value' (p. 22).

LEADERSHIP

The notion of leadership, while remaining to be a source of interest and even fascination for many educational and corporate theorists, is elusive. Definitions and descriptions of what leadership is and what it entails are as varied as the individuals who engage in its study. Over time, explanations based on trait, behaviour, situation and contingency approaches have all been considered. Dimensions, styles and types of leadership have been explored. Yet leadership remains, as Burns (1978) suggested, one of the most observed and least understood phenomenon on earth.

School effectiveness research consistently identifies leadership as one of the key variables making a positive difference in students' experience of school. Assuming the importance of leadership, and its multi-faceted nature, do school principals share any common understanding of what leadership is, and how it is different from other types of behaviour in which they may engage?

Rost (1985) attributes the confusion and uncertainty surrounding leadership to the fact that in many instances, management not leadership has been the focus of enquiry. Clear separation between leadership and management behaviours is not obvious. Many executive actions are characteristic of both. It may, therefore, be more fruitful to look for differences in intent and purpose rather than differences in action and behaviour. For example, both leaders and managers must communicate. As a leadership action, the communication will be value driven. As part of management, it will be task or production oriented. That is, there are times and instances when the delivery of the message is the overriding priority of the communication. In this instance, the action is more ends than means motivated. Delivery of the message serves a pragmatic function. If, however, the principal uses the need to transfer information to serve two agendas, one to deliver the message and one to build morale, provide feedback, or reassert school priorities, then the communication is instrumental and value laden. Communication occurs and the opportunity to reinforce the value priorities, the culture, and the vision of the school has been seized. The same act or decision may be taken for different reasons and to different ends, which helps to make tentative distinctions between leadership and management as well as between items on the value agenda.

Writing in the North American context, Hodgkinson (1978) equates leadership with administration and specifies a distinction between administrative and managerial practice. He distinguishes between the two by suggesting that management includes 'those aspects of the role which are more routine, definitive, programmatic and susceptible to quantitative methods' (p. 5).

Leadership, or administration on the other hand, is 'the art of influencing men to accomplish organizational goals' (p. 5).

Similarly, Sergiovanni (1990) recognizes the relationship of leadership and managerial actions. He views leadership in an inclusive sense, that is leadership includes the functions, tasks and responsibilities of management: 'Leadership combines management know-how with values and ethics' (p. 28). From this perspective, it is the manager who ensures that the school functions in a competent manner, but 'no matter how competently managed a school may be, it is the extra quality of leadership that makes the difference between ordinary and extraordinary performance' (p. 18). Sergiovanni (1990) discusses *transactional* and *transformational* leadership. A transaction mode of operation attaches primary importance to managerial skills. The leader manages, and individuals 'do their job'. This creates a separation between leaders and followers in that the work relationship is based on doing, as Sergiovanni suggests, 'a fair day's work' (p. 39). This separation reinforces a traditional 'us–them' relationship. It is a task for school administrators in the 1990s to break down the 'us–them' thinking that haunts many systems. A transformational style of leadership is a move in this direction. Here, staff 'do a fair day's work', but not solely as an obligation of a work contract but because they feel a level of commitment to, and gain satisfaction from, their involvement. A leader who seeks to support and build this climate among staff stands to create a more unified mindset in the school.

Professional development serves as an example of the difference between the two approaches to leadership. A principal who is a *transactional leader* may judge staff requests for professional development based on the individual choices staff members make. Teachers would then pursue self-identified needs and interests. One may attend an in-service activity for science, another for direct teaching, and a third for computer literacy. The *transformational school leader* is more likely to have created and developed the climate of the school such that staff begin to focus on individual needs and interests within the context of school-level objectives and priorities. A more concerted effort on a narrower range of topics is probable.

A *transformational leader* seeks to build a culture where individual members of staff strive to support and advance mutually determined outcomes for students. Here, it is more likely that staff are informed about budget possibilities and constraints and have an active role in planning and allocating monies.

Sergiovanni supports the claim made in the effective schools' research that leadership is somehow 'grander' or more 'encompassing' than management and contributes to the distinction between competent and excellent schools. He suggests that:

> If the principal is viewed as leader of leaders and responsible for helping teachers, parents and others assume a greater share of responsibility and

obligation for what happens in the school, then her or his role becomes decidedly more "executive" than "managerial". (p. 110)

This executive nature involves activities which deal with the identification and articulation of purpose, the value issues and the human component of the organization. This is not a small task. Single, absolute positions do not exist. Worldwide trends such as the erosion of traditional social values, the loss of automatic consensus due to increasing recognition of cultural, racial and religious diversity, loss of public trust in regard to the effectiveness of schools, the resulting demand for increased accountability, changing expectations coupled with diminishing resources and support, and changing norms for leadership expectations, have significant impact on the role of the principal. As societal and educational trends continue, the role becomes more and more complex. It is not a single dimension, single focus task, but rather, a multi-faceted phenomenon.

The restructuring movement brings with it system-level implications and pressures for open enrolments, competition for students, entrepreneurship, marketing, emphasis on exam and test results. The task of facilitating unity amongst disparate groups can be enormous. Staff, parents and school councils/governing bodies may well hold views which differ from one another and from the system perspective. As individuals, principals may struggle in the role of leader which increasingly requires the ability to mediate between ever multiplying sets of values. As Burns (1978) suggested over a decade ago, the difference between leadership and management is that the latter is *doing things right*, while the former is *doing the right things*. The choice of the 'right things' is based on values.

VISION

The significance of vision in school life was a recurring message in educational research literature in the 1980s. Much of the effective schools' research concluded that vision was an important aspect of school success and identified the school leader as the critical contributor to its development and implementation: 'Through living out the vision the leader breathes a sense of purpose and excitement into the routines of daily life in the school' (Duignan, 1987, p. 211). While vision has been defined and discussed in many different ways, there is general agreement in the literature that it seems to be vital to success.

Vision is a statement of what the organization ought to be: the ought, the should, the values, which guide practice. Colton (1985) suggests that vision defines not what we are but rather what we *seek to be or do*. While on the one hand, it 'can make dreamers of us all' by letting us 'see feelingly' (p. 18) there is also a practical, purposeful role for vision to play. Vision expresses a view of what is desirable but it must do so in a way which can 'inspire and motivate people to work towards improvement' (Duke, 1990, p. 26).

The utility of a vision derives from its degree of defensibility and from the meaning it has for those affected by it. A useful, defensible vision is the product of careful thought, systematic effort and continuous evaluation and refinement. It is also the basis for proactivity, for determining priorities about how to spend time now, for setting clear goals and for other aspects of planning – coming to agreement about the value priorities. A clearly articulated vision guides decision making and problem solving so that situations are resolved in a way that is consistent with the goals, priorities and direction of the school. Vision moves from a 'dream state' to a practical, daily hands-on guide when it includes the goals staff hope to accomplish for, and with, students.

Vision is grand; it is bigger than the daily routine tasks which operate at the 'how-to' level. While the vision must have a sense of the how, the what and the why are the powerful dimensions of it. It is the what and the why that are reflections of values. A values orientation to school leadership endorses the importance of vision. From this perspective, vision is a shared, public statement of values.

Of equal importance to the vision as *product* is the *process* through which the vision statement is developed and communicated. The process may unfold in a number of ways. Two influences critical to the process are leadership style and personal values. The context and nature of the managerial orientation of the school also have an important role to play. A transactional leader, for example, may publicize values in the form of a vision, which is a statement of personal values. The pursuit or imparting of a personal vision is not the nature of effective schools; it is *common* understandings and messages which make a critical difference. Since participation is a valued component of school-based management, it is a clear dynamic of vision elaboration and articulation. Hence the transformational leader pursues a *common* vision to impart to the wider community, and addresses both the product and the process agendas.

The vision statement can take many forms. It may be referred to as the school's mission, objectives, aim or purpose. In Western Australia, a statement of purpose is one of six components which make up the School Development Plan (SDP) (Ministry of Education, Western Australia, 1989). The policy indicates that the school purpose should be stated 'in terms of the outcomes it intends for its students. Students' cognitive, social and personal development must all be considered in establishing a purpose' (p. 3). Within these broad system-wide parameters, it is the responsibility of each school community to formulate and agree upon an SDP.

As vision statements can take different forms, so can the means for arriving at them. Drawing again from the Western Australian context, the process is to be participatory, where the SDP is 'produced by a school's staff and community' (p. 3) and where 'Principals have the responsibility of enabling staff to participate' (p. 1). This emphasis on shared development is consistent with involvement which is cited as a factor in the effective schools' research. Traditional organizational characteristics of authority, one-way communication, limited access to information and hierarchical decision making have given way in effective schools to processes of involvement, participation and collaboration. A premise of school-based management is that involvement and ownership are important to the 'oneness' and commitment of staff.

The existence of a clearly thought out and stated vision statement can simplify the decision making and action which takes place in the swamp. The Western Australian Ministry (1989) indicates that an SDP 'should be a working document that helps to focus teachers' efforts constructively. It is produced by a school's staff and community in order to guide decision making' (p. 3). Because development plans and vision statements represent a degree of consensus about the direction and priorities that the school acknowledges, situations can be handled within the pre-established framework provided by the vision statement. A vision statement, like a policy, provides guidance and bounds the number of possible alternatives for action. Often conflicts which arise in the school setting are conflicts of values – different standards in discipline between teachers on a staff or between a particular teacher and a parent, for example. It is a value conflict which is at the basis of the disagreement, not the superficial differences evident in implementation of the homework policy. Potentially swampy situations can move towards the high ground through application of a clearly articulated vision statement. Useful visions, like the values they embrace, provide a guide to action.

Achilles (1987) sees that school leaders face a threefold task:

> They must know why we need an education and good schools. They must know what is needed to improve schools. They must know how to administer the school to achieve the desired results. As a starting point, principals must envision better schools, articulate this vision to others and orchestrate consensus on the vision. (p. 18)

Value questions are raised by Achilles' comments. First, if, as he suggests, it is important to know why we need an education, an exploration and selection of value priorities is called for. A principal's ability to administer involves both managerial and leadership tasks. Striking the right balance between the two and matching the balance to the needs of the school community are integral features of the effective school. Holmes and Wynne (1989) propose that in past decades, school leaders suppressed their philosophies and beliefs to become *value-free* managers who supposedly could run any school with equal efficiency. This clone-type thinking sees schools as one and the same, and teachers and administrators as similar. What the effective schools' research reveals, however, is that what schools need most is a clear sense of purpose and direction, and an individual identity. The vision must reflect the unique aspects of the school and the community which it serves. This can be accomplished through a process of school development planning which involves all significant stakeholders. The principal's role is to initiate and maintain the process as well as to provide input. The process is more likely to be successful if there is a match or similarity of the core values of major players. What level of congruence exists between the value priorities of the system, the principal, and the school community? Agreement presupposes overt and conscious awareness of value issues by the interested parties. Before agreement can be reached, all parties must have an opportunity to express their preferences and priorities. This implies that the stakeholders have clarified their own views on the nature of education and are prepared to articulate and discuss their position.

Independent schools have a tradition of making their value positions known. School community beliefs and values are usually clear to administrators, staff, parents, students and the community at large. It is often on the basis of the publicly stated position that staff and parents make their school-related choices. What values does one school embody in comparison with another and which of those positions best fit the view of potential parents, students and staff? In government systems, staff are typically assigned to schools according to criteria unrelated to value preferences and students generally attend the school nearest to their home. It is predictable, therefore, that a more diverse range of priorities and preferences will be represented by the school community. Conflict and diversity complicate the creation of a vision. Since the potential for value conflict is high, the need for input and participation is crucial. Implications for the role of the principal include:

- the necessity and importance of a conscious personal value position
- recognition of the importance of negotiating the position
- the need to seek input and participation from significant stakeholders in the school community
- contact with, and awareness of, the value position of colleagues and neighbouring schools
- cognizance of the system perspective
- skill in the task of facilitation
- skill in listening, consolidating and guiding the process of value articulation and vision creation.

To be truly useful, while drawing *what is to be*, vision must be cognizant of *what is*. McDonnell (1989) identifies four trends in education which undoubtedly have direct implications for schools. They include: greater decentralization of authority; increased public accountability; changes to content and process of classroom instruction; and a move towards stronger links between school and community. These trends, in themselves, are statements about value preferences, values espoused at levels other than the school. McDonnell writes from his experience of the context of schools in the United States but the relevance of these trends for systems in other Western countries is apparent. When a principal's value position is in serious opposition to the system or community view, leading and mediating a process of school development and vision creation cease to be options. The individual should be advised to seek an alternative placement or assignment, inside or outside the system, which provides a closer match of value positions, thus reducing conflict.

A growing recognition of the contribution to be made through community participation is consistent with the trend towards devolved systems evident in many Australian states. This devolution includes a move to local-level decision making which invites input from all significant stakeholders in an effort to accommodate local needs and differences. Statements in the Western Australian Ministry of Education's (1989) SDP policy reflect this relocation of control: 'Throughout the public sector there is a trend towards less centralized and more participative decision making which has the potential to be more responsive to local needs' (p. 2).

It is signalled in the Ministry of Education's (1987) *Better Schools* document in Western Australia and in similar reports elsewhere in Australia, North America and England and Wales that the responsibility and accountability for the process of teaching and learning must rest in close proximity to where the process unfolds – in schools. If part of leadership is 'doing the right things' then a leader must operate within the context of his or her vision of where the organization is going and the rationale for that choice. The local school community is in the best position to judge the appropriateness of decisions and actions which impact upon the delivery of quality education. As Peters and Waterman (1982) found in their study of excellent corporations, one lesson learned by the successful corporate leaders interviewed was the importance of being 'close to the customer'. It is at the workface that professionals are best able to make choices and implement decisions. School leaders, not central office educators, are at the workface of school life.

As Duke (1990) suggests:

> Some principals are more effective than others because they have a better sense of what to do – and what not to do. No one can do it all, and one of the keys to effective leadership is knowing which things to leave undone. Too many school leaders try to do too much. The value of vision is that it helps us prioritize our use of time, and never has the need been greater. (p. 25)

The vision of a school must be embedded in, and compatible with, the culture. When the culture does not support the vision, problems are likely to arise resulting in many hours in the swamp for the decision makers. If, for example, through its ceremonies and symbols a school honoured the achievement of only males in science while purporting in its vision statement a policy of equality in relation to gender and to discipline, a mismatch between the rhetoric and the reality would be evident. Vision statements must and can be more than rhetoric – they can be working guides to practice. In effective schools, the cultural and the visionary messages are consistent, as are the ensuing actions.

CULTURE

The *culture* of a school is the revelation and demonstration of the school community's 'conception of the desirable'; the practice. The school culture reflects value preferences and priorities, influences and differences. Exploration of the composition of culture and its underlying value themes is one way of possibly unravelling and understanding the differences between schools perceived to be excellent or 'less than excellent'.

Sergiovanni (1984) characterized culture as 'the collective programming of the mind that distinguishes the members of one school from another. Cultural life in schools is constructed in reality' (p. 9). The reality of a school's staff, students, internal environment, external environment, priorities, structures, procedures and programmes determines and shapes what it is to be 'school x' rather than 'school y'. The cultures are built subjectively and as Duignan (1987, p. 210) suggests, 'through the everyday business of school life'. Everyday activities are the medium for value display. Writers in both corporate and educational sectors agree that organizational cultures are comprised of key elements such as values and beliefs, shared meaning, heroes, rites and rituals, ceremonies and cultural networks.

As facts are viewed through a value filter, so too are the components of culture. Separate components form a hierarchical configuration with values as the base. That is, choice and recognition of heroes, for example, occurs within the cultural boundaries identified through the value filter. This important aspect of culture is recognized within the boundaries of established value priorities. The accomplishments of those individuals who come to be regarded as heroes are compatible with the cultural emphases. If the school culture espouses all-round excellence, then sporting heroes will not be the only students honoured. Social, academic and artistic heroes will be equally recognized.

Within the culture of the school, two domains are active, one *professional* and one *bureaucratic*. Values underpin both. Differences between schools can be highlighted through attention to the balance or proportion of each domain and perhaps the degree of excellence can be identified through similar means. The practices of school-based management initiate a negotiation of time and importance between the domains. As processes become more collegial and are controlled from the school rather than the system level, the balance between bureaucratic and professional alters. Principals have a significant role to play in shaping the choices that are made in regard to the development of the culture domains in their school. In moving towards a better understanding of the implications of this role, there is value in viewing the domains through the lens of coupling theory.

The concept of coupling has been part of administrative theory for some time. Events or structures can be tightly or loosely coupled. Weick (1976) suggested that coupled events are responsive, but that each event also preserves its own identity and some evidence of its physical or logical separateness. In an organization with clear-cut tasks and standards, consistent inputs and identified outcomes, tightly coupled structures are warranted and workable. Each event retains evidence of its separateness; for example, the supply of raw materials remains identifiable from the production task, yet the two are connected: 'Loose coupling connotes weak or infrequent ties between any things that are minimally interdependent' (Weick, 1976, p. 5). Weick's position has application to a variety of situations. It is used here with respect to aspects of organizational life. From this perspective, organizations are characterized by ambiguous goals, unclear technology, changing participation, uncoordinated activity and loosely connected structural elements. The ambiguity of goals may occur due to the absence of a specification process, or as a result of value conflict, that is the identification of different priorities for school outcomes by different stakeholders. The diversity of teachers, students and circumstances makes the validity of any simplistic statement about the superiority of particular teaching methods, techniques and approaches more questionable. The influence of time, place and subject are critical to the selection of methods and requires the professional judgement of the educator. Consequently, teaching is closer to an art than to a science and is characterized by unclear, rather than clear and absolute, technology. Given the desirability of the school community reaching consensus on important issues, these four elements may stand as obstacles to that end. Mediation and negotiation processes will centre around issues embodied in these elements.

If we accept that schools are non-rational places of high uncertainty and situation-dependent circumstance, what relevance does tight coupling have? Typically, the *bureaucratic domain* of the culture is tightly coupled. Hoy and Miskel (1987) suggest that attention in the bureaucratic domain focuses on mediating between school and community, implementing law, administering internal affairs, procuring and allocating resources and mediating between students and teaching. Programmes and procedures may be standard from one school to another. A tightly linked and cohesive structure usually exists for the completion of these tasks. That is, procedures and routines are established, understood and acted upon. As individual situations arise, precedents have been established for dealing with the situation. Teachers and administrators are on the high ground.

If these procedures and routines have been established in consultation with staff and community, the likelihood of conflict is reduced. Assuming that, in effective schools, stakeholders have contributed to the development of policy and procedures, the level of understanding among staff and parents is increased. Consequently, the devolution of decision making within school-based management increases understanding through involvement and thus reduces mixed messages.

The activities of the *professional domain* focus on the process of teaching and learning and the collegiality which surrounds the process. Educators know that much of what is involved in schooling is ambiguous and needs to be negotiated by interested stakeholders. The goals of the organization are varied, as are the dimensions of power, decision making, external environment and teaching. The professional relationship among teachers, between teachers and their administration, and the links between a system and its schools, are typically more loosely structured than bureaucratic functions. The professional role is, by definition, autonomous and self-regulating. It also presupposes participation, involvement and sharing. Attention to the professional role develops a professional culture. A professional domain in the true meaning of the term belongs to, and is created and shaped by, the participants. If conditions, practices and policies are inherited rather than created, then Cooper's (1988) question 'Whose culture is it?' becomes relevant. Cooper suggests that:

> If teachers are told what to be professional about, how, when, where, and with whom to collaborate, and what blueprint for professional conduct to follow, then the culture that evolves will be foreign to the setting. They will once again have 'received' a culture. (p. 47)

It is relevant to consider three variables with respect to the domains of culture. First, the relative position of each on the *coupling continuum*, second, the driving force of each domain, and third, the balance or division between the bureaucratic and the professional domains. The variables interact in different configurations depending on the extent to which school-based management practices are operating in the organization.

The bureaucratic domain is typically positioned towards the tightly linked and cohesive pole of the coupling continuum. If this domain becomes too rigid and opportunities for adaptation and flexibility are reduced, alienation among teachers is likely. The professional sphere is typically more loosely structured and sits closer to the opposite pole. Here, teachers have and use discretion to make professional judgements about the teaching–learning process. If these professional judgements are thwarted, participation and commitment will be threatened.

The second variable to consider is the focus or the underlying motive for action within the domain. Is the motivating force one which is focused in a way which serves the shared values of the school community, or is it aimed at serving personal ends and priorities? To what extent is the focus a shared one? Does the nature of the coupling relationship become an end in itself, or is it a means to serve and promote organizational values in order to support and enhance culture and school effectiveness? Is the driving force a 'conception of the desirable' or a pragmatic choice? Reflection on the issues raised by these questions provides an opportunity for school principals and their school communities to clarify their value position and examine the motivating force which inspires them.

Consideration of the first two variables in tandem creates four possible configurations which detail the final variable; balance. Each option produces different opportunities and challenges and may have application to the notion of excellence versus competence or incompetence in schools. Describing organizations according to the following types: ineffective, efficient, classroom effective, school effective, may enhance our understanding.

In Type One, *Ineffective* Schools, the professional is dominated by the bureaucratic. These are highly bureaucratic schools with limited professional input to the actions and decisions which flow from a hierarchy. Here, while bureaucratic procedures are tightly coupled, the intent of action is loosely focused. These schools tend to be authoritarian organizations driven by bureaucratic procedures which lack a clear and overall educational focus.

Like the first, Type Two represents a school culture which values the structures and procedures of the bureaucratic domain more than the participation, involvement and collegiality which are characteristic of the professional domain. Schools of this type (*Efficient* Schools), are more clearly focused than their Type One counterparts. While the focus may be unduly concentrated on questions and issues of procedure, focus does exist. There is shared understanding of bureaucratic domain issues, but rationales for action in the professional domain are determined on an individual basis. A Type Two school, while efficient in its operation, is not effective in its practice.

In schools characterized by effective classrooms (Type Three – *Classroom Effective*), the autonomy of the professional domain supersedes any school-level focus or shared intent among staff. Teacher creation and determination of the professional–bureaucratic balance within their own classrooms is the norm. When this balance is not coupled with, and tuned to, a common school focus, excellent practice resides at the classroom level. While cooperative planning and team involvement will be characteristic of teacher work in Type Three schools, individual and collaborative efforts will be focused upon classroom, not whole-school excellence. The contribution that strong bureaucratic processes can make to an organization's efficient operation are not utilized to the best advantage in Type Three schools. The opportunities of coupling and of focus are not maximized.

The effective school (Type Four – *School Effective*) is defined by an emphasis on the professional domain and a collective focus of intent, purpose and action. In this school, staff have opportunities to operate in a manner defined as professional yet they benefit from the presence of bureaucratic structures which exist to support the professionalism through shared intent and purpose. A high degree of agreement concerning the focus of practice means that staff are clear about, and committed to, the direction in which the school is moving; there is clarity with respect to the purpose and priorities of the organization. This clarity is due to the contribution made by staff and community to the vision and objectives for student learning and school programmes. Through the participation and collegial practice common to effective schools, a balance which is consistent with, and reflective of, the school development plan and its vision can be struck and maintained between the two cultural domains. The Type Four school has 'collective effectiveness'; that is, it is more than the sum total of its effective classrooms.

A FINAL STATEMENT

Principals most assuredly influence the coupling relationships which characterize their schools. For some, the influence is intentional; for others, incidental, but it does exist. The balance struck between the professional and bureaucratic domains, and between the clarity of focus and the state of the coupling relationship, has implications for levels of efficiency and effectiveness. In effective schools, the balance tips towards the professional with the bureaucratic domain existing as a support to teaching and learning. The focus of professional and bureaucratic actions and decisions is clear, consistent and shared among significant stakeholders of the school community.

Peters and Waterman's (1982) research in the corporate sector reveals that successful corporations hold tight to their core values. Core values are also the touchstone of effective schools. Through the principal's leadership the vision, grounded in facts and values, shapes the culture. The vision and the culture are valued, as are the processes of identifying, articulating and sharing both. These processes, characteristic of school-based management, include participation, involvement, devolved control and decision making, and school-level planning and practice. Through the effort and direction of the principal, values, leadership, vision and culture are distinguishable and consistent. In an effective school, each element supports and enhances the others.

THE CONTEXT FOR SCHOOLS IN THE 1990s

Organizational contexts are rapidly changing. Both the nature and rate of change have an effect on structure, process and product within the organizational structure. As Handy (1989) suggests:

> The world of work is changing because the organizations are changing their ways. At the same time, however, the organizations are having to adapt to a changing world of work. It's a chicken and egg situation. One thing, at least, is clear – organizations in both private and public sectors face a tougher world – one in which they are judged more harshly than before on their effectiveness and in which there are fewer protective hedges to shelter them. (p. 87)

Schools do not escape the impact of this changing and demanding context. Some of the harsh judgements to which Handy refers are particularly evident in the education sector. The changing context is characterized by public concern over the quality of education, increased scrutiny and calls for accountability, competition between technical and professional approaches, the stronger voice of minority and pressure groups, and a move towards an information-driven era where power is based on knowledge.

A more competitive context for schools is foreshadowed, given increased demands on, and diminishing resources for, schools. Shopping for the best product, price and service is becoming as widespread in education as it is in the purchase of food, transport, clothing, housing, and professional advice. Parents will inform their consumer choice by judging the practice and promise of schools. Given the contextual factors of the 1990s, many parents will *shop* to find a school community which shares or accommodates their view of educational priorities. In the past, schools in large, centralized systems have typically not had to make their values explicit and formal. Schools of the 1990s will need clear statements of aims, goals and directions as well as practice which is consistent with these. Parents will consider their educational options in light of the school's stated purpose.

The restructuring movement brings to education a paradox of top-down policies endorsing school-based management. While central policies commend involvement and shared decision making at the school level, involvement and shared decision making at central levels are, at best, limited. Schools are expected to consult with their communities yet the system rarely consults effectively with its community of professionals. Centralized policies rely upon individuals at the workface for their implementation. The success of implementation will be influenced by the message of the policy content as well as by the message of the policy development process. This 'do as I say, not as I do' characteristic of centrally formulated policy exposes rifts and differences in value preferences and priorities. A gap exists between values inherent in the policy process and in the policy message.

THE CONTENT OF SCHOOLS IN THE 1990s

Organizations used to be perceived as gigantic pieces of engineering, with largely interchangeable human parts. We talked of their structure and their systems, of inputs and outputs, of control devices and of managing them, as if the whole was one large factory. Today the language is not that of engineering but of influence or power rather than control, of leadership not management. It is as if we had suddenly woken up to the fact that organizations were made up of people.

(Handy, 1989, p. 89)

Handy names power, influence, leadership and people skills as important components in the new view of organizational life. These critical elements apply to the organization of the school and contribute to the enormity and complexity of the role of principal. The substance or content of the role is varied; the demands and expectations, fluid. The shape of school leadership in the 1990s must be inclusive. In practical terms, the content of the role is too immense for one individual. A solution lies in the involvement and assistance of others. Given that a principal has limited resources and tries to meet unlimited demands and tasks, the pooled resources of a team of school leaders is a realistic and necessary option. A shared or team approach can enhance the efficiency and effectiveness of leadership.

In order to work effectively in a team structure, principals of the 1990s will be recognizing and assessing staff strengths. There will be a need to match the talents of members of the team to those responsibilities related to the priorities and directions specified in the school plan. Specific knowledge about the skill breadth and depth of staff and the ability to encourage and support members of the team in their efforts, become important elements of the principal's role. This necessary support and encouragement relates to the view of empowerment put forward by Bennis and Nanus (1985). They suggest that leaders 'empower others to translate intention into reality and sustain it' (p. 80). Empowerment is not power over others, but power with others. Members of the school team must have opportunities to contribute to the vision and culture of the school and principals must create the opportunities for this to happen. Such action contributes to the development of the school's professional domain.

Traditionally, principals in centralized systems have not been encouraged to make their own values explicit or to elicit the value preferences held within the parent group. Articulating the values which underpin the activities and processes of the school organization is central to the work of the school-based manager. This is consistent with the view of Bennis and Nanus (1985) who indicate that:

> Leaders articulate and define what has previously remained implicit or unsaid; then they invent images, metaphors, and models that provide a focus for new attention. By doing so, they consolidate or challenge prevailing wisdom. In short, an essential factor in leadership is the capacity to influence and organize meaning for the members of the organization. (p. 39)

The meaning referred to can be organized through continued reflection, discussion and debate at individual, staff and community levels and will involve negotiation and mediation between points of view.

In the 1990s, the role of the principal must be focused on value specification, articulation and exhibition. Principals will need to engage in these activities on a personal level initially, in order to clarify their position. Then, it will be important for them to develop and/or utilize skills which enable them to help others do the same. A third step will be aimed at finding the middle ground where all stakeholders of the school community can be satisfied that the school will in fact make a difference to the educational development of its student body and to the professional lives of its educators.

REFERENCES

Achilles, C.M. (1987) 'A vision of better schools', in W. Greenfield (ed.) *Instructional Leadership: Concepts, Issues and Controversies*, Boston: Allyn & Bacon.

Bennis, W. and Nanus, B. (1985) *Leaders – the Strategies for Taking Charge*, New York: Harper & Row.

Burns, J.M. (1978) *Leadership*, New York: Harper & Row.

Caldwell, B.J. and Spinks, J.M. (1988) *The Self-Managing School*, London: The Falmer Press.

Colton, D.L. (1985) 'Vision', *National Forum* 65(2): 33–5.

Cooper, M. (1988) 'Whose culture is it, anyway?', in A. Lieberman (ed.) *Building a Professional Culture in Schools*, New York: Teachers College Press.

Duignan, P. (1987) 'Leaders as culture builders', *Unicorn* 13(4): 208–13.

Duke, D.L. (1990) 'School leadership for the 90s: A matter of time and vision', *Principal* 69(4): 22–7.

Greenfield, T.B. (1986) 'The decline and fall of science in educational administration', *Interchange* 2(2): 57–80.

Handy, C. (1989) *The Age of Unreason*, Boston: Harvard Business School Press.

Hodgkinson, C. (1978) *Towards a Philosophy of Administration*, Oxford: Basil Blackwell.

Holmes, M. (1985, June) 'The revival of traditional thought and its effect on educational administration: The case of decision making', Paper presented at the Annual Meeting of the Canadian Society for Studies in Education, Montreal.

Holmes, M. and Wynne, E.A. (1989) *Making the School an Effective Community: Belief, Practice and Theory in School Administration*, New York: The Falmer Press.

Hoy, W.K. and Miskel, C.G. (1987) *Educational Administration, Theory, Research and Practice* (3rd edn), New York: Random House.

Kluckhohn, C. (1951) 'Values and value-orientations in the theory of action: An exploration in definition and classification', in T. Parsons and E. Shils (eds) *Toward a General Theory of Action* (pp. 388–433), Cambridge, MA: Harvard University Press.

McDonnell, L. (1989) *Restructuring American Schools*, New York: National Center on Education and Employment.

Ministry of Education (1987) *Better Schools in Western Australia: A Programme for Improvement*, Perth: Ministry of Education.

—— (1989) *School Development Plans: Policy and Guidelines*, Perth: Ministry of Education.

Patterson, J.L., Purkey, S.C. and Parker, J.V. (1986) *Productive School Systems for a Nonrational World*, Alexandria, VA: Association for Supervision and Curriculum Development.

Peters, T. and Waterman, R. (1982) *In Search of Excellence*, New York: Harper & Row.

Purkey, S. and Smith, M. (1983) 'Effective schools: A review', *Elementary School Journal* 83(4): 427–52.

Rokeach, M. (1973) *The Nature of Human Values*, New York: The Free Press.

Rost, J.C. (1985) 'Distinguishing leadership and management: A new consensus', Paper presented at the Symposium on Transforming Leadership at the Organization Development Network National Conference, San Francisco, California.

Schon, D.A. (1983) *The Reflective Practitioner: How Professionals Think in Action*, New York: Basic Books.

Sergiovanni, T.J. (1984) 'Leadership and excellence in schooling', *Educational Leadership* 41(5): 4–13.

—— (1990) *Value-Added Leadership*, Orlando, FL: Harcourt Brace Jovanovich.

Weick, K.E. (1976) 'Educational organizations as loosely coupled systems', *Administrative Science Quarterly* 21: 1–19.

Chapter 6

Delegated financial management and school effectiveness

Brian Knight

Whether the delegation of financial management to schools leads to improved school effectiveness is one of the key questions raised by restructuring. The speed with which delegation of financial management to schools is spreading in Western countries suggests legislators and administrators think it does, or should, lead to improved school effectiveness. They sometimes produce a rationale for this benign linkage, as if school-based financial management *per se* is a solution to many current problems besetting school systems.

But what is the evidence to support this view? The first part of this chapter looks at the problems underlying a search for links between financial delegation and school effectiveness. The second part examines the evidence now emerging on the effects of financial delegation first upon the school process, and then on school outcomes.

PROBLEMS OF LINKING FINANCIAL DELEGATION WITH SCHOOL EFFECTIVENESS

Many proposals for financial delegation have focused upon *managerial efficiency and effectiveness*. Here financial delegation is seen as pushing decisions down to those who are best informed and motivated to take them, and closer to the clients whom the decisions should benefit. Three examples of this rationale follow:

> The Commission considers that more delegation of authority and responsibility to the local level will result in better value for money and avoidance of waste.
>
> (UK Audit Commission, 1984, p. 49)

> Good management requires the identification of management units for which objectives can be set and resources allocated; the unit is then required to manage itself within those resources in a way which seeks to achieve the objectives; the performance of the unit is monitored and the unit is held to account for its performance and for its use of funds.
>
> (Coopers and Lybrand, 1987, p. 7)

The efficiency and effectiveness of the system can be improved only if schools have sufficient control over the quality of education they provide....
To maintain a system of education which responds to changing Government and community priorities and which can use Government funds most efficiently, individual schools must become the focus for the administration and delivery of education.

(Western Australian Ministry of Education, 1987, p. 5)

Others have focused upon the idea of *empowerment* giving teachers, and also parents and local citizens and employers, greater participation in school decision making. Such empowerment has usually involved delegation of financial management, but has not centred on it. Indeed in some schemes it has been very limited in scope:

school-site management alone does not guarantee administrative decentralization ... the issue is not simply *how* to achieve school-site management but how to achieve *collegial* and *collective management at the school level*.

(Conley and Bacharach, 1990, p. 540)

School-based management is only one way to restructure decision making and planning at the school site so that day-to-day administration and teaching can be collaborative and collegial.

(Taylor and Levine, 1991, p. 394)

Other approaches, however, see financial delegation as just one of several conditions necessary to create a competitive *market economy* for schools. These stem from a politico-economic belief in the efficiency of free economic markets to deliver goods and services effectively to consumers and provide them with choice. In 1990, the then Secretary of State for Education and Science in Britain espoused the market economy argument, thus:

The only importance of pupil-led funding will be seen in the effect it will have on educational standards. It will lead to a competition for excellence. There will be a clear incentive for schools to attract more pupils. We want to reward success. Popular schools – not hampered by artificial admission limits – will attract more pupils, grow and receive more money. In short, we shall have a much more responsive system and greater customer orientation. There will be two reasons for this: because management decisions will be closer to the ground and because there will be a financial incentive to improve standards.

(MacGregor, 1990, p. 1)

A further analysis is provided by Bowe *et al.* (1992) in relation to developments in the education system of England and Wales:

The educational process becomes the production process, teachers are producers, parents are consumers, knowledge becomes a commodity and the educated student the product, with a minimum specification laid down by the National Curriculum.... For the government, the essence of LMS is buried within the move to market driven funding. This encourages schools to enter a new era of self-help, entrepreneurialism, cost-effectiveness and consumerism. In the "natural environment" of the market, free from the "contamination" of a system, schools should release the "natural" gifts of individuals' enterprise, initiative and the instinct for survival. The 'successful' schools will be those that become self-determining enterprises, promoting innovative and cost-effective approaches to fulfilling consumer demand. Removing the constraints of the system will allow the schools to "do what should come naturally".

It is clear, however, that the nature and emphases of policies differ between countries. One could regard many of the schemes in Canada and Australia, the Netherlands and Belgium, and England and Wales before the 1988 Education Reform Act, as being more concerned with *managerial efficiency and effectiveness*; many of the schemes in the USA as more concerned with *empowerment*; and the current LMS (Local Management of Schools) developments in the UK, plus those in New Zealand and the Dutch vocational schools, as centred upon a *market economy*.

However, these are not either/or situations. Many, though certainly not all, managerial schemes are also concerned with empowerment through participation. Empowerment schemes assume that greater involvement of teachers and community will lead to greater effectiveness. And the market schemes certainly require managerial efficiency, and involve school empowerment, although not in the sense in which the term is used in the USA.

Recently a new category of financial delegation has appeared, namely *cost transfer*. In April 1992 *white* schools in South Africa were invited, and most agreed, to take full responsibility for all their non-salary costs (that is, all premises maintenance, energy and water costs, grounds, rates and taxes, insurance, furniture, equipment, books and materials and other supplies and services) *and to raise the funds for them*. Schools may raise funds and generate income in the usual way, but may also legally charge fees to parents. These fees are likely to average 500 to 1000 rand per child (equivalent to US $350 to $700).

This is the first example of which this writer is aware of a Western school system delegating responsibility for supply as well as expenditure. It has arisen from economic pressures and budget reductions, but there is another motive. This *topping-up* of state finance will allow ethnic communities to produce different models of schools beyond the standard multi-racial provision. Of course, in developing countries and in the black communities of South Africa, delegation of part of the funding of schools to local communities is already commonplace.

WHAT KIND OF FINANCIAL DELEGATION?

Even a superficial glance at financial delegation schemes worldwide shows that they differ enormously: in scope, administration, structure and implementation. In *scope*, the categories of delegated expenditure vary widely. Few schemes delegate the full range of financial responsibilities. With regard to *administration*, regulations are the key. An apparently flexible scheme rapidly becomes rigid if regulations are unduly restrictive or fussy. With regard to *structure*, key aspects include the governance of schools (for example, the influence of governing bodies or school councils and provision for consultation); the arrangements for allocation of funds to schools, usually by some kind of formula; and the treatment of special factors such as small schools and special education, social or ethnic needs. With regard to *implementation* there can be great differences in phasing, transition and training. It is clear that financial delegation has no standard form.

SCHOOL RESPONSES TO FINANCIAL DELEGATION

How a particular scheme affects an individual school depends considerably on the school's stage of development, institutional culture and individual circumstances. Some schools quickly develop the skills and practices necessary for successful financial delegation; others flounder. Devolution can accentuate differences between schools, both by unplanned factors, such as the quirks of formula allocation or fixed costs, and from different school reactions to the opportunities for planning, entrepreneurship and income generation. In a competitive market economy, some schools seem to react much more positively than others.

The different ways in which schools respond to the same scheme of delegation is neatly illustrated by Thomas (1987, p. 229). He describes how four schools in Solihull took very different stances to the opportunity to vire (or switch) funds out of teacher salaries into other areas of expenditure. Of four headteachers interviewed, one had vired funds from teaching to non-teaching staff; two would consider doing so, but not in the current situation; one was opposed on principle.

A vivid illustration of different school reactions within a common scheme is provided by Levacic and Marren (1991). They describe in detail the spending decisions of 11 schools in one LEA during the first year of delegation. The abiding impression is of the individuality of each school. Schools took contrasting decisions about:

- changes to teacher staffing
- supply teaching and non-teaching support
- premises maintenance and improvement
- learning resources
- lettings of premises and income generation

- longer-term planning

Such variations in school responses to financial delegation arise from factors such as the personality and values of the principal; the views of senior staff, or the staff as a whole, and the governing body; the effectiveness of the school's management; the previous experience and tradition of the school; and its perceived needs. They remind us that schools do not necessarily exercise choice rationally.

Another major factor in a school's response to financial delegation is its current financial position, in particular whether it sees itself as *winning* or *losing* under the formula, as facing rising or falling enrolment, and expanded or reduced central funding. It is easier to be adventurous on a rising tide.

It is clear that financial delegation is not an automatic solution to improving schooling. Evidence of its effects needs to be set clearly in particular contexts. That one effect occurs in one situation is no guarantee that it will occur in another. The research findings assembled below need to be seen in that light.

THE NATURE OF THE RESEARCH EVIDENCE

Initial research findings on the school effects of financial delegation are beginning to accumulate in the early 1990s. Brown (1990) conducted a survey of the earliest surviving scheme, Edmonton School District, Alberta, which began a pilot stage in 1976 and was fully operational in 1980, together with Langley, a suburban area outside Vancouver, which introduced delegation fully in 1985. He conducted other interviews in two rural British Columbia districts, Peace River North and Fort Nelson and in Cleveland, Ohio.

The earliest schemes in the UK were introduced in Solihull in 1981 and Cambridgeshire in 1982. Both schemes involved full delegation, first to pilot schools and then to others. Each had an external evaluator, Hywell Thomas and Tyrrell Burgess, respectively. Levacic (1989) provides case studies of three schools joining the Cambridgeshire scheme for LFM (Local Financial Management) in 1988, and several headteachers have described their experiences in detail (Downes, 1986; Stenner, 1988; Thomas, 1989).

In the USA early schemes were established in the 1970s in Florida and California. The movement lost impetus, however, by 1980. Schemes revived in a number of states after 1986, and some research information is now appearing, but this focuses mainly on empowerment and participation rather than financial delegation.

The state of Victoria, Australia, introduced programme budgeting to over 2000 schools in 1984, linked to school improvement plans. The collaborative model used was trialed and operationalized at Rosebery District High School in Tasmania, and is described in Caldwell and Spinks (1988). Western Australia set out a blueprint for delegation in its policy document, *Better Schools* (1987).

The first phase of financial delegation began in 1990, with increasing financial responsibilities due to pass to schools in each successive year.

In England and Wales a full market economy model was introduced with the Education Reform Act (DES, 1988) and associated legislation, to affect 25,000 schools by 1994, but with schemes beginning only in April 1990. Research evidence (Levacic and Marren, 1991; Thomas and Bullock, 1991) is now appearing on the first year of LMS (Local Management of Schools).

There is only limited research evidence to date from the above countries. Much of the data available relate to pilot schools or schools in the first year or two of delegation. Moreover, these data are often gathered by case studies involving small samples and are reliant on anecdotal evidence given in interviews with principals and administrators. For these reasons and the substantial differences in purpose and character of the various schemes, considerable caution is necessary in comparing and generalizing from specific findings.

THE EFFECTS OF FINANCIAL DELEGATION: RESEARCH EVIDENCE

School management

Financial delegation highlights the need for efficient school management. Indeed, the term *management* is central to the concept of financial delegation as is indicated in the range of terms used – school-based management, site-based management, local management of schools, the self-managing school, local financial management. In recent years there has been an explosion in school management training and literature, and in school development planning. Financial delegation has certainly contributed to this, although some of the impetus comes from elsewhere. School development planning, for example, partly derives from the school improvement movement.

There is the possibility that financial delegation has some adverse effects for school managers, although research evidence is presently insufficient to draw conclusions. To what extent does financial management distract the focus of principals, deputies, and other senior staff away from other key tasks, such as instructional leadership? Does financial delegation *bureaucratize* relations between principals and staff and create a less caring climate? Clearly, all these things *can* happen – what we do not yet know is the extent to which they do.

Roles

The principal

There seems to be general agreement that the importance of the principal increases significantly with financial delegation. In Edmonton, for example, Smilanich (1990), the Associate Superintendent, reports:

The principal has the unenviable task of arbitrator – of soliciting the needs and wishes of staff and community (often conflicting and in competition) and being the final authority on planning decisions reflected in the proposed budget. The principal is now very much viewed as an extension of the Superintendent of Schools at the school level. (p. 7)

This is echoed in the American context by Conley and Bacharach (1990): 'Even today, many schools that fit the criteria commonly ascribed to school-site management (e.g., decentralization of resources) are managed by a single person: the principal' (p. 540).

Most research implicitly acknowledges the importance of principals by frequent reference to their views and actions. However, power has not grown unchecked. Participation and involvement of staff, the enhanced role of governing bodies and increased accountability, all discussed below, have provided some limitation.

There is conflict about whether the principal becomes more of an administrator and less of a manager. The Sheffield City Polytechnic (1986) evaluation of delegation in Lincolnshire, based on interviews with the seven pilot school principals, found:

All seven heads were agreed that the scheme had increased their workload and changed its pattern. As one head put it, 'I spend a considerable amount of time on matters not strictly educational ...'. Four heads commented that this change in role meant less contact with pupils and staff, and a number expressed some worries about such a change in role, although all except one felt that the time spent on the scheme was of benefit to his school in terms of providing better working conditions for pupils and staff. (p. 7)

Burgess (1986) found less of a shift to administration in the Cambridgeshire pilot schools:

People in Cambridgeshire feared, at the start of the pilot scheme, that questions of finance and administration would come to dominate educational decisions, that heads would become merely book-keepers. The reverse is what has happened. All the heads have found themselves able to make financial responsibility serve their educational objects; they have become better educational managers, because of their management of finance. (p. 23)

How principals respond to these new powers and responsibilities depends partly on their attitude to their role. Levacic (1989) suggests:

A significant issue which emerges from the case studies is the relationship between a head's management style and the way in which financial management is undertaken. In terms of the headship style taxonomy adopted by Hall et al. (1988), the teacher–educator head is predisposed to minimize involvement with financial management. This is then taken up by a more enthusiastic deputy, or collectively, by heads of departments. In contrast, the chief-executive-style head welcomes the powers and responsibilities offered by financial delegation and takes on the additional role of budget officer which reinforces the chief-executive role. How the professional–leader head is likely to respond to financial delegation is less obvious. The case studies suggest that such heads may well respond with enthusiasm to financial delegation because of the enhanced ability it gives to pursue their educational aims. (p. 72)

Senior school staff

The role of deputy principals is more difficult to interpret. Levacic (1989), for example, shows how, in her three case studies, one deputy was associated with financial delegation although the head took the key decisions; in another, 'the head's policy of sharing financial management with the heads of departments is perceived by most of the staff interviewed ... to have side-lined the deputies' (p. 66); in the third, where the head was not in favour of financial delegation, 'responsibility for LFM has been shared with the deputy head, who takes particular responsibility for it' (p. 68). This variation, almost a mirror image of the principal's position, seems typical.

In England and Wales a number of secondary schools have bursars (senior administrative officers) as do some clusters of primary schools. These generally have been considered of great value, with demands for their extension to more schools. However, the cost efficiency of providing bursars has not been evaluated.

There is evidence that financial delegation tends to trickle down to departments in secondary schools, and to class teachers in primary schools. This is partly through the process of consultation, but also because the logic of *subsidiarity* (that is, decision making at the lowest point appropriate) implies delegation beyond the principal. A number of such examples are quoted by Brown (1990, pp. 168–75). There are, however, some strong examples to the contrary, where the personality of the principal resists further delegation.

Governing bodies/school councils

In most restructured schemes governing bodies or school councils are given an enhanced role. In some, these bodies have been specially created for this purpose; for example, the school councils in Victoria, Australia. Where governing bodies have a long history, as in England and Wales, their powers and responsibilities have been expanded. However, as with principals, the response to new situations varies from one governing body to another. Based on anecdotal evidence the following taxonomy for governing bodies in England and Wales may be suggested:

- Trustees ('We are really watchdogs, and trust our headteacher to run the school unless we have some reason to be concerned.')
- Partners ('We want to work alongside our school staff, sharing ideas and expertise.')
- Board of Directors ('We take the strategic decisions, but leave executive action to the managing director (headteacher) and his or her colleagues.')
- Activists ('We are the masters now, elected to run the school on behalf of the parents.')

Time demands

Burgess (1986), evaluator for the Cambridge pilot scheme, reported that:

the heads have discovered that their burdens were different, but not greater. To put it crudely, it proved less burdensome to take a decision than to get a decision out of 'the office'. The heads did not report that they spent significantly more time on administration: nor did any significant demand arise for additional administrative staff. (p. 21)

The headteachers of two of the schools quantified the demands.
First, a primary headteacher:

The workload is not onerous and time spent on LFM averages out at about one and a half hours a week over the school year. At budget time more hours are needed but in other weeks, none at all.

(Stenner, 1988, p. 64)

Then a secondary headteacher:

The pattern of work seems to be that I have a short burst of concentrated work and then never give it another thought for several weeks. The busy time is when the budget for the following year has to be worked out and when the staffing allocation for the following year is known. Other than that, the regular monthly printouts need to be checked and matters followed up. I have to attend meetings of my own financial management committee and the LFM review group in Cambridge. I work with my accountant and the deputy head at the time of the capitation requests and distributions. My general impression is that I spend less time on LFM than outsiders expect.

(Downes, 1986, p. 6)

The views of these headteachers of volunteer pilot schools are probably too sanguine. A more typical response is that expressed by Brown, citing Alexandruk (1985), who found that both principals and teachers in Alberta identified the *time factor* as the greatest weakness of school-based management (see Table 6.1 below):

Respondents ... expressed a view that school budgeting is a time consuming process for teachers and principals and that it has an impact on instructional and teacher preparation time. Comments from teachers and principals indicate that there is insufficient time allocated to the planning and budget preparation process. Principals' responses indicate a need for additional administrative time allocation, and that this is being achieved via the budgeting process in the allocation of resources within the school.

(Brown, 1990, p. 166)

The conclusion drawn by Brown appears well balanced: 'Generally, workloads for administrators (that is, principals) appear to have increased, although many appeared to be willing to accept the additional burden' (Brown, 1990, p. 186).

However, it can be argued that, as financial delegation establishes itself and principals gain greater experience, the workload becomes lighter. Simplification of procedures and regulations and extension of information technology reduce the burden of administration. The greater involvement of senior school staff and members of governing bodies and school councils in school finance might also tend to decrease the time principals devote to financial matters. Nevertheless, if principals do spend more time on finance, they will either be working longer hours or shedding one or more of their previous tasks.

Participation and consultation

Brown (1990) found considerable interest in staff participation in the Canadian and American school districts he surveyed, but also great variation in practice:

What have the interviewees told us about participation? Two things: First, there are clear expectations that principals are to involve school staffs in their planning and decision making. However, principals do not permit decisions to be made when they disagree with them. Their reason is simply that they, not their staffs, are held accountable to their respective associate superintendents. Second, responses to the request for involvement vary according to preferences of the principals. (p. 172)

This dependence on the view of the principal is creating problems in the USA, where the late 1980s threw up strong beliefs in the value of greater teacher participation. Conley and Bacharach (1990) argue that 'without such participation the power to make decisions may well be decentralized to the school level, but the information that legitimizes these decisions will be limited, and school-site management will be no more successful than any other system of centralized control' (p. 540).

It seems likely that, over time, exhortation will prevail against resistant principals. Some delegating authorities have mandated schools to organize participation. Cambridgeshire, for example, in the mid 1980s insisted that all schools set up consultative procedures (Downes, 1988). Thomas (1988) describes a consultative process in operation:

> staff in this middle-management area now feel that the discussions are comprehensive in their meetings. Papers are produced, costings made, rival claims discussed and at the conclusion a decision is reached and ultimately introduced.... Thus in preparing the budget for 1986/87, the year GCSE [The General Certificate of Secondary Education] was introduced, real arguments ensued as to whether greater capitation [books, equipment and materials] or more ancillary support staff was required. (p. 78)

A description of a fully collaborative model is provided by Stenner (1988), head of a Cambridgeshire primary school:

> The procedures for deciding priorities for next year's budget and for allotting any underspend were improved after the second year by having joint meetings for all the governors and staff to make the decisions together. The model of decision-making which has evolved is partly collegial and partly based on a 'market-system', in that individual teachers and governors put in bids for sums of money. They have to convince the others that the bid is sound for reasons of development, current deficiencies, or whatever it might be, and then a decision is made by everyone about priority order or, if ideas race ahead of resources, which projects are to be deferred. (p. 66)

Undoubtedly the best known collaborative model is that adopted by Rosebery District High School in Tasmania, and fully described in Caldwell and Spinks (1988).

In general, financial delegation tends to involve wider participation and reduce autocracy, though not universally. It creates a need to legitimize decisions, enlist enthusiasm or expertise, delegate responsibilities and obtain cooperation.

Planning

Financial delegation has a similar relationship with school development planning. It does not require it – some of the early delegation schemes, as in Solihull, were solely about financial management – but it does imply it. It highlights the need for priorities and a rationale for expenditure. Thomas (1989) remarks, 'because the school now controls its finance it is inevitable that we look at the most cost-effective manner of implementing the curriculum policy' (p. 91). In detailing an example, Thomas describes how, 'in the academic year 1985/6 after considerable discussion in the Board of Studies it was decided that a modern language subject should be provided for all pupils in the school [years 7–11]' (p. 92). He then describes how the books and equipment needed were purchased, classrooms improved acoustically, and funds spent on extra foreign language assistants and teacher relief to allow frequent testing of pupils. The proportion of students gaining a GCSE award grade A–C in a modern language rose from 17 per cent to 49 per cent of the cohort.

As an illustration of the evolution of delegated budgeting, Stenner (1988) describes how her primary school began with a 'save-then-spend' pattern, but in 1986 constructed the budget as a 'quantitative statement of a plan of action'. However, linking a school development plan to the delegated budget is technically not easy. The schools studied by Levacic and Marren (1991) identified priorities for their first year of LMS, but only one had a full development strategy.

The current position in England and Wales seems to be that some schools use their school development plans to shape the budget, but most only use it to establish priorities, or just as a paper exercise. The operational link, however, between school development plan and budget may improve with experience. Schemes using programme budgeting, as in the state of Victoria, Australia, have this linkage built in.

Administration

Financial delegation should mean less work at the centre. Does it therefore lead to a reduction in central administration costs? Brown (1990) quotes a research study comparing four centralized districts and four matched decentralized ones in British Columbia. Of seven secretary–treasurers responding, none 'perceived a significant reduction of central office costs in either school-based managed or conventional managed districts and only one ... in a school-based managed district ... perceived a minor reduction' (p. 188).

The early schemes in England and Wales involved an actual increase in central administration, but this was associated with phased implementation of delegation. The influential Coopers and Lybrand report (1988) stated:

> Perhaps the most important resource implication for the LEA is that, while we would expect LMS to lead to increased effectiveness in the use of resources, it is unlikely to lead to reductions in overall expenditure and may well, certainly in the transitional period, require increases in expenditure. (p. 30)

It suggests that ongoing central costs include an enhanced role for advisers and inspectors; advice to, and monitoring of, schools on financial matters; and possibly loss of economies of scale. It accepts that some central functions will become obsolete but concludes:

> In some authorities these savings will more than balance the extra long-term costs, in many it will be the other way round. Our approach has not enabled us to form a definitive view about the net balance over all authorities, but we would be surprised if it turned out to be a net saving.
>
> (Coopers and Lybrand, 1988, p. 31)

If administration has not reduced at the centre, it has certainly increased in the schools. Evidence for this lies in the increased workload of principals and the demand on time discussed above, the general demand for increased clerical support in schools and the increase in bursars and administrative officers. The load has undoubtedly been increased in some schemes by unnecessary regulations, forms, returns and procedures.

Overall, it appears that administration involved in financial delegation does not cost less, and often costs more. Whether it is more efficient depends on some of the other considerations discussed below. An important factor seems to be the pressure on the delegating authority. Schools with delegated budgets tend to become curious about the amount of 'their' money spent at the centre and press for its reduction and subsequent transfer to school control. A government drive to achieve this is often necessary to ensure the transfer. Currently in England and Wales central government extracts statistics from each LEA showing the percentage retained for central administration, issues 'league tables' and castigates the laggards.

Information technology

An unintended result of financial delegation has been a rapid extension of information technology for school administration. This was less true of the earlier schemes, some of which operated on manual records at the school and monthly printouts from the centre. But in more recent schemes IT has been seen as important, both for efficiency and as an alternative to additional clerical support.

Initially the main use of information technology was seen as the immediate availability of financial and other information to the school's administration, but later its value for modelling the financial costs of alternatives has become more prominent. Where on-line facilities are provided, immediate transfer of information to and from the centre is possible. Each school is then able to know much more about its finances, but then so does its delegating authority! Central monitoring is, at least in theory, more easily achieved.

In another respect, however, information technology has created problems. There are widespread complaints in many schemes of problems with miscoding, debits 'without warning', incomprehensible printouts and so on. This should only be an initial problem, though it seems to take years rather than months to put right.

Flexibility

Flexibility emerges strongly as the greatest gain for schools. Brown (1990) provides a summary of Alexandruk's (1985) work, which surveyed principals and teachers in Edmonton on the main advantages and disadvantages of school-based management (see Table 6.1).

Table 6.1 Advantages and disadvantages of school-based management
(adapted from Alexandruk and cited by Brown (1990))

	% Principals (n = 77)	% Teachers (n = 398)
Leading advantage		
Subsidiarity	35	19
Flexibility	31	25
Efficiency, effectiveness & staff awareness of programme needs and costs	13	12
Staff involvement in decision making	12	23
Other	17	21
Leading disadvantage		
'The time factor'	32	22
Allocation of resources	23	15
Stress	10	14
Increased authority of principal	–	13
Other	33	22

Since subsidiarity also implies more school flexibility, the emphasis on flexibility is very strong. It is further illuminated by numerous interview responses of principals quoted by Brown (1990). For example, 'the heart of the matter is the ability to respond to the unique needs of the school. You can now do the little things in your school for people that make the job that much better.' He concludes : 'When asked about the flexibility of decision making provided them under school-based management, principals emphasized that they operated under fewer constraints than under centralization. They saw they had a greater ability to adapt to school needs with greater speed. Their scope of decision making was wider than previously' (Brown, 1990, p. 157).

Identical comments emerge from evaluation of English schemes. Humphrey and Thomas (1986), for example, report on the ten pilot schools in the Solihull scheme:

> several institutions commented very favourably on the power autonomy gives in deciding priorities within programmes, particularly with regard to maintenance [of buildings].... One of the implicit criteria by which schools judge the benefits of autonomy is in terms of the opportunity provided to respond to their own perceived needs, as and when they arise. (p. 513)

Numerous examples of the benefits from flexibility are noted by Levacic (1989), Levacic and Marren (1991), Downes (1988) and Thomas (1989).

Innovation

There is little evidence to date of financial delegation encouraging major innovation. There are certainly examples of schools doing things they were not able to do previously. Smilanich (1990), for example, comments: 'It is interesting to note that every school now offers computer related programs without a single edict ever being issued from central services.... Schools moved on a broken front when their staffs were ready and consumer (parent) demand suggested' (p. 9). There are few, if any, examples of schools inspired by financial delegation embarking on major, breakthrough innovation. The evidence so far is that financial delegation has had minimal influence on existing attitudes to change. There are financial mechanisms which seem to encourage innovation – specific or targeted grants, competitive tendering, competition for grants ('honeypot management', see Knight (1987)) – but straight delegation is not one of them.

Accountability

The management literature stresses accountability as an important consequence of delegation. If you manage it, you are accountable for it. Principals are accountable for their delegated budgets.

But this does not really amount to very much. Balancing a budget is not difficult, and it certainly is not an indication of effectiveness or efficiency. Overspending, or underspending to save for a major project, might be better indicators. This may be the reason why, in Alexandruk's survey above, accountability scored low as an advantage or disadvantage of school-based management.

There is little evidence that principals yet feel, or are, much more accountable for the outcomes of their schools, apart from this additional financial responsibility. There is movement in that direction; the evaluation of, and reporting on, school development plans, the painful struggle to develop useful performance indicators, the tighter definition of roles (for example, in Edmonton the introduction of the 'one-boss' rule). It appears that financial delegation may eventually make principals and staffs more accountable, but at present accountability exists more in name than fact.

In one sense delegation does make school staffs feel more accountable. They are certainly much more cost conscious. Many interviews and case studies report to this effect: Stenner (1988), for example, comments, 'value for money is an imprecise term, but whatever people mean by it, that is what they feel they are aiming for and achieving' (p. 68). Likewise, Humphrey and Thomas (1986) conclude that 'schools also feel that they are able to maximize their assets and to make sure that they are getting value for money' (p. 513); and Brown (1990) quotes a Langley principal in his survey who describes teachers as now more conscious of energy costs.

More local management means more scope for misappropriation. Few, if any, major scandals have yet come to light. Delegating authorities have been careful to establish strong audit controls and financial regulations. However, as decentralization spreads, and if familiarity breeds slackness, it seems likely that there might be some good tales to tell.

The level of funding

Fears have been expressed that financial delegation could lead to a delegating authority failing to fund schools adequately now that it is no longer immediately responsible for their budgets: what the UK Audit Commission has called 'abdication of blame'. This could occur overtly, through retrenchment, or covertly, by failure to finance new needs adequately or to offset inflation fully.

This is difficult to assess, since it is virtually impossible to prove what the level of funding would have been if the system had remained centralized. There has been some evidence in England and Wales of LEAs in financial difficulties cutting delegated budget allocations more freely than they would probably have cut a central budget. It is certainly easier to do this, since it involves just one painful decision over the value of 'pupil-units', rather than a series of hard-fought battles over each individual cut.

However, there is also evidence that school principals and governing bodies are now much better informed about school finance and more adept at arguing their case. They are becoming a stronger lobby. This new power will certainly be put to the test. Schools are entering a more capital-intensive stage, requiring increased investment in educational technology and its support, maintenance and replacement. It is not at all certain that delegating authorities will increase budgets adequately for this.

Augmentation of funds by income generation

It is difficult to distinguish income generation which would have occurred anyway from that which has been encouraged by financial delegation. Certainly in England and Wales there has been a marked increase in fund raising since the introduction of LMS. This has taken the forms of industrial sponsorship and sale of school services to business, appointment of school development or marketing officers, as well as appeals for donations, often covenanted, to parents or community.

This apparent acceleration of an existing trend of income generation is enhanced by a market economy context. It is promoted by greater awareness of the school improvements extra funds can realize, a need to offset underfunding of *loser* schools under the formula, and greater use of public relations and marketing. There are two important underlying issues. First, does income generation actually augment existing funding, or just compensate for underfunding? Second, it raises strong questions of equity, since schools located in wealthier areas will have much more income-raising potential than those in less fortunate areas.

Allocation of funds between schools

The shift to formula funding has been generally welcomed as being more open, understandable and more equitable. There seems to be a general dislike of the importance of lobbying and personal influence in centralized funding. In England and Wales the approach to decentralized funding was summarized in the DES Circular (1988):

> The basis on which resources are allocated to schools ... will need to be clear and explicit, so that all concerned with the scheme are aware of its effects; and it will need to be based on objective needs rather than simply on historic spending, in order to ensure an equitable allocation of the available resources between schools. (paragraph 99)

Unfortunately, assessing objective needs is a subjective process. All schemes base the formula largely on a per-pupil allocation; the *dollar follows the child* rule. Most include an age-weighting element, and this varies considerably, often to reflect tradition or accommodate previous historic allocations. Thomas (1990) notes that English and Welsh LEAs in 1990 proposed a percentage difference in *pupil-units* between pupils in the last year of primary and first year of secondary school ranging from less than 5 per cent to 95 per cent; and between pupils aged 7 and 16–18 ranging from 80 per cent to 175 per cent.

In England and Wales LMS has led to fierce discussion of this primary–secondary differential, focusing on the degree to which secondary schools should be better funded per pupil than primary schools. Overall this has led to a slight shift towards improved primary funding, with the suggestion of more to follow. Significantly, in Edmonton, Canada, the differential has now almost disappeared.

Agreement on the other factors to be included in the formula is also difficult. One such element is the allowance for small schools. But here a conflict with efficiency arises. Subsidizing small schools can only be at the expense of larger ones, and the larger the subsidy, the less the incentive to rationalize the system. Despite frequently expressed intentions to protect small schools, in practice they seem to be disadvantaged. Thomas and Bullock (1991) report for the first year of LMS in England and Wales:

> There appear to be size thresholds, the crossing of which is a key determinant of the scale and likelihood of winning and losing. In the primary sector this threshold is 200 pupils, schools with less than that number [being] more likely to be losers... two thirds of [secondary] schools with fewer than 700 pupils lose with the change of funding. (p. 8)

In Edmonton, Alexandruk found:

Respondents [both principals and teachers] perceived the allocation formulas as being inadequate and resulting in severe restrictions on small schools and small programs.... [They] indicated that as school size decreases, the amount of flexibility in the educational program declines rapidly. The view was expressed that, while school budget allocation formulas have established a degree of equity among schools in the district, the formulas have not sufficiently addressed the particular needs of small schools or schools with unusual mixes of educational programs or needs.

Other special factors include special educational needs; problems arising from social deprivation; children needing extra tuition in the prevailing language; and high premises costs. Most of these have been accommodated in formulae, but nowhere adequately, partly because it is difficult or time consuming to create an objective but simple assessment. Thomas (1990), for example, analysing the proposed LMS formulae of 90 LEAs in England and Wales, points out the difficulties: 'There is a real concern that the socio-economic deprivation of individual pupils has a close correlation with their learning difficulties, but most [LEAs] are very uncertain which methods are best able to assess such disadvantages. Most are unable to use any better index than free meals' (p. 29). Free school meals in fact have been shown to be a poor indicator of socio-economic deprivation and educational need.

Another factor which needs consideration is fixed costs. Most formulae make some allowance for them, often in the form of a fixed *starter allowance*. However, fixed costs are actually a larger element in a school's budget than is generally realized, between 10 and 20 per cent in most schemes. (This problem is discussed in Knight (1983, pp. 155–62).) They are also connected with enrolment, since they weight less heavily as rolls rise and more heavily when rolls fall. If two schools have the same number of pupils and the same formula allocation, and if one then grows in number and one shrinks, the latter will have less of its budget per pupil free to spend on classroom resources compared with its peer.

Although financial delegation makes allocation of funds to schools *apparently* more equitable, it is not certain that it actually does. Assume the worst case scenario: a small school with a high proportion of pupils with special educational needs, needs for tuition in the native language, and problems arising from social deprivation; on a split site with buildings costly to maintain and energy inefficient; underoccupied and with falling rolls. On the evidence available, and given current formulae, it is doubtful whether any existing scheme will give the pupils of this school as equitable a share of available resources as their peers in less disadvantaged schools, or probably as they would have received in a previous centralized scheme.

Allocation of funds within schools

The evidence that financial delegation results in a more beneficial allocation of funds within schools is more positive. Nevertheless, some schools claim improvements under financial delegation which are really circumstantial. For example, funding for pilot schools is often unduly favourable. Furthermore, one school's improved funding under the formula may be at the expense of another. If the global budget is constant in real terms, the gains of *winning* schools will be offset by the losses of *losers*. Whether the global budget increases or decreases in real terms, the real issue is the part financial delegation plays in influencing the size of the total budget and its allocation to each school.

More *research* evidence is needed of economies, better value-for-money or revised priorities making possible the virement of funds to areas more closely related with learning, or better targeting of funds for the curriculum. There is presently an abundance of *anecdotal* evidence that this is happening in schools experiencing financial delegation.

Commonly, most savings made by schools are in energy and water costs, while good examples of better value for money secured by schools relate to buildings and grounds maintenance. Substantial savings are often made in the relief teachers' budget, and from the covering of short-term vacancies by existing staff. In fact, examples can be found of savings made somewhere, to virtually every budget heading – advertising vacancies, interview expenses, stationery and equipment, refuse collection, cleaning, postage and telephone – and commonly several of these in one school. Stenner (1988), for example, reports for her primary school:

> Economies were achieved by such means as using cheap telephone time, pupil post, arrangements for evening classes which did not involve heating the entire school for one flower club, installing gadgets in the urinals which saved hundreds of gallons of metered water during weekends and holidays, and more thoughtful use of electricity. The supply underspend was generated by the head and a part-time teacher covering for absence whenever possible, a direct saving to the school of £50 a day. (p. 65)

The shift in allocating resources to activities at or close to the chalkface has been almost universal. There are reports of schools appointing additional teachers, awarding additional allowances or enhancing salaries, hiring additional technicians and increasing clerical support. Commonly there is additional funding of in-service training. For premises there are examples of long-term maintenance programmes, improved redecoration, enhancement of public areas and quicker responses for emergency repairs. Most schools report additional expenditure on books and equipment, sometimes substantial.

Brown (1990) describes how one Edmonton school saved 4 per cent of its budget and allocated this to updating the library, purchasing curriculum materials, physical education equipment and microcomputers, and sending teachers and aides on training programmes, to conferences and on interschool visits.

Downes (1986) describes the shift in his large secondary school, thus:

The amount of money notionally moved from one heading to another in the course of a year has always been under two per cent and the general direction of the moves has been to:

- increase ancillary staffing
- increase teacher staffing
- increase supply teacher [relief] cover
- set up our own in-service training account. (p. 4)

A shift of 2 or 3 per cent in a budget may sound marginal. However, a school's expenditure on books, stationery, equipment and educational materials will commonly total less than 4 per cent of the total budget. Financial delegation therefore makes possible an improvement of 50 per cent or more in capitation expenditure or consumables. Humphrey and Thomas (1986) were able to quantify this shift:

An analysis of the 1986/87 budgets of seven of the autonomous schools shows planned virement ranging from 2 per cent to 3.5 per cent in secondary schools and 2.3 per cent to 5.4 per cent in primaries. In cash terms, this amounts to virement ranging from £19,900 to £41,200 in the case of secondaries and £5,800 to £11,400 for the smaller primary school. (p. 513)

DELEGATION OF CENTRAL SERVICES

A more recent trend in a few restructuring schemes is the delegation of central services. Edmonton, Canada, introduced a pilot scheme in 1986 for subject consultancy services. In England and Wales central government is pressing LEAs hard to delegate the funds for most central services. Schools can then decide whether they wish to purchase these from the LEA, or find an alternative supplier, and in what quantity or quality.

Generally this seems a desirable principle. It makes apparent the cost of services, previously a 'free gift' from the school's viewpoint, and allows comparison with other external providers and with in-house provision. There is risk, however. If some schools decline to use these services the cost to other schools may increase. This is particularly dangerous for services with high fixed costs, such as library and museum loans, and special centres for science, technology, audio-visual aids, foreign languages and so on. There is also a risk of diseconomies of scale. This has been the case in Western Australia, where the ministry grants substantial funds to schools which then individually invest them. However, investment of the total funds centrally would save time and effort and provide a better financial return. The disadvantage of central investment from a school's viewpoint is, as one Western Australian principal stated, 'we'd never see that money!'.

It is highly likely that the trend towards a breaking down of the central monopoly of support services will continue. Central services, faced with competition, will become leaner and probably more efficient, and more hard-nosed. Schools appreciate the opportunity of choice, although they will often prefer to choose the central rather than a private provider. In some cases, particularly in-service work, schools may decide to provide more of their own in-house training.

In England and Wales the situation in relation to premises and grounds maintenance, cleaning and catering has been further complicated by a government requirement for competitive tendering. This process seems to be lowering costs, but can have adverse effects on quality and be very time consuming for school administrators.

MANAGEMENT OF TIME AS A RESOURCE

A number of restructuring schemes, particularly in North America and the UK, allow schools to determine their own school day. Although currently there is considerable experiment with new patterns of day (see Knight, 1989, chapters 3 and 4), it is difficult to see actual links with financial delegation. Potentially, however, there is clear linkage, as in Figure 6.1.

The penultimate stage, conversion into *resource hours*, is often taken for granted. A school can hire teachers, construct buildings or buy equipment, but it cannot *use* them until it has converted them into resource hours, usually through the school timetable. The present school day is a very poor converter.

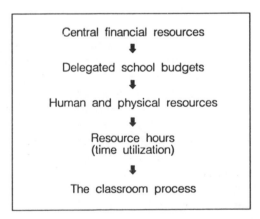

Figure 6.1 Linkage between financial delegation and teaching and learning time

It seems inevitable that as schools receive delegated budgets and become keener to achieve value for money and cost effectiveness, they will turn their attention to more effective and efficient forms of organizing the school day, which will provide a better return on their financial investment. Initially, this may manifest itself in terms of changing the arrangements for teaching and learning; for example, maximizing the use of premises and equipment and increasing total teacher-time (see Knight, 1991).

Headteachers or principals with fully delegated financial responsibilities are beginning to talk of *teacher-hours, supply (relief) days* and *dollars/pounds per pupil*. Eventually the logic of financial delegation implies that schools will cost outcomes, and so compare the costs of alternative learning methods. Hence the cost of teaching *n* students to a certain standard in a specific subject could be compared with the cost of the same outcomes secured by alternative learning strategies, such as supported self-study, computerized learning or distance learning. At present, delegation does not spark such innovation, but its financial logic may do so in the future.

CURRICULUM

The foregoing sections suggest that financial delegation to schools not so much generates curriculum change as facilitates it: by providing extra learning resources, by enhancing the teaching or non-teaching establishment, by financing minor modifications to premises, and by investing more in in-service training. While the overall effect seems to be marginal, the effects in some schools are considerable. However, schools with less proactive management or with more severe financial problems seem to find less scope for curriculum change.

COMMUNITY EDUCATION

In theory financial delegation encourages school interaction with the local community, including the provision of community education. Schools have greater management and financial flexibility and often enjoy greater parent or community involvement as a result. In practice, however, regulations created by the delegating authority can inhibit flexibility over charging policies, programmes and payment of staff.

A specific problem arises over premises costs. It is often difficult, particularly in countries with heavy heating costs, to isolate the cost of premises use for an individual activity. In the past some lettings were hidden loss-makers; with devolved budgets their cost can be seen as a drain on the school budget.

In some schemes a technical problem arises with the community education budget. Should it be treated as quite separate from the school budget, or linked with it in some way, either feeding the school budget or fed by it? The former is more beneficial in the long term to community and school, but in England and Wales, for example, is excluded by the 1988 Act.

Overall, it seems reasonable to believe that more opportunities for community education *should* follow from financial delegation. There is little evidence of this, however, and in reality the reverse may be more accurate, since the present regulations of some schemes (in England and Wales, for example) forbid the cross-subsidization of school and community education.

THE OVERALL EFFECTS OF FINANCIAL DELEGATION

Drawing generalizations about the effects of, and reactions to, financial delegation from such a spread of data is not easy, particularly when such data are contextually dependent. Nevertheless, the general drift is positive. Anecdotal evidence, largely from England and Wales and Canada, points to the enthusiasm of principals, and to a lesser extent other school staff and governing bodies and school councils. Schools are keen to enter pilot schemes, and only one school known to this author has dropped out of a pilot project. There is no move anywhere to reverse financial delegation.

Clearly, devolution makes schools more aware of the need for more effective, purposeful management. There are strong links between financial delegation, more purposeful management and school development planning.

The role of headteacher or principal becomes more important. There is not yet much evidence that they become engulfed in administration. In general, principals feel more in control of the destiny of their schools. With some exceptions, financial delegation leads to increased participation by other staff and governing bodies. The use of information technology for school administration is accelerated.

The feature of financial delegation which schools most highly value is the flexibility it provides. The school can more easily direct its funds to meet its perceived needs. Information technology can help in long-term planning and aid school management in making quick responses where necessary. Although often there is virement of only about 2 or 3 per cent of budgets, there is evidence that more resources than before are directed to classrooms, with visible effect. It also generates increased expenditure directly relevant to curriculum development. Overall, financial delegation probably improves the school climate, but with exceptions where it is badly implemented or where the school suffers from the switch to formula funding.

With regard to other effects the evidence is less certain. Although financial delegation appears to give schools greater freedom for major innovation, there is little evidence yet of this occurring. In theory schools become more accountable, and they claim greater awareness of accountability, but how this accountability is linked to school outcomes awaits evidence in the future.

There is as yet no evidence that financial delegation improves, or worsens, the overall level of funding. The total cost of administration, central and devolved, is probably increased. Formula funding, which financial delegation requires, is generally felt to be both more open and more equitable, but in practice it is not clear that it is actually any fairer to schools with severe needs or problems. It may be less equitable. Financial delegation should encourage the growth of community education, but there is no evidence of this, and in some instances the attendant regulations are actually restricting it.

The least popular feature of financial delegation is the additional time required for financial management in schools, and the pressure this creates. Beyond that, there is the possibility that there may be negative changes in the style of school principals and their relationships with staff; that financial delegation may distract principals and governing bodies from the educational purpose of the school; and that existing mismanagement may be magnified.

All of these are serious potential problems, but there is not yet evidence of their development on any scale. It is possibly fair to conclude that financial delegation has, overall, beneficial effects on the management and the educational processes of most schools. But is this evidence strong enough to claim that financial delegation affects student learning outcomes?

THE EFFECT OF FINANCIAL DELEGATION ON SCHOOL OUTCOMES

There is really no solid evidence that financial delegation has improved school outcomes. Brown (1990) looked for this in his Canadian studies. In Langley, although there was regular testing, it was considered too early in 1988 to determine learning effect changes since school-based management was only generally adopted in 1985. In an interview the superintendent felt there was no hard evidence that learning outcomes had improved. In Edmonton, with district-wide delegation since 1980, there are no general yearly examinations. The only evidence found by Brown was the annual survey of parental and student satisfaction. Between 1979 and 1983 parent response improved for 64 per cent of the survey items, and only deteriorated for 4 per cent. The equivalent student responses were 72 per cent of items up and 1 per cent down. Gallup polls of citizen (not just parental) satisfaction for Canada as a whole for 1979 and 1984 showed absolutely no change. However, since the Edmonton district embarked on a programme of improvement measures much broader than just financial delegation, it is difficult to prove that this was the decisive factor.

In the state of Victoria, Australia, there is no evidence to date linking devolution, let alone financial delegation, with improved school outcomes. There is a similar lack of evidence in the USA. Nor can there yet be in England and Wales for the large-scale changes of the 1988 Act, since these only affected schools in April 1990 (and not all schools until April 1994). The same holds for New Zealand.

There is, however, some anecdotal evidence, typified by two headteachers of Cambridgeshire schools which commenced financial delegation in 1982. Stenner (1988) records for her primary school:

> An evaluation at the end of the pilot scheme showed that governors and staff believed that it had had significant value in bringing considerable educational, financial, social and organizational benefits to the school. While it would be rash to claim that improved reading averages and the like can be attributed necessarily to LFM (Local Financial Management), it has most certainly created better conditions for learning. At the most basic level children no longer have to share a maths textbook between three and the school is better resourced than it has ever been. It has turned savings made under non-educational headings into books, computers, instruments, equipment, furniture and it wants for very little of that nature. The teachers can make curriculum decisions in the knowledge, not just the hope, that they can be resourced and extra teaching and ancillary hours are financed each year. (p. 67)

Downes (1986), headteacher of a large secondary school, replies to sceptics of financial delegation who ask for proof that it has benefited pupils in his school by claiming that it has enhanced teaching and learning conditions:

> People who are unconvinced by the philosophical arguments behind LFM often ask me to 'prove' that it has made education better for the pupils in my school. I am unable to do so in any clear and statistical way. Instead I would point to what has been done and I would argue that these actions have brought significant advantages to the education of the pupils, mainly through making teaching conditions better for their teachers. For example, the fact that we now have a part-time librarian means that the libraries are open more often and the books better organized than before. The fact that we have a reprographics assistant means that teaching staff have to spend less time duplicating their own teaching materials. We can point to specific items of equipment, particularly in the sphere of technology and comput- ing, and say that we would not have been able to buy those when we did had it not been for LFM. I can indicate that we have been able to reduce the occasional over-sized class by buying-in an extra couple of teaching periods to enable a class to be split.
> Perhaps the important, yet intangible, advantage to the school as a whole is that ... we are to a much greater extent masters of our own destiny. This helps to foster a pride in our own establishment and encourages initiatives and a measure of independence of action. In a word, it can produce, at all levels, greater job satisfaction. (p. 6)

However, these were pilot schools with some windfall advantages, and with two very capable and experienced headteachers. While we can see what *can* happen to the school process, we are still no clearer about what *does* happen to student outcomes.

It appears that decentralization in general (and financial delegation in particular) has a *facilitating* and perhaps a *gearing* effect on the schools that experience it. It facilitates because of the flexibility and additional choices that it offers; and gears because it tends to strengthen school management, planning and participation. It does not necessarily alter the values, aims, expectations or classroom practices of the school. It is not an alternative to school improvement programmes, but rather an extra element. This was the final conclusion of Taylor and Levine (1991):

> School-based management can be an important component of school improvement projects. By itself, however, it does not provide a comprehensive model for bringing about fundamental reform in elementary and secondary schools. (p. 397)

But there is more to be said. At present decentralization is seen as providing schools with freedom to spend money on different inputs. What if it were used to spend on different outcomes? You pay for what you get, not for what you put in.

Schools with delegated budgets, and no hampering regulations, could contract with an external provider, or an in-house group, to supply education or training for an agreed level of outcomes, say in modern language teaching, or technical training, or adventure experience, or catch-up coaching. Clearly, outcomes for students could not be specified definitively, but schools could change suppliers if they were not satisfied with the results.

Financial delegation also enables schools to examine the cost effectiveness of alternative learning strategies:

- variations on traditional forms of teaching
- *free school* learning approaches
- individualized learning and supported self-study
- computer-assisted learning
- distance learning
- learning using the total resources of the community.

Such alternatives coincide with current thinking about the need to 'break the mould' – to build learning systems for the twenty-first century and the Information Age.

However, schools will not necessarily act logically to maximize efficiency and effectiveness. Faced with the threat of innovation, the reverse may be more likely. A mechanism to encourage them to adopt outcome-led financial management may be necessary. Supporters of the market economy believe it is a sufficient mechanism to induce outcome-led financial management. However, innovation is not usually advanced as one of the main merits of the market economy approach to education, and serious doubts exist about the effectiveness of problem or ailing schools in a market context. However, other mechanisms besides the market economy are available: for example, 'honeypot management' (see Knight, 1987), the most striking current example of which is the America 2000 Education Strategy, where communities and schools will bid for funds to develop 'new age' schools; national awards; specific grants payable on attainment of specified innovative criteria; group innovation, of which there are a number of current examples, including Washington State's Schools for the 21st Century and, in the UK, Education 2000; or government support for alternative schools, as in the free schools in the Netherlands, or city technology colleges in the UK. All of these could encourage expenditure linked to outcomes. Not 'the dollar follows the child', but 'the dollar pays for student achievement'.

Overall the conclusion is that financial delegation substantially and progressively affects the school process and mainly for the better. Currently, it is probably improving student experience through better funding of chalkface activities but not sufficiently to achieve any measurable improvement in student outcomes. Ultimately, it could be an essential element in alternative approaches to school effectiveness by linking finance to school outcomes. Predictably, financial delegation will remain a facilitating and gearing device, its true value and impact lying in the hands of the user.

REFERENCES

Alexandruk, F. (1985) 'School budgeting in the Edmonton public school district', Unpublished Masters Thesis, Department of Educational Administration, University of Alberta, Edmonton.

Audit Commission (1984) *Obtaining Better Value in Education: Aspects of Non-teaching Costs in Secondary Schools*, London: HMSO.

Bowe, R., Ball, S.J. and Gold, A. (1992) *The Educational Reform Act, 1988: From Policies to Practices*, London: Routledge.

Brown, D.J. (1990) *Decentralization and School-based Management*, Lewes: Falmer Press.

Burgess, T. (1986) 'Cambridgeshire financial management initiative for schools', *Public Money*, June.

Caldwell, B. and Spinks, J. (1988) *The Self-managing School*; London: The Falmer Press.

Conley, S. and Bacharach, S. (1990) 'From school-site management to participatory school-site management', *Phi Delta Kappan* March: 540.

Coopers and Lybrand (1988) *Local Management of Schools: A report to the Department of Education and Science*, London: HMSO.

DES (1988) *Circular 7/88. Education Reform Act: Local Management of Schools*, London: Department of Education and Science.

Downes, P. (1986) *Local Financial Management*, Huntingdon: Hinchingbrooke School.

—— (ed.) (1988) *Local Financial Management in Schools*, Oxford: Blackwell.

Humphrey, C. and Thomas, H. (1986) 'Delegating to schools', *Education* 168 (24).

Knight, B. (1983) *Managing School Finance*, London: Heinemann.

—— (1987) 'Managing the honeypots', in H. Thomas and T. Simkins (eds) *Economics and the Managing of Education: Emerging Themes*, Lewes: Falmer Press.

—— (1989) *Managing School Time*, Harlow: Longman.

—— (1991) *Designing the School Day*, Harlow: Longman.

Levacic, R. (1989) 'Managing a delegated budget: Three schools' experiences', in R Levacic (ed.) *Financial Management in Education*, Milton Keynes: Open University Press.

Levacic, R. and Marren, E. (1991) 'Implementing local management of schools: First year spending decisions', A paper given at the Annual Conference of the British Educational Management and Administration Society, September 1991.

MacGregor, J. (1990) 'A message from the Secretary of State for Education and Science', in *The Education Management Exhibition Newsletter 2*, The Court House, The Square, Wiveliscombe, Somerset.

Sheffield City Polytechnic Department of Education Management (1986) *Study of the delegation component of Lincolnshire's 'Project 7'*, A report to the Lincolnshire LEA.

Smilanich, R. (1990) 'Devolution in Edmonton public schools: Ten years on', Mimeographed paper, Edmonton School District.

Stenner, A. (1988) 'LFM in a primary school', in P. Downes (ed.) *Local Financial Management in Schools*, Oxford: Blackwell.

Taylor, B. and Levine, D. (1991) 'Effective schools project and school-based management', *Phi Delta Kappan* January: 394.

Thomas, G. (1988) 'LFM in a secondary school', in P. Downes (ed.) *Local Financial Management in Schools*, Oxford: Blackwell.

—— (1989) 'LFM at St Peters secondary school', in B. Fidler and G. Bowles (eds) *Effective Local Management of Schools*, Harlow: Longman.

—— (1990) *Setting up LMS – A study of local education authorities submissions to DES*, Milton Keynes, Centre for Educational Policy and Management: Open University.

Thomas, H. (1987) 'Efficiency and opportunity in school finance autonomy', in H. Thomas and T. Simkins (eds) *Economics and the Management of Education: Emerging themes*, Lewes: Falmer Press.

Thomas, H. and Bullock, A. (1991) 'School size and local management funding formulae', A paper given at the Annual Conference of the British Educational Management and Administration Society, September 1991.

Western Australian Ministry of Education (1987) *Better Schools in Western Australia*, Perth: Western Australian Ministry of Education.

Chapter 7

School development and review in an Australian state education system

Peter Cuttance

This chapter describes the framework for reviewing the effectiveness of schooling in South Australia and for auditing the performance of management in the system. The fundamental aim of regular reviews and audits is to improve learning opportunities for students. The chapter describes the basis of the reviews and audits undertaken by the Education Review Unit (ERU) and the relationship between the work of this Unit and the development and delivery of education through other parts of the system.

Suggestions for a programme of school reviews have been discussed at various times since the demise of the former Inspectorate in South Australia in the early 1970s. The Committee of Inquiry into Education in South Australia produced two reports – an interim and a final report (Keeves, 1981, 1982) – recommending the establishment of a system of school reviews. It also discussed the concept of school development programmes and the links between these and school reviews. Further, in the context of in-service work in schools, the Schools Commission *Report for the Triennium 1982–84* argued that:

> school communities [should be] encouraged to assess their school's performance, examine its organizational arrangements, consider its overall offering and the special needs of its pupils, and devise plans leading to modifications and changes that substantially improve the quality of the service offered.
>
> (Schools Commission, 1984, p. 205)

During the early years of the 1980s some district superintendents worked with schools to undertake reviews initiated by those schools. Guidelines for school evaluation were published by the Department but this work was not actively supported as a high policy priority. The onus for initiating such reviews lay with schools as part of an earlier policy transferring authority for school operational issues from the Education Department of South Australia (EDSA) to schools themselves (EDSA, 1970).

Although many successful school reviews were undertaken, the process never spread systematically to all schools in the system. The Keeves Report indicated that this system of school evaluation had not been successful, in particular:

• There was a weak linkage between these reviews and the directorates responsible for development and operational activities in the system. This meant that the review process was separated from the planning processes of the system and failed to provide any basis for systemic accountability.
• There was a strong tendency for the reports from the evaluations to remain confidential documents. This tended to stifle change in the practices, programmes and policies of schools, and defeated the purpose of the reviews as a basis for the public accountability of schools.
• The review reports were generally not made available to the officers of the central and regional administration; hence, they did not assist in building up a wide professional perspective of the effectiveness of the school or of its policies and curricula.
• Some of the evaluation studies were time consuming and costly, and as a consequence there was a degree of disillusionment with the value of such exercises (Keeves, 1982, p. 202).

The Keeves Report recommended the development of a system of prospective reviews of schools that would provide a basis for assessing:

• the needs of individual schools
• the success with which they had operated in the past
• the quality of their plans and products for the future (Keeves, 1982, p. 204).

In addition, the report recommended the development of a regular review of the system every ten years; a programme for monitoring student performance; and a series of curriculum and teaching studies to map curriculum and teaching practices.

The recommendations on school review and development in the Keeves Report were not acted on and the issue of school development and review was not raised for widespread discussion again until the *Report of the Review of Superintendents* (Cox, 1987). This report discussed what it called School Achievement Plans as an extension of the Curriculum Plans that schools were expected to prepare for the Department in response to the policy statement, *Curriculum Authority and Responsibility* (EDSA, 1985). This policy statement described the means by which the Director-General's responsibility for curriculum plans is discharged. It described the organizational and functional framework within which curriculum is approved at a systemic level and the process of curriculum plan approval for individual schools.

The Curriculum Authority and Responsibility policy requires schools to produce, for approval, a curriculum plan which consists of the following elements:

- A statement of the overall aims and objectives of the school consistent with *Our Schools and their Purposes* (EDSA, 1981).
- A statement of the subjects or areas of study available to students at the various year levels, and their respective time allocations.
- Documentation of the subjects or areas of study, including reference to Education Department guides, used as the basis for planning and instruction. Documentation [is also to] indicate the major teaching resources being used.
- The school policy on the assessment of student learning – both general policy and policies for individual curriculum areas.
- A statement of the means by which the school monitors, evaluates, reviews and revises its curriculum plan (EDSA, 1985, p. 12).

The Cox Report (1987) recommended that:

- The Curriculum Plan required by the Curriculum Authority and Responsibility process be extended to form the School Achievement Plan. The report outlined the proposed functions and responsibilities of each of the groups of superintendents in relation to the School Achievement Plan and included a proposal to establish a Quality Assurance Unit.
- The School Achievement Plan was to provide a framework for the school to meet its stated objectives. It was to be a working document, practical in its outline and written so as to be easily understood with an emphasis on brevity.
- Each school was to develop a three-year School Achievement Plan with specific objectives, means by which they were to be addressed and indicators against which achievement could be gauged. The plan was to be prepared in cooperation with the school's staff, the school council and, where relevant, the students. It was to be a public document. The plan and the processes used to develop it were to be central to the determination of quality achievements by schools.
- The plan was to include statements which indicated:
  - the involvement of the school council and the opportunities provided for parents to play a part in developing the plan
  - consideration of the school environment, taking into account safety, health and welfare issues for students
  - equality of outcomes for all students
  - the proposed processes, timetable and timeline for accommodating policy and management directives from the Director-General or Minister
  - special activities which provide opportunities for the school community to celebrate aspects of educational achievement or important community and social events
  - the monitoring of the effectiveness of classroom practice

- the proposed strategies and timeline for the professional development programme for the school's staff

• These extensions were in addition and complementary to the five components of the existing Curriculum Plan, described in the Curriculum Authority and Responsibility process, and elaborated earlier.

Finally, the report recommended the establishment of a Quality Assurance Unit to convene/coordinate a series of team visits to schools on a regular basis to assess the schools' achievement plans. The discussion of proposals for school development and review in the Keeves Report (1981, 1982) and the Cox Report (1987) bear many similarities to those discussed in the UK during the 1980s (for a discussion of the issues raised in the UK, see Cuttance (1989a, b)).

Early in 1989 the Education Department's draft *Three Year Plan* was released. It required that all schools formulate a School Development Plan. The policy statement *School Development Plans*, issued by the Director-General of Education in October 1989 (EDSA, 1989), described the school development plan (SDP) as a 'statement of the key things which the school wants to change and improve (objectives); how these things are to be achieved (strategies); and what the impact will be (outcomes) to improve education for students'.

The statement outlined the responsibilities of various participants in relation to the school development plan, delegating to Area Directors the responsibility of approving such plans. It also referred to the relationship between the school development plan and the external review process to be carried out by the newly established Education Review Unit (ERU).

The review framework developed by the ERU explicitly recognized that the effectiveness of schooling depends on both the processes that directly influence student learning in schools and the effectiveness with which schools are supported by services provided at other organizational levels in the system. For this reason the review framework has been designed to support two types of reviews. The first assesses the development and progress of individual organizational units such as schools, development and other service units, and area and central directorates. The second cuts across organizational units to evaluate the effectiveness of the Department's policies and programmes, and of practice in various domains.

The programme of reviews aims to contribute to the effectiveness and development of education by building on the practices of the most effective schools in the system. The reviews of individual schools, service and development units, directorates, and policies and programmes are undertaken by teams which draw on the skills of school-based and other professional staff. In so doing, the reviews assess the effectiveness of the practices and functioning of individual units and of their development and processes for change. The review system also enables the dissemination of effective practice among schools.

Reviews of schools as individual organizational units focus on school development plans. The development plan for each school is set within the context of the wider goals that are described in that school's vision statement. School development plans focus on the development and change that schools intend to implement in order to improve teaching and learning, and the reviews of schools assess the extent to which this objective has been met.

REMIT OF THE ERU

The ERU conducts regular reviews of the effectiveness of individual policies and programmes, and of individual units – schools, directorates, and development and support units – in the education system. These reviews are based upon audit and review techniques for evaluating programme performance, compliance with regulations, and organizational effectiveness. They take account of the objectives set out in the Education Department's *Three Year Plan*, Departmental policies and guidelines and of the development plans of individual units.

The guiding principles that have informed the development of the review programme and methodology can be stated as follows:

- that reviews must serve the dual purpose of accountability (proving quality) and development (improving quality)
- in order to serve accountability purposes, the review programme must be as independent as possible from operational and development functions in the system
- the reviews must focus on issues of the management of quality throughout all schools, development and support units, and systemic functions, rather than simply assessment of the outcomes of schooling
- the reviews must make a constructive and timely contribution to the development of schools and the management and development of other units and functions
- there must be a primary focus on the practices and functioning of schools and units as they affect student learning outcomes.

The work of the Education Review Unit supports the development and improvement of schooling by:

- reviewing the effectiveness of individual policies and programmes and making appropriate recommendations for their improvement
- providing a basis for identifying effective practices and disseminating knowledge about them
- supporting the effective management and development of schools and other parts of the system through external review
- providing a framework for the accountability of schools and the education system

- providing externally validated information on the effectiveness of individual schools and of other units in the education system.

The progress of individual units towards the attainment of the objectives set out in their development plans is the subject of regular internal and external reviews, as shown in Figure 7.1. These reviews aim to locate the areas of effective and ineffective practice and provide a basis for revising their operation.

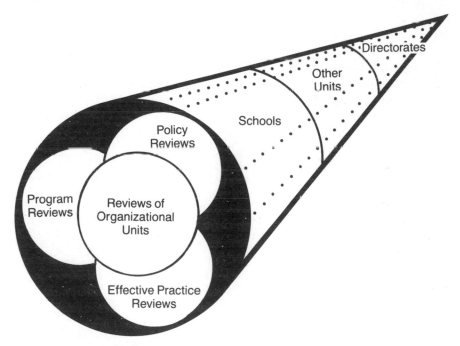

Figure 7.1 Framework for reviews of organizational units and systemic reviews

Reviews are conducted within guidelines established by the ERU in consultation with the education community. The development of schooling requires that all aspects of the education system be subject to regular review. The review programme for schools is integrated with reviews of other units and directorates to assess the performance of the system as a whole.

In addition to reports on the effectiveness of individual schools, other units and directorates, the ERU produces regular reports on progress towards the attainment of the objectives stated in the systemic *Three Year Plan*. It provides an important source of information for the refinement and development of strategies both to attain these objectives and address emerging issues in education. In addition the review programme satisfies the requirements for an accountability framework for the system.

Figure 7.1 indicates that the various types of review overlap within units at each level and that the programme integrates reviews across the various operational levels in the system. At the school level there will be a review of the school as an organizational unit. Other organizational units in the system will also be subject to regular reviews.

The review activities in schools also encompass reviews of systemic performance. In particular, the effectiveness of departmental policies and programmes is reviewed. Systemic performance is monitored through a series of reviews in schools of effective practice in four domains: teaching and learning, organization and management, ethos and culture, and equal opportunities and social justice. Other systemic reviews assess the effectiveness of the Education Department's policies and programmes in providing a better learning environment in school.

The different types of review are discussed in more detail after the next section, which addresses the relationship between school development plans and the Department's *Three Year Plan*.

In summary, the system addresses performance at all organizational levels:

- individual school
- other units involved in the support of schools
- central and area directorate
- the system as a whole.

The following types of review are undertaken to review the effectiveness of the system:

- school development
- effective practices in schools
- the effectiveness of educational programmes and policies
- the implementation of regulations and requirements and the effectiveness of management practices
- the performance of directorates and other units.

The first three of these will review schools as individual units, and the last will likewise review the performance of other individual units and directorates in the system. The remaining one will contribute to the review of the performance of the system as a whole. Because all policies and practice are ultimately aimed at the support of pupil learning, much of the review activity is school based. Systemic programme and policy reviews incorporate reviews of the contribution of other units responsible for supporting the work of schools.

SCHOOL DEVELOPMENT PLANS

School development plans state ways in which schools aim to improve student learning. They set out how schools pursue the development of their curriculum, teaching practice, management and the school community (EDSA, 1990a).

School development plans set out the primary objectives that schools plan to address each year over a three-year period; the strategies to be employed in attaining these objectives; and the outcomes expected from successful implementation.

The stated objectives and implementation strategies chart a development path for the school. The objectives often require different strategies for implementation at whole-school level, sub-school level and classroom level. Outcomes specify the behaviours and events that meet the objectives at the appropriate level within the school. Thus, school development plans facilitate focused long-term development in schools.

An annual internal review of progress in meeting school development plan objectives is required in each school. As part of good management practice schools are expected to monitor their development on a continuous basis, so that they are able to make appropriate ongoing adjustments to their development plan. As part of the process of rolling forward the three-year school development plan the annual internal review also reassesses the next two years. Thus, at all times schools have a development programme that extends over three years. The level of detail in the third year of any plan is generally less than that for the first two years. The third year of the plan indicates the objectives that the school intends to set for that year, but these may be subject to later modification. The school development plan provides a plan for the development of the school but it must also be capable of responding to substantial changes, such as changes to the school's staffing, that may occur over a three-year period.

Schools consult their communities in considering their priorities for development. A collaborative process involving the school principal, staff and the community encourages commitment to the school development plan. Through joint ownership a school development plan can remain as the development plan for the school even if there is a change of principal. A new principal might legitimately seek to influence the future development of the school through the internal review process or by making the implementation process more effective, but the essential continuity and coherence of the planning and development process is important.

SELECTION OF OBJECTIVES

School development plans do not replace the school's overall goals. Figure 7.2 indicates that a vision statement of a school overarches the planning and management objectives. In other words, the school development plan sets out the process by which the school moves towards its overall vision through the specification of a set of more immediate objectives and the strategies by which the vision will be pursued.

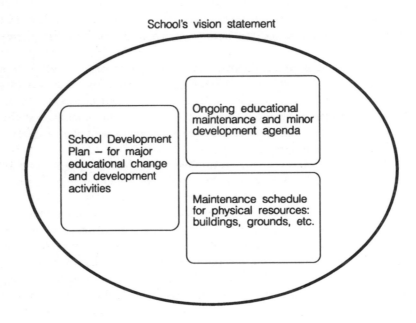

Figure 7.2   School development plans in relation to the school's vision and ongoing maintenance activities

Development is separate from educational and resource maintenance in school management. Schools' maintenance agendas address ongoing work in school management, although they may also contain some minor development and change activities. The important distinction between the school develop-ment plan and other management and planning agendas in schools is the focus on the core development activities in the former, compared with ongoing work of the school in the latter. Thus, once a programme of development has been completed and the changes resulting from it have been embedded in the ongoing activities of the school, its continued maintenance becomes an item on the school's educational or resource maintenance agenda.

NUMBER AND TYPES OF OBJECTIVES IN A SCHOOL DEVELOPMENT PLAN

The aim of school development plans is to facilitate focused and planned development through the specification of objectives that can be attained in each year. Programmes of development that are to be pursued over a period of more than one year are specified as staged, sequential objectives that can be achieved in each year. This assists the management of development by setting appropriate targets for each year of the programme.

The number of objectives addressed in each year of the plan takes account of the capability of the school to achieve effective outcomes for all of them – the total number of objectives in each year depends on their scope and the size and complexity of the school. Schools are advised to limit the number of objectives addressed, rather than attempt a large number of objectives, if this is likely to mean only partial achievement of their intended outcomes. Many schools tend to overstretch resources and capabilities. Schools are expected to consider addressing more than six objectives in each year of their plan only if they are confident of achieving them. This requires that schools synthesise their needs and priorities so as to address their key aspects through a limited number of objectives.

The objectives specified in school development plans are of two types. One type is drawn from the Department's systemic development objectives for the year – as targeted in Area Directorate Plans – as described through particular programmes and policies. The specification of systemic objectives requires the Department itself to take a developmental perspective of schooling. Further, it requires the Department's forward planning, as embodied in the systemic *Three Year Plan* and Area Plans, to provide a clear framework and timetable for the provision of materials and support for the implementation of the Department's programmes and policies in schools. Thus, a precondition for effective planning is coordination between central directorates responsible for development work and area directorates responsible for implementation and support in schools. This coordination ensures completion of the development work necessary for new programmes and policies prior to their implementation in schools.

Therefore, the systemic *Three Year Plan* is viewed as an overarching statement from which the central directorates responsible for development work construct management plans. Area Plans then reflect the planned priority and flow of development work from central directorates through area support and services to schools.

Figure 7.3 indicates the relationship between the Department's systemic *Three Year Plan*, central directorate plans and operational plans for the support of programmes and policies through Area Plans. The solid arrows indicate the normal path through which the Department's programmes and policies flow through the system to their implementation in the development plans of individual schools. The direct path between the systemic *Three Year Plan* and area directorate plans, however, indicates that in terms of new programmes or policies there may be some systemic priorities which do not require prior development work in the central directorates. This is, though, expected to be a rare occurrence as most programmes and policies have resource implications related to curriculum, personnel or physical resources which require to be addressed by central directorates prior to their implementation in schools. There may also be exceptions where an objective from the systemic *Three Year Plan* can be translated directly to school development plans without any prior need for central or area directorate support.

The broken lines in Figure 7.3 indicate the feedback loops in the system for the revision and roll-forward of the systemic *Three Year Plan*. The requirement that the Department complete the development and resourcing of priorities in the systemic *Three Year Plan* prior to their implementation in schools depends upon establishing a clear set of priorities for implementing major objectives for education in South Australia.

Schools' planning processes will also be facilitated by requiring that the Department specify its primary development objectives for each year. The Department's priorities will need to be specified three years in advance. Schools will then be in a position to plan their development in the knowledge that they will not be overloaded or overwhelmed by additional major departmental objectives specified after their plans have been drawn up.

In addition to the systemic objectives, schools specify further objectives according to their particular needs and context. These objectives must also be consistent with the Department's *Three Year Plan* and with Departmental policy. Whereas the systemic objectives reflected in Area Plans ensure that all schools address particular areas of development, the local objectives in school development plans facilitate the individual response of schools to the needs of their local communities.

The individual response of schools to the needs of their communities is shown in Figure 7.3 by the reciprocal paths between school development plans and the development priorities of school communities. These communities are also to be consulted in the process of revision of the systemic *Three Year Plan*.

STATEMENT OF OUTCOMES AND PERFORMANCE LEVELS

In their development plans schools seek to indicate the expected outcomes for each of the objectives in a way that readily allows them to assess whether they have attained the objective. Performance levels indicated in outcome statements are set at a level which encourages school staff to achieve high levels of performance, but not so high that they deter staff from attempting to reach them. The external review process takes account of the level of expectation embodied in schools' development plans when reviewing their progress.

STRATEGIES IN SCHOOL DEVELOPMENT PLANS

How a school chooses to address a particular development objective is an issue of professional practice and the responsibility of school staff. Thus, school development is necessarily linked to professional development in schools.

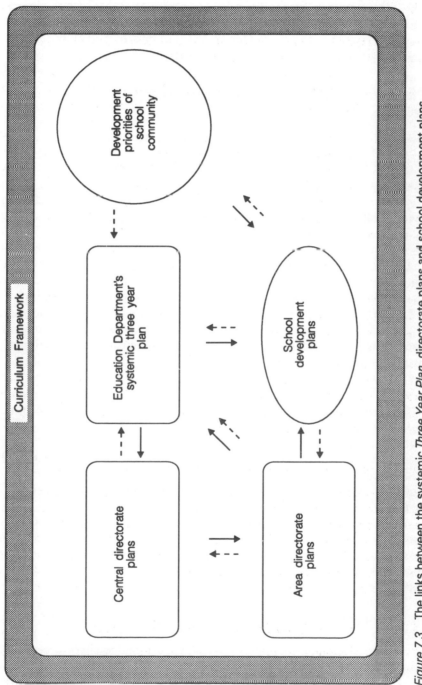

Curriculum Framework

Development priorities of school community

Education Department's systemic three year plan

Central directorate plans

School development plans

Area directorate plans

Figure 7.3   The links between the systemic *Three Year Plan*, directorate plans and school development plans

The Education Review Unit works with operational directorates to strengthen networks for the dissemination of strategies that schools choose in addressing their development objectives. The framework for dissemination is an open system which provides for exchange of information on the effectiveness of particular strategies for specific situations.

TRAINING AND DEVELOPMENT TO SUPPORT SCHOOL DEVELOPMENT

Although the support structures for school development are not the responsibility of the Education Review Unit, it is important that the external review activities, for which the Education Review Unit has responsibility, provide maximal support for development in schools.

Area directorates have responsibility for school staff training and development. Research on teacher training and development suggests that these activities are most effective if they are based on a teacher–teacher, rather than an expert–teacher, model. The integration of professional development with the needs identified through internal reviews in schools is particularly important in the area of curriculum development and teaching practices. It is essential that schools build on the effective and efficient management and development structures that already exist. Schools need to evaluate the skills and knowledge required for planning and managing the development process. The planning process requires leadership, peer group communication and collaborative problem-solving skills. Further, interpersonal skills in providing feedback on performance between individuals and groups is required. In many cases schools develop external cluster networks to share experience and expertise.

Schools assess their training and development requirements in relation to the strategies that are specified in their school development plans. A brief statement of these from each school provides a basis for planning appropriate programmes for delivery through area directorates. As an adjunct to the roll-forward of schools' plans each year, these statements provide advance notice of major areas of training and professional development required in order for schools to carry out their plans.

The designation of school staff to coordinate the planning and implementation of development activities is necessary. Newly created leadership positions created as a response to industry restructuring provide schools with increased flexibility in the selective targeting of a range of areas for development through their school development plans.

Schools are encouraged to involve staff in internal reviews who have served in Education Review Unit teams or internal reviews in other schools. This confers a perspective from outside the school while providing a valuable professional development opportunity for the external teachers through their consultancy role in the review process. The professional development of teachers through their participation in internal and external reviews also makes an important contribution to the skills and knowledge required to achieve school development objectives.

APPROVAL OF SCHOOL DEVELOPMENT PLANS

Area directors, and district superintendents as their advisers, are responsible for the approval of school development plans. Approval requires school development plans to conform to the guidelines that have been set by the Department, and schools to set themselves realistic outcomes. Outcomes which embody high expectations, but which are attainable, are considered realistic in terms of school development.

REVIEW OF SCHOOL DEVELOPMENT PLANS

The review process associated with school development plans consists of both internal and external reviews of progress and of the management of the development process. Schools conduct their own annual internal review of progress in terms of their school development plan. In addition, this internal review process assesses potential areas of development that the school needs to address in its current forward plan or at the end of the present three-year development cycle. This provides schools with time to plan and introduce new development strategies and coordinate them with the strategies contained in their current school development plans.

THE RANGE OF REVIEWS UNDERTAKEN

The Education Review Unit external review programme consists of three components: school reviews, reviews of other organizational units and reviews of individual policies and programmes. The reviews are conducted against published criteria indicating standards of performance in a range of relevant aspects of schooling and the management of education. These performance criteria have been established in close consultation with the educational community.

In order to provide objective reviews that are independent of sectional interests the review and audit process must be substantially independent of the political processes in the organization. In order to achieve this the Education Review Unit is provided with the authority to review any organizational units, programmes or policies that it so determines. In addition, the Department, through the Director-General, may request reports on specific units or areas of concern. These reports may lead to reviews if the inquiry cannot be answered from extant sources of information.

Reviews of directorates and other units

Reviews of directorates and other units responsible for the development and support of programmes and policies in schools is conducted on similar lines to school development plan reviews. In addition, such units are reviewed in terms of a series of key performance indicators covering their practices of management, decision making, personnel practices, resource utilization and so on.

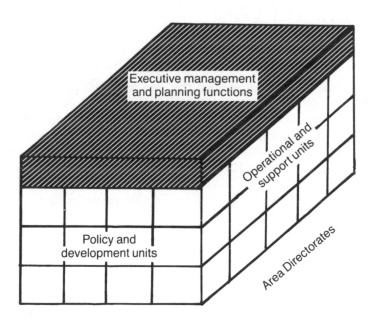

Figure 7.4   Structure of reviews of directorates and other units

Directorates carry out either policy and programme development or operational and support functions (Figure 7.4). They consist of an executive structure responsible for their overall management and planning, plus internal units responsible for development and support activities. The internal units in directorates are reviewed as part of the programme of *other unit* reviews. Reviews of directorates utilize information from the reviews of their internal units, in addition to further information obtained from a strategic focus on management and planning.

School reviews

Reviews of schools by the Education Review Unit (as shown in Figure 7.5) consist of a review of the school development plan, an audit of selected regulations and requirements, and an optional school-initiated component of review. These external school reviews are conducted on a three-year cycle to ensure that all schools are reviewed within four years of their previous review.

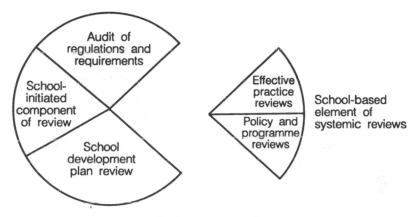

Figure 7.5   The components of school-based reviews

School development plan reviews

The Education Review Unit undertakes an external review of each school's progress in terms of the objectives and outcomes stated in their school development plan. This review assesses the effectiveness of the strategies adopted by the school to achieve its particular objectives. The review also examines the planning and management processes associated with the development and implementation of the school development plan. The objective of these external reviews is to complement schools' internal reviews of their school development plans.

AUDIT OF REGULATIONS AND REQUIREMENTS

This audit assesses the implementation of statutory regulations and the Department's mandatory requirements, including curriculum provision, for the operation of schools. A selected number of regulations and procedures are audited in each school. These audits provide information on the extent of schools' compliance with particular regulations and requirements; hence they serve accountability purposes.

SCHOOL-INITIATED COMPONENT OF REVIEW

Schools are offered an opportunity to indicate a particular aspect of their operation or development which they wish to review in collaboration with the review team. The purpose of this component of the review is to provide schools with the opportunity to utilize the skills of the review team to obtain an external perspective on some additional aspect of their operation or development. In many cases this centres on some aspect of the development of the school that has already been identified through the school's internal review as a priority area for development.

SYSTEMIC REVIEWS

Systemic reviews are undertaken in order to provide an evaluation of the performance of the school system as a whole. The information collected for this purpose within schools is not intended to be of sufficient scope to make representative statements about the performance of individual schools, but by selecting a representative sample of schools across the system the information sustains valid statements about the system as a whole. These reviews are based on clearly defined criteria and relate to three types of activity: effective practices, programmes and policies (see Figure 7.5). Systemic policy and programme reviews will assess the effectiveness of both schools and other organizational levels in the Education Department.

EFFECTIVE PRACTICE REVIEWS

The primary purpose of this type of review is to report on performance with respect to particular practices across the system as a whole. Effective practice reviews are conducted in four *domains*: teaching and learning, organization and management, ethos and culture, and equal opportunities and social justice (Figure 7.6). Each domain addresses five to eight *areas* of school activity. Three to five *aspects* of performance have been developed to report on each of the areas of activity reviewed. In total this provides about 100 profiles of performance across the four domains of practice. In general, only one of the four domains of effective practice is reviewed in each school. Further information on these reviews is available in EDSA (1990b, c, 1991).

Effective practice reviews are conducted using criteria established through a series of consultative working parties, one for each of the four domains of effective practice. The performance criteria developed by these working parties are disseminated to all involved with schooling. The information obtained from effective practice reviews is used to diagnose problems and monitor trends in the education system as a whole. Further, it offers summative information on the standard of practice that exists in the system. This information provides important input into policy formulation, and operational

Figuro 7.6   Tho four domains of effective practice reviews

decision making and resource allocation. It also contributes to the annual revision of the Department's *Three Year Plan*.

The Education Review Unit monitors and revises its descriptions of effective practice in light of feedback from practitioners in schools and from an evaluation of the relationship between various practices and student learning. The latter builds on departmental approaches to student assessment to evaluate the relative importance of different practices on the educational development and progress of students.

REVIEWS OF THE DEPARTMENT'S PROGRAMMES AND POLICIES

Programme and policy reviews are conducted according to criteria and procedures established and agreed before each review takes place. These criteria are established through consultations with the various parties involved in the development, delivery and support of the particular programme or policy. Programme and policy reviews require a clear statement of the aims and objectives of the programme or policy and a statement of expected outcomes.

Reviews of the effectiveness of programmes and policies are conducted across units and organizational levels in the system. In terms of Figure 7.7 these reviews assess the development and implementation of a programme or policy across organizational levels, from the school level to other units and directorates responsible for programme and policy development and operational support to schools. That is, the effectiveness of programmes and policies is

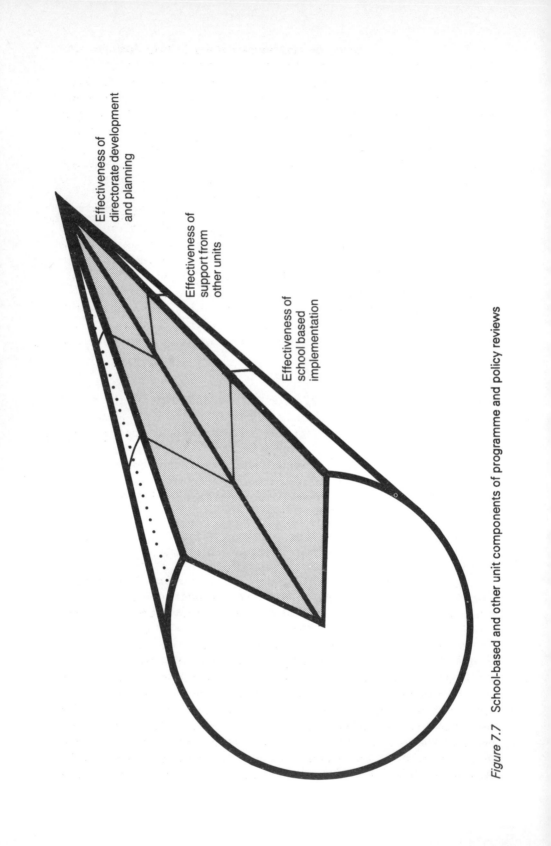

Effectiveness of
directorate development
and planning

Effectiveness of
support from
other units

Effectiveness of
school based
implementation

Figure 7.7   School-based and other unit components of programme and policy reviews

evaluated through the support provided by the various organizational levels in the system to schools, as well as the effectiveness of schools in implementing them. The selection of programmes and policies for review will be based on the standard audit concept of risk analysis. The establishment of review priorities will thus be determined by evidence on the performance of programmes and policies. The primary mechanism for providing information that will allow the appropriate assessment of risk will be the effective practice reviews.

An analysis of the Department's policies and programmes as they relate to each of the four domains of effective practice has been undertaken as part of the development of the review instruments. Practices with a weak performance profile provide evidence that particular programmes or policies are failing to achieve their objectives. This information provides the basis for selecting programmes and policies for review.

Each programme and policy review is managed by a review team with experience and expertise in the various aspects of the programme or policy. Stakeholders are consulted as part of the procedure of drawing up the criteria for these reviews.

COMMISSIONED REVIEWS

In addition, other reviews may be commissioned by the Director-General on the advice of the officers of the Department. These reviews may be of individual units or of particular programmes or policies.

REPORTING AND RESPONSIBILITIES FOR ACTING ON REPORTS FROM REVIEWS

School reviews

Written reports from school reviews focus on the review of the school development plan plus the audit of regulations and requirements. The reporting procedure for the school-initiated component of the review is capable of adaptation to the purposes for which the school sought the review and may therefore be confidential to the school.

The report of the school review is the joint responsibility of the principal of the school and the Education Review Unit superintendent leading the review team. In addition to school staff and students, the audience for the review is parents and the school council, the area director responsible for the school and the Director-General. School reports are public documents. The reports from school reviews highlight areas of achievement in schools and provide feedback on progress in terms of the objectives set out by the school in its development plan, including an assessment of the effectiveness of the strategies employed. Further, reports provide feedback on the planning and management processes associated with the development and implementation of the school development plan.

School principals are responsible for acting on the recommendations put forward in reports from school reviews, and area directors have responsibility for ensuring that principals take appropriate action. Area directors also have responsibility for providing advisory and other services to individual schools in response to the resourcing implications of school reviews.

Other unit reviews

The reporting for other units is the responsibility of the superintendent leading the review, in consultation with the unit manager. The unit manager and director are responsible for responding to the recommendations from the review.

Systemic reviews

Reports from systemic reviews – effective practice reviews, programme reviews and policy reviews – are aggregated across schools and integrated with review information from other units in the system. This information provides regular and comprehensive reports to the Department for further action, where necessary.

CYCLE OF REVIEWS

School reviews

School reviews are conducted on a three-year cycle. This is to ensure that the external review of schools makes a timely contribution to school development. Each school undertakes a number of different reviews, including those of the whole school, one or more components from the domains of effective practice, the school programme and policies in process at the time.

Other unit reviews

The reviews of administrative development and support units, and of directorates, is undertaken on a five-year cycle in line with Treasury guidelines for departmental reviews of their programmes.

Systemic reviews

Effective practice reviews are based on about 60 schools in each domain of effective practice. Programme reviews are based on up to 50 schools, depending on the nature of the programme, and policy reviews are also based on a sample of about 50 schools.

The chart in Figure 7.8 shows the structure of the overall programme of reviews. Each two-year cycle includes school reviews consisting of a review of the school development plan, an audit of regulations and requirements, and a school-initiated component of review. The review activities in each school also include one or more systemic review components. In addition to reviewing each of the four domains of effective practice, a combined total of ten policy and programme reviews is undertaken in each two-year cycle. Reviews of other units are additional to this programme of school-based reviews. The programme described in Figure 7.8 envisages that each superintendent in the ERU will lead a school-based review panel in 30 weeks of each year. The reviews of other units will be scheduled for periods when schools are not in session.

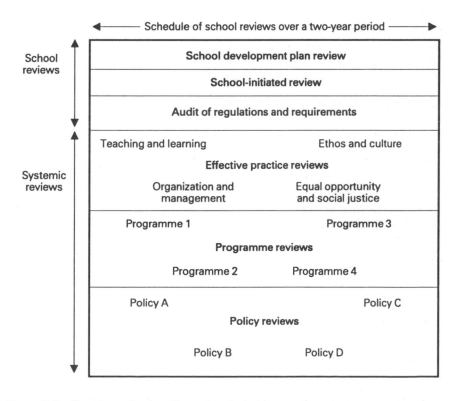

Figure 7.8 Structure of school-based review programme

REVIEW TEAMS

All members of review teams receive training in review methods. The ERU requests expressions of interest from appropriate individuals for training. The parameters of the selection process are designed to meet the needs of review teams and, over time, ensure that all schools have staff trained in review methods. The opportunity to work in review teams provides school-based staff with a valuable training opportunity which is directly relevant to school planning and development.

The composition of individual review teams is determined primarily by the skills and expertise required to undertake the various components of the review programme. In general, school-based reviews are conducted by a team led by an ERU superintendent, a community representative, a school principal, one or two school-based teachers, and the principal of the school under review. Where required, teams may include other staff, such as district superintendents, or others with specialist knowledge. With the exception of the home school principal, all members of the panel are external to the school under review.

REFERENCES

Cox, I. (1987) *Report of the Review of Superintendents in the Education Department of South Australia*, Adelaide: Education Department of South Australia.
Cuttance, P. (1989a) *Performance Indicators for Schooling*, Edinburgh: Scottish Education Department.
—— (1989b) 'School development and review', Paper prepared for a conference of Principals and Superintendents held at the Regency Park Centre, Adelaide.
Education Department of South Australia (1970) *Freedom and Authority in Schools*, Memorandum from the Director-General, A.W. Jones, to Principals of all Department schools.
—— (1981) *Our Schools and their Purposes*, Adelaide: Education Department of South Australia.
—— (1985) *Curriculum Authority and Responsibility*, Adelaide: Education Department of South Australia.
—— (1989) *School Development Plans*, Adelaide: Education Department of South Australia.
—— (1990a) *Guidelines for School Development Planning*, Adelaide: Education Department of South Australia.
—— (1990b) *Review Program of the Education Review Unit*, Adelaide: Education Department of South Australia.
—— (1990c) *School Reviews*, Adelaide: Education Department of South Australia.
—— (1991) *Guidelines for Internal Review in Schools*, Adelaide: Education Department of South Australia.
Keeves, J. (1981) *Education and Change in South Australia* (First Report), Adelaide: Education Department of South Australia.
—— (1982) *Education and Change in South Australia* (Final Report), Adelaide: Education Department of South Australia.
Schools Commission (1984) *Report for the Triennium (1982–84)*, Canberra: Schools Commission.

Chapter 8

The changing role of the school principal

A review of developments in Australia and New Zealand

Brian J. Caldwell

THE NEW REALITIES IN EDUCATION

The scope and pace of change in education at the start of the 1990s is nothing short of breathtaking. In the United States, the so-called 'second wave' of reform is apparently sweeping over the nation, with virtually every aspect of schools and systems which direct and support schools under critical examination. The key word is *restructuring* and it is being applied to curriculum, pedagogy, administrative structures, governance, teacher training and retraining, and to the teaching profession itself. In Britain, England and Wales now have, for the first time ever, a national curriculum framework and provision for nationwide tests at the primary and secondary levels. All secondary schools and most primary schools have total control of their budgets, with schools having the power to opt out of control by their local education authorities on the majority vote of parents. A national system of education in New Zealand has been, literally, turned upside down (or should it be downside up?) with the dramatic empowerment of boards of trustees at the school level in what was already a relatively decentralized system. Remaining to provide a framework is a small central authority which includes a powerful review and audit function. Many Australian states which underwent radical decentralization in the 1970s and 1980s are now building stronger frameworks of direction and support while others, notably New South Wales, Queensland and Tasmania, are just starting on a major programme of reform. At the same time, the elements of a national curriculum framework are starting to emerge and a national initiative to restructure the teaching profession is underway. The pioneering system of self-management in Canada, the Edmonton Public School District in Alberta, continues to evolve, with a vision of empowerment at the student level now emerging. There is evidence of similar far-reaching change in virtually every nation in the Western world with the first signs of change now appearing in other groups of nations.

Among structural changes alone, what has occurred thus far is historic. In Britain, for example, there is no precedent for each of the major elements in the 1988 legislation: never before has there been a national curriculum nor have there been nationwide tests at primary and secondary levels. While schools have always had some authority in respect to resource allocation, never before have they had total control over their budgets. Schools have never had the authority to opt out of control by their local education authority.

The scope of change in Australia is best summarized by Hedley Beare, Professor of Education at the University of Melbourne and one of the nation's most respected commentators:

> The overwhelming impression left by the most recent round of reconstructions is that there has been a profound reconceptualization of the organization of Australian education, in schools no less than systematically. Bluntly, there has been a paradigm shift.
>
> (Beare, 1990, p. 18)

R.J.S. Macpherson was a participant–observer in the preparation of the Picot Report which led to the reform of education in New Zealand and has subsequently written of these experiences and those of a similar nature in the state of New South Wales, Australia (Macpherson, 1990a), where he assisted in the review of administration conducted by Brian Scott. He characterized events in New Zealand as a 'political intervention into education on a scale never before seen' (Macpherson, 1990b). William Lowe Boyd, another scholar who has written widely on developments in the United States and in other countries, notably Australia, has observed that 'Since 1983, American public schools have been experiencing the most sustained and far-reaching reform effort in modern times' (Boyd, 1990, p. 42).

The purpose of this chapter is to describe and appraise critically the impact of these changes on the role of the principal in two of these countries, namely Australia and New Zealand, drawing on the author's experience as a consultant to governments in both countries, especially in relation to the professional development of principals; and on two nationally funded research projects which have given particular attention to the roles of principals and other leaders at the school level. These were the Effective Resource Allocation in Schools Project, funded by the Australian Commonwealth Schools Commission (1983–6), and the Exemplary Schools Study Project, funded by the Australian Research Council (1989–91).

THE CHANGING STRUCTURE OF EDUCATION IN AUSTRALIA AND NEW ZEALAND

Australia

Education is a state responsibility in Australia and, for more than a hundred years until the early 1970s, public education at primary and secondary levels was administered in each state through highly centralized state government departments of education. Curriculum was for the most part determined centrally, with tight control exercised through an inspectorial system and state-wide external examinations at the end of secondary schooling. Most funds for education came from state sources, with centralized allocation of resources which provided little money for discretionary use by schools other than that raised by voluntary contributions from parents and the local community. The federal government provided very limited support until the 1960s when aid for libraries and science facilities in both public and private schools was introduced.

There have been dramatic changes to this pattern of governance since the early 1970s. The federal government became involved in a very significant way through the Australian Schools Commission established in 1973. A comprehensive grants scheme administered by the Commission for both public and private schools was designed to achieve greater equity among schools and equality of opportunity for students. The task of administration in state departments of education became immediately more complex, with several states, notably Tasmania, decentralizing to the school level decisions related to a substantial portion of recurrent grants received from the Commission. The early 1970s were also marked by administrative decentralization of education departments through the formation of regional units in several states. South Australia and the Australian Capital Territory led the way in providing greater freedom and autonomy for schools, with provision in both instances for school-site councils or boards having advisory and limited decision-making powers. The concern for equity was evident in the grant structure of the Australian Schools Commission. A movement towards decentralization was associated in large part with increasing complexity in the administration of education. Political values in the form of a desire to participate in decisions were also evident in the positions taken by some parent and teacher organizations. A wish to match authority with responsibility and to locate power to make decisions closer to the classroom was part of the management philosophy of several leaders of state departments of education.

The trend to a decentralized system of school governance continued most markedly in Victoria. Administrative decentralization to regional units proceeded throughout the 1970s and 1980s. In 1975, the state government required all public schools to establish school-site councils of teachers, parents and other members of the school community. A variety of models was offered as a guide, with most providing powers of advice only to the principal and staff. These initiatives in regionalization and decentralization to the school level were taken by a relatively conservative Liberal government. In 1983, however, the election to government of the Australian Labour Party saw a dramatic change, with substantial commitment to devolution ('devolution' is the preferred term in Victoria for describing what is generally termed 'decentralization' in other places). Towards the end of the 1980s, however, a significant shift of a centralizing kind occurred in this state as the government called for the building of state-wide curriculum frameworks, the development of state and regional strategic plans, and a system of accountability linking school, region and state. The national government now requires much tighter account-ability in respect to outcomes at the state level of nationally funded initiatives.

The Victorian experience was, in many respects, the reverse of that in the United States in the 1980s. The former experienced a strong decentralizing trend followed by a centralizing 'correction'. The latter, in the first wave of reform, experienced the centralizing trend, with the second wave, including interest in school-site management, having a strong decentralizing thrust.

Most other states and territories are now adopting similar patterns to Victoria, with leaner but more powerful central functions in terms of the formulation of goals, the setting of priorities and the building of frameworks for accountability, but with a clear shift towards school-site management in terms of operational decision making, including budgeting and community involvement. Ten goals of schooling have also been adopted by the Common-wealth and state governments, with recent interest in a national curriculum framework.

New Zealand

New Zealand has had a national system of education since 1877 but there has traditionally been a relatively high degree of decentralization. Secondary schools have had Boards of Governors that worked within a framework of curriculum and resource policies determined at the national level. Elementary schools have received advice and support from school committees but were largely controlled on a district basis by an Education Board.

In 1988, the national government accepted (Lange, 1988) the major recom-mendations of the Picot Report (Picot, 1988) which called for a virtual transfer of decision making from the national system to the school level. Since late 1989 each school has had a school board, a majority of whom are parents, with a charter which, once approved by the Minister, provides a framework for operations. More than 90 per cent of the costs of running each school have been decentralized to the school level in a school-based budget. The long-term plan is for staff to be selected and employed by the school board at the site level.

There will be a national curriculum framework in New Zealand but the number of staff employed at the system (national) level is now relatively few in number, serving mainly to monitor (or audit) operations at the school level and to provide support to schools, especially in the area of special education services.

Implementation is proceeding in New Zealand, with many of the concerns noted elsewhere in relation to developments in other countries also evident. The background to the changes has been well documented by Macpherson (1990b). In general, the pattern is similar, with a decentralizing initiative towards school-site management accompanied by a centralizing thrust, with a smaller central agency determining goals, priorities and frameworks for accountability.

THE IMPACT OF SOCIETAL CHANGE ON STRUCTURES IN EDUCATION

Restructuring education in Australia and New Zealand, as elsewhere, is an outcome of the interplay of forces which are evident more broadly in society. What follows is a brief examination of these forces and an exploration of their implications as far as leaders in education are concerned.

Concern for quality and strategic capability in education

In both Australia and New Zealand, it is apparent that central authorities, whether at national or state levels, have adopted a powerful but sharply focused role. It is essentially one of determining goals, setting priorities and building frameworks for accountability.

A major factor underlying this centralizing trend is concern about quality. This concern is clear from OECD reports, including one devoted exclusively to the issue which stated that 'concern for the quality of education in schools is today among the highest priorities in all OECD countries. It will remain so for the foreseeable future' (OECD, 1987, p. 123).

There is, however, a broader concern for quality that is having an impact on patterns of management in education. This is the concern for general quality in life which is determined in large measure by the capacity of a nation to perform well in a global economy. There is a sense in which Australia and New Zealand may fall behind and that, to become more competitive, they must ensure a highly responsive economy which calls, in turn, for a highly responsive system of education that equips citizens with required knowledge, skills and attitudes. This relationship between education and economic needs has, of course, always existed. Education has always made a significant contribution to economic well-being. The recent rhetoric of governments has simply brought the relationship into sharper focus, with a stridency and urgency that many educators find discomforting. Nevertheless, it is currently a reality which accounts in part for the stronger role governments are taking in many areas of policy in education.

Apart from gaining an understanding of the scope of the change and its underlying reasons, there are a number of implications for leaders in education. For those at the national, state or system levels, it means the development of a capacity to set goals, establish priorities and build frameworks for accountability. These capacities have not always been well developed in the past when education was relatively stable and such direct connections between education and the economy were not stated so clearly or were subject to such rapid change. Administrators at the system level were then able to perform a range of functions within the bureaucratic structure which was, in many respects, highly appropriate in an age of stability. Management in a climate of continuing change demands a large measure of *focused flexibility*. Leaders at the school level require the capacity to manage within a centrally determined framework, something which, to a degree, has always been the case, except that more recent developments involve adaptation to a changing set of priorities and a more demanding set of accountability requirements.

Schools in the 1990s thus require a high-level capacity for strategic planning; that is, to see the 'larger picture' and, on a continuing basis, set and reset priorities in a simple strategic plan which will provide the framework for the annual operational plan.

Perhaps the most important strategic capability is concerned with curriculum, which is expected to be highly responsive to the needs of the nation. This has always been so but, whereas these needs in the past tended to be relatively stable from year to year, there may now be considerable change from one year to the next. The notion of national curriculum which has a high level of specification will not satisfy this requirement. What is required is a curriculum framework within which these changes can occur. It is interesting that what has started as an exercise in national curriculum has invariably ended with the publication of a broad framework. That was the outcome in England and Wales and is the likely end of a process in Australia which has seen, first, a statement on national goals and, second, an effort to *map* the curriculum across the different states and territories.

At the student level, the curriculum is seen as affording the individual an opportunity to acquire the knowledge, skills and attitudes to participate productively and satisfyingly in a world of work which will see continuous change. It seems that the basics in education will be expanded to include problem solving, creativity and a capacity for lifelong learning and relearning.

Another important strategic capability is concerned with learning and teaching. At one level this calls for a range of approaches at the school level to match the curriculum and this may mean change in situations where, for example, problem solving and creativity have not been emphasised in the past. At another level, however, is the need to utilize the wealth of learning opportunities which have been created by advances in telecommunications and computers. Computers can now be utilized across the curriculum, including the arts, and learning of a kind which was once laborious or difficult can now occur with ease in any location. Students will have access to information sources around the world. With the increasing use of lap-top computers, this information can be acquired quickly and unobtrusively without jeopardy to patterns of human interaction which we hold to be so important in the educative process.

EQUITY, RESOURCE ALLOCATION AND THE EMERGENCE OF A *DE FACTO* EDUCATIONAL VOUCHER

Strategic capability in respect to curriculum and learning is being shaped by a core value which is influencing public policy in most fields on a global scale, namely equity. In educational terms, this means that every child, regardless of circumstance, should receive an education which will enable the full development of capability. This value has underpinned much of the rhetoric of public education in Australia and New Zealand for a hundred years or more but there is increasingly an insistence that this rhetoric be brought to realization. The particular outcomes or indicators of outcomes which have been specified in public policy pronouncements have varied, but these include an increase in retention rates of students, at least to the end of secondary school, implying a reduction in failure rates at key stages of secondary schooling. The particular processes of policy implementation have included approaches to resource allocation, since an implication of the foregoing is that schools shall be provided with the resources to enable them to meet the individual learning needs of every student. This suggests a form of decentralized school-based budgeting in contrast to centralized, relatively uniform approaches to allocating resources to schools which, in the past, were assumed to be equitable.

The author has been a participant–observer in several countries where efforts have been made to introduce related approaches to resource allocation, especially in Britain through the Local Management of Schools (formerly known by a title which emphasized its focus on resources: Local Financial Management); in New Zealand; in Australia, especially in New South Wales and Tasmania; and in Edmonton, Alberta, where school-based decision making, formerly known as school-based budgeting, has been in place for more than a decade. It has taken time in each place to determine the criteria for allocating resources to schools. It is essentially a process of determining what it costs to provide different educational experiences to students with different educational needs and then devising a schedule of grants to schools which are combined to form a school's total allocation.

One perspective on this process is of interest. The total resource allocation to a school is, in effect, determined by the number of students who attend the school, the educational needs of those students, and the kind of educational programmes they will undertake. Expressed simply in stark financial terms, *the money follows the student*. The process is accomplishing in important ways what the so-called educational voucher was intended to achieve. The voucher has never been implemented in the manner originally proposed: in its original form it was a sum of public money given to parents who would then pay for the education of their children according to their choice of school. What is emerging, however, is a situation where, to use an image offered by Thomas (1988), the student is, in effect, the voucher, but where equity objections have been satisfied through differentials in grants to schools in school-based budgets which take account of the educational needs of students. The educational voucher may become a reality but not in the form originally envisaged by its proponents.

SELF-MANAGEMENT AND THE COLLAPSE OF BUREAUCRACIES IN EDUCATION

There are a number of arguments and factors accounting for the trend to school self-management in Australia and New Zealand but recently, however, the case has been put rather bluntly on the grounds that it is simply more efficient and effective in the late twentieth century to restructure systems of education so that central bureaucracies are relatively small and schools are empowered to manage their own affairs within a centrally determined framework of direction and support. Two arguments have usually been offered: one is concerned with responsiveness, the other with priorities for resource allocation in times of economic restraint or budgetary crisis.

An example of a powerful argument on grounds of responsiveness is that offered by Brian Scott following his review of the Education Department in the government school system in the Australian state of New South Wales, one of the largest education systems in the world. The following are excerpts which focus on the lack of responsiveness:

> Many problems in school education in this State today are directly attributable to the fact that systems have rigidified. The Department has not recognized the full extent of the challenge of accelerating change in today's society. Nor has it been sensitive to the fact that in the modern world we now live in, school education – its curriculum, its teaching and learning processes, and its delivery systems – should be in a continual state of adaptation.
> The message ... is clear enough. While many of the same questions need to be asked about content, structure and delivery of school education as in the past, the assumption that has guided the development of the New South Wales State school system for more than 100 years – namely, that the quality of school education is best achieved through a centralized system – is no longer valid for a modern, technologically-advanced state. The inflexibility of the Department's structures and procedures has made it unresponsive to the real educative needs of students and teachers.
>
> (Scott, 1990, xiii)

Another factor accounting for the shift towards school self-management has been the resetting of priorities for government expenditure, especially in times of financial restraint or budgetary crisis. In a general sense, governments the world over have found it increasingly difficult to resource public enterprises. Costly technology advances and high public expectations, the latter now more powerfully articulated than ever before through highly skilled lobbying efforts, make it difficult for governments to satisfy the demands of all. Consider, for example, the very high cost of maintaining a public health service, especially one which can now provide a much higher quality of medical attention through an impressive array of elective services. Consider also the high cost of increasingly sophisticated approaches to law enforcement, defence, transportation and education. To provide all of these services at the same time that the public is demanding reductions in levels of taxation makes the task of government even more difficult. In countries like Australia and New Zealand, with high levels of foreign indebtedness and unfavourable terms of trade, the problem is acute. It becomes almost unmanageable, as in Victoria, Australia, where the recession of the early 1990s is more severe than elsewhere in the country and the government is faced with high losses from the collapse of public enterprises, such as the State Bank. Another Australian state, Tasmania, is experiencing similar difficulties. The response by government is to make more severe cuts in educational expenditure at the central level than at the school level. Essentially, then, when faced with the need to set priorities under conditions of constraint such as those described here, governments are opting to support schools at the expense of the centre.

THE SERVICE ETHIC

An important function at the central and regional levels of school systems in Australia and New Zealand has been the provision of support for schools in the areas of curriculum, teaching, management and student services. It has generally been considered more efficient and effective to locate these services at central and regional locations, given that the resources and needs are insufficient to place them in individual schools. For some services, a high level of specialized expertise is required with relatively small numbers of people available.

The extent and need of these services has been challenged as systems have moved to self-management. Two factors have been evident. One is associated with the economic plight described in the last section: when priorities have been reordered or where reductions in expenditure have been made, a curtailment of central and regional services has been a more acceptable course for governments to take than cut-backs at the school level. This has forced governments to examine the nature and extent of central and regional support services to determine those which meet the greatest needs. In effect, these service units have been called on to justify their existence. In some instances, notably in New Zealand and more recently in Victoria, proposals for change have initially been sweeping and campaigns in the defence of services have been mounted. In the final resolution of these matters, some services proposed for cut-back or elimination have been restored, especially those which concern the provision of support for students with special learning needs.

Another factor has been the response of schools once they have acquired a capacity for self-management. Where school-based budgets allow schools to select the source of special assistance, experience has shown that they will frequently acquire support from sources other than that previously provided at the central or regional levels (see an account of the Edmonton experience in Caldwell *et al.* (1988)).

The effect of both factors is to focus attention on the quality of service provided to schools. Where the existence of the service was once more or less taken for granted, there is now evidence of more careful design and delivery, often manifested in the formulation of mission statements, strategic plans, needs assessments, careful costing of services, negotiation of relatively explicit contracts between centre or region and schools, and appraisal of the quality of service following its delivery. In several states in Australia, services were arranged in what have become known as school support centres, essentially *one-stop shop* facilities for a wide range of support. In Victoria, after achieving some measure of stability over three years, the level of service and the number of centres were greatly reduced in the 1990 state budget, resulting in a new round of critical reviews as to the worth of the service provided. These developments are evident in other fields of public service to the extent that it is now appropriate to refer to a new ethic or culture of service in the public service.

EMPOWERMENT

The final theme that is evident in these developments is that of empowerment in the sense that certain groups of people in the school community now have the opportunity to influence the course of events in the life of a school to a greater extent than in the past. There are several sources of power in a school, including authority and expertise. For the first of these, a person or group of people acquire power because of the authority they have been granted. Throughout most of the history of large government or public school systems in Australia and New Zealand, this kind of power has been exercised by professional educators at the centre of school systems and in schools. In Australia, particularly since the early 1980s, there has been a widening of the source of power at all levels, especially in respect to a role for the community at the school level. Most states now require, or are encouraging, the formation of school councils or school boards with powers to set policies, approve budgets and evaluate the programmes of the school. Teachers and, in some instances, students have also been empowered in this manner.

Another source of power is expertise. An individual or group can influence the course of events by virtue of the expertise they can bring to bear. There is now broad acceptance of the need for teachers to engage in ongoing professional development, thus acquiring a broader range of knowledge and skill in the areas of curriculum and teaching. There are also programmes for parents, especially to help them acquire the knowledge and skill to contribute fruitfully in decision-making processes but also, to a lesser extent, to support teachers in matters related to learning and teaching. Thus a wider range of people in the community of the school have the opportunity to influence the course of events through the acquisition of knowledge and skill.

In general, these developments are a movement away from hierarchical controls on schools and their programmes, although some hierarchical structures for the exercise of power remain through the centralized arrangements described earlier.

THE PROFOUND CHANGES TO THE ROLE OF THE PRINCIPAL 1970–90

The changes in the role of principal in Australia and New Zealand are profound. Expressing the contrast in the starkest terms, in 1970, the principal was working in a highly centralized system with a stable and centrally determined curriculum. Society was relatively homogeneous and parents were largely excluded from decision-making processes. Hierarchical patterns of authority predominated. There was little opportunity at the school level for influencing the way resources were allocated to the school and within the school. While rhetoric suggested otherwise, there was little pressure at the secondary level to ensure that the educational needs of all students were addressed; there were high failure and drop-out rates. Both countries were still dependent on primary industry in a secure international market. There was little need for the principal to plan ahead. Compared with the period since 1970, the tasks of the principal were relatively straightforward. There seemed to be little need for professional development or training and little was provided.

By 1990, there had been radical change in almost every aspect of the role as described for 1970. The principal is now working in a highly decentralized setting although the centrally determined framework is more sharply focused than before. Rhetoric must be brought to realization in terms of meeting the needs of all students. Society is no longer homogeneous, with both countries now broadly multicultural. Most states in Australia and all of New Zealand require a form of parent participation in decision making. Hierarchical forms of decision making are quickly disappearing, with principals now expected to consult and reach consensus with a wide range of individuals and groups. There is continuous change and the school which attempts to respond to everything is quickly overwhelmed. Strategic planning and a capacity to *take charge of one's own agenda* are important, yet responsiveness to a national agenda is unavoidable if each country is to maintain its standard of living. Being a principal is a challenging and complex assignment: pre-service teacher education programmes offer inadequate preparation; and ongoing professional development and training are critically important but increasingly difficult, given the economic circumstances of each country.

PROFESSIONAL DEVELOPMENT AND TRAINING OF PRINCIPALS

The author has been extensively involved in professional development and training programmes for principals since 1984 as the trend to self-management has taken place. This work has been shaped by a nationally funded research and development effort from 1983 to 1986, with ongoing refinements based on experience in the international consultancy arena from 1986 to 1990. The following is a brief account of this work and the manner in which it responds to the profound changes in the principalship described above. A more detailed treatment is provided by Caldwell and Spinks (1988, 1992).

The initial research was carried out in 1983 in the Effective Resource Allocation in Schools Project in Tasmania and South Australia. The work was funded by the Commonwealth Schools Commission as a project of national significance. Its purpose was to identify the knowledge and skill required by principals in schools deemed to be highly effective in a general sense and in the way in which they allocated their resources. Tasmania and South Australia were selected because in these two states school-site budgeting had been encouraged. An outcome of this research was a professional development programme for principals and others.

The professional development programme was immediately utilized from 1984 to 1986 in Victoria, Australia, where the government wished all schools to adopt a form of school-based programme budgeting in the context of substantial decentralization of authority and responsibility as described earlier in this chapter. The major feature of the programme was a model described as the Collaborative School Management cycle, which incorporated an integrated cyclical approach to goal-setting and needs identification, policy making and the setting of priorities, programme planning, programme budgeting, implementation and programme evaluation, with clearly defined roles for a policy group, known as the school council in Victorian schools, and programme teams, being groups of teachers working in discrete areas of learning and teaching. Working with Jim Spinks, Principal of Rosebery District High School in Tasmania, which furnished the model as it was identified in the initial research, the author conducted more than 100 workshops for approximately 5000 principals, school councillors, teachers and students representing about 1100 schools. Subsequent surveys have revealed a high rate of adoption and adaptation. A detailed account of the model, refined and retitled a model for school self-management, is provided by Caldwell and Spinks (1988).

International comparative studies by the author (Caldwell, 1990a, b) suggested the relevance of the model to developments in other places, especially Britain, New Zealand, Canada and the United States. It was also apparent in the intervening years that schools everywhere were struggling under the weight of apparently continuous change, with multiple often conflicting agendas set by school systems and local communities. To a large extent, of course, this describes the general environment in all fields of public service throughout the Western world as described earlier. Consequently, the model for self-management was refined further for utilization in an extensive round of training programmes for principals and others in New Zealand and Britain. The author worked with Jim Spinks in New Zealand in 1989, mostly with principals and representatives of school boards, as the government proceeded with the implementation of the Picot Report. Workshops, seminars and other presentations were conducted for about 10,000 people. Jim Spinks worked in Britain throughout much of 1989 and 1990 on training programmes for principals, governors and officers in about one-quarter of the local education authorities in England and Wales. Approximately 10,000 people participated. The feature of the refined model was the incorporation of a capacity for strategic planning and a sharper focus on learning and teaching. The refined model is described by Caldwell and Spinks (1992).

Further research is now underway in Tasmania in the Exemplary Schools Study Project, an initiative funded by the Australian Research Council. The intention is to provide comprehensive portraits, utilizing Lightfoot's (1983) imagery, of the way in which outstanding schools have achieved their success. Preliminary findings confirm a capacity for leadership along the lines outlined below.

LEADERSHIP IN SELF-MANAGING SCHOOLS IN THE 1990s

A unifying concept in terms of restructured schools is that of self-management. A self-managing school (Caldwell and Spinks, 1988, p. 5) is a school in a system of education where there has been significant and consistent decentralization to the school level of authority to make decisions related to the allocation of resources. This decentralization is administrative rather than political, with decisions at the school level being made within a framework of local, state or national policies and guidelines. The school remains accountable to a central authority for the manner in which resources are allocated.

Resources are defined broadly to include knowledge (decentralization of decisions related to curriculum, including decisions related to the goals or ends of schooling); technology (decentralization of decisions related to the means of learning and teaching); power (decentralization of authority to make decisions); material (decentralization of decisions related to the use of facilities, supplies and equipment); people (decentralization of decisions related to human resources, including professional development in matters related to learning and teaching, and the support of learning and teaching); time (decentralization of decisions related to the allocation of time); and finance (decentralization of decisions related to the allocation of money).

Attention is drawn to the breadth of this concept of self-management in that it goes beyond the relatively narrow focus on finance which was evident in the 1970s and 1980s in developments known as school-based budgeting or school-based management (Canada and the United States) or the local financial management of schools (Britain). There is also a distinction between self-management and other concepts which have been used, such as self-governance and self-determination, these implying the lack of a centrally determined framework for the management of schools. While some scenarios suggest that such schools will emerge over the next decade, self-management is the more accurate descriptor for what is happening in systems of government and non-government schools in Australia and New Zealand.

There seem to be four facets to the leadership role of the principal as it is emerging in the self-managing school in Australia and New Zealand: cultural leadership, strategic leadership, educational leadership and accountable leadership (following the classification of Caldwell and Spinks (1992)). These are in addition to the management role implied in the basic model for self-management, namely the establishment of the structures and processes for an ongoing cycle of goal-setting and needs identification, policy making and priority setting, programme planning, programme budgeting, implementation and programme evaluation.

Cultural leadership is essentially a capacity to work with others in the school community to create and sustain a culture of excellence, defined broadly to include equity.

Strategic leadership is the capacity to *take charge of one's own agenda* which involves the principal:

- keeping abreast of trends and issues, threats and opportunities in the school environment and in society at large, nationally and internationally; and anticipating their impact on education generally and on the school in particular;
- sharing such knowledge with others in the school's community and encouraging other school leaders to do the same in their areas of interest;
- establishing structures and processes which enable the school to set priorities and formulate strategies which take account of likely and/or preferred futures; being a key source of expertise as these occur;
- ensuring that the attention of the school community is focused on matters of strategic importance; and
- monitoring the implementation of strategies as well as emerging strategic issues in the wider environment, facilitating an ongoing process of review.

Educational leadership involves what may be described as *the nurturing of a learning community*, with the community including students, teachers, parents and others with a stake and interest in the school. The focus is, of course, the processes of learning and teaching and the support of learning and teaching but there is a much longer agenda for action than there was a few years ago. Training programmes for teachers in a wider repertoire of approaches to learning and teaching, the restructuring of the workplace for teachers, the development of social capital in the sense of strong mutually supporting relationships among the different constituencies in the school community, all make for a substantial educational leadership role for the principal. Clearly, this will require a capacity to build a team of educational leaders in the spirit of Sergiovanni's (1984) concept of 'leadership density' that pervades the model for self-management.

Accountable leadership refers to the capacity of the principal to work with others to demonstrate that the school has indeed been responsive to the needs of the student, the local community and society at large within the particular framework of responsibility of self-management which applies to the school. Accountable leadership incorporates and broadens the notion of accountability which characterizes the delivery of public services in the 1990s.

It seems that authorities in Australia and New Zealand are only now coming to grips with the magnitude of the task, both generally in respect to restructuring in education, and specifically in terms of the preparation and professional development of principals. There has been much greater discussion and debate in the United States, as evidenced by papers at successive meetings of the American Educational Research Association, than there has been in Australia and New Zealand. It is regrettable that this discussion and debate is getting underway at a time of severe economic difficulty, when there will be few resources to mount large-scale programmes of professional development.

THE NEXT DECADE IN AUSTRALIA AND NEW ZEALAND

There have clearly been substantial changes to the role of the principal in Australia and New Zealand since 1970. It seems unlikely that the rate of change will abate. Trends of the kind described seem to have sufficient momentum and direction that what is likely to emerge over the course of the next decade can be described with a reasonable degree of confidence. Two approaches may be adopted, utilizing the concepts of megatrends and scenarios.

THE CONCEPT OF MEGATREND

John Naisbitt coined the term *megatrends* to describe broad social, economic, political and technological changes which influence in very powerful ways the direction of change in different fields of endeavour. He foreshadowed a number of trends which he believed would occur in the 1980s (Naisbitt, 1982):

- from an industrial society towards an information society,
- from forced technology towards a 'high tech/high touch' people-oriented use of advanced technology,
- from reliance on a national economy towards involvement in a world economy,

- from preoccupation with the short term towards consideration for the long term,
- from centralization towards decentralization,
- from institutional help towards self-help,
- from representative democracy towards participatory democracy,
- from communication and control in hierarchies towards networking,
- from a concentration of interest and effort in the north (developed countries) towards concern for the south (developing countries), and
- from consideration of either/or towards a multiple option range of choices.

While the outcomes have been uneven, it is fair to say that most have occurred in the manner foreshadowed by Naisbitt. Their effects in education are evident, especially in regard to trends towards an information society, decentralization, self-help, participatory democracy, networking and multiple options.

Naisbitt was joined by Patricia Aburdene in describing megatrends in the 1990s. Again, ten megatrends were identified, with many being a continuation of, or development from, those set out earlier (Naisbitt and Aburdene, 1990):

- a booming global economy,
- a renaissance in the arts,
- the emergence of free-market socialism,
- global lifestyles and cultural nationalism,
- the privatization of the welfare state,
- the rise of the Pacific Rim,
- the decade of women in leadership,
- the age of biology,
- a religious revival, and
- the triumph of the individual.

It is likely that most will influence or be associated with developments in education in the 1990s, with implications for the management of education in each instance.

MEGATRENDS IN EDUCATION

Trends in education of the kind described earlier in the chapter have been underway for a sufficient period of time and have sufficient depth and strength that they might be considered megatrends in education. They seem to be broadly evident in Western countries, including Australia and New Zealand. Ten are offered here, with each stated in the future tense although current strength is evident in most instances (see Caldwell and Spinks (1992) for a detailed exploration of these possibilities).

- There will be a powerful but sharply focused role for central authorities, especially in respect to formulating goals, setting priorities and building frameworks for accountability.

- National and global considerations will become increasingly important, especially in respect to the curriculum and education systems that are responsive to national needs within a global economy.
- Within centrally determined frameworks, government (public) schools will become largely self-managing, and distinctions between government and non-government (private) schools will narrow.
- There will be unparalleled concern for the provision of a quality education for each individual.
- There will be a dispersion of the educative function, with telecommunications and computer technology ensuring that much learning which currently occurs in schools or institutions at post-compulsory levels will occur at home and in the workplace.
- The basics in education will be expanded to include problem solving, creativity and a capacity for lifelong learning and relearning.
- There will be an expanded role for the arts and spirituality, defined broadly in each instance; there will be a high level of *connectedness* in curriculum.
- Women will claim their place among the ranks of leaders in education, including those at the most senior levels.
- The parent and community role in education will be claimed or reclaimed.
- There will be unparalleled concern for service by those who are required or have the opportunity to support the work of schools.

SCENARIOS

We may be on safer ground if we contemplate the future by describing some possible scenarios. Four are sketched out here for illustrative purposes. Only the major distinguishing features are identified; combinations of some features will suggest other scenarios.

Scenario 1: The Market Model

School self-management within a central framework will become school self-government in a nation of free standing schools, with public schools receiving their core funding directly from the treasury. There will be a national curriculum framework and national testing but little else in terms of central direction and support. The capacity of schools to enrol students will be the chief determinant of their survival. Schools will purchase support services in a largely private market. Staff will be employed by their schools. Elements of this scenario are discernible in England and Wales, with the demise of local education authorities being foreshadowed.

Scenario 2: The Charter Model

A system of self-managing schools will emerge, with a charter becoming the key mechanism for resourcing and accountability. Public schools will, quite literally, be chartered in the sense that a formal agreement is reached between government and school council on the arrangements at the school level for addressing state and national policies and priorities on the one hand and local policies and priorities on the other. Agreement provides a guarantee of resourcing and a focus for accountability. Minimal support is provided. Staff are employed by their schools within a national framework of salaries and working conditions. The major features of this scenario are evident in New Zealand.

Scenario 3: The Local Support Model

The recent trend in some states of Australia and in New Zealand to establish clusters of schools and school districts will gain momentum, with these arrangements being the means of providing schools with support services more efficiently and more effectively than if schools were to seek such services independently. This scenario has similarity with some aspects of school systems in Canada and the United States, especially in respect to support arrangements but not in respect to funding and staffing which would remain centralized except for staff selection, which would be local.

Scenario 4: The Recentralization Model

This scenario responds to a continuing concern that schools do not serve the national need. There are large numbers of students who do not complete their secondary schooling; knowledge, skills and attitudes do not create the clever country. The outcome is a national system, tightly monitored and extensively supported through a network of arrangements at all levels, with a rebuilding of structures at the state level which were steadily dismantled in the late 1980s and early 1990s.

A lively debate will result from efforts to identify which scenario or combination of scenarios is the most desirable, the most feasible or the most likely. The policy process will be crowded with participants and the values of accountability, excellence, effectiveness, efficiency, empowerment, equity, quality and uniformity will be fiercely contested.

More than 200 participants at the Annual Conference of the Australian Council for Educational Administration in 1991 were invited to rank the scenarios in terms of probability and desirability. Mean rankings were similar in each instance with the Charter and Local Support Models ranked highest, followed by the Market Model. The Recentralization Model was lowest in these mean rankings for both probability and preferability.

IMPLICATIONS FOR PRINCIPALS

The particular ways in which these megatrends and scenarios affect developments in particular schools and in particular roles will, of course, vary from setting to setting. Some effects may not be immediately evident. The view expressed here is that, over the long term, there will be a local pattern which reflects the broader megatrends and each of the scenarios other than that conceptualized in the Recentralization Model.

What are the implications for schools and, especially, principals? What actions might be taken now or anticipated in the near future in order to take advantage of the opportunities or deal with the threats?

- Principals will have a high-level capacity for strategic planning; that is, to see 'the larger picture' and, on a continuing basis, set and reset priorities in a simple strategic plan which will provide the framework for the annual operational plan.
- Principals will have a high-level capacity for marketing, with a broader range of potential competitors than in the past and a need to describe in more precise terms the nature of their educational programmes.
- The educational voucher will appear in the 1990s although not in the form originally conceived and advocated, providing schools with a new focus for marketing and restructured source of public funding.
- Schools will offer programmes and services to meet a wider range of student and community needs.
- Many schools will operate from an initial position of strength in respect to breadth and connectedness of curriculum, but major effort will be required to sustain the advantage.
- Schools will become part of a lifelong educational movement to a greater extent than is currently evident.
- Schools may become centres for the delivery of school support services.
- The autonomy of schools may be curtailed to some extent with the emergence of national (and possibly international) curriculum frameworks.
- The community will be more actively involved in the decision-making process than has often been the case in the past.
- Rhetoric must become reality as far as intentions and outcomes of schooling are concerned, for we will have a highly educated community which will search out and insist on the best for its students.

CONCLUSION

What emerges is a rather daunting but exciting role for the principal in the 1990s. But, as Drucker observed at the start of the last decade, when writing of management in turbulent times, 'a time for turbulence is also one of great opportunity for those who can understand, accept and exploit the new realities. It is, above all, a time of opportunity for leadership' (Drucker, 1981, p. 10).

REFERENCES

Beare, H. (1990) 'Educational administration in the 1990s', *Monograph*, 7, Australian Council for Educational Administration.

Boyd, W. (1990) 'The national level: Reagan and the bully pulpit', in S. Bacharach (ed.) *Education Reform: Making Sense of it All*, Boston: Allyn & Bacon.

Caldwell, B. (1990a) 'Educational reform through school-site management: An international perspective on restructuring in education', in S. Bacharach (ed.) *Advances in School Management and Educational Policy*, Vol. 1 (pp. 303–33), Greenwich, CT: JAI Press.

—— (1990b) 'School leadership in a new era of management in public education: Implications for preparation and professional development', in P. Thurston and L. Lotto (eds) *Advances in Educational Administration*, Vol. 1, Part B: Changing perspectives on the school (pp. 41–71), Greenwich, CT: JAI Press.

—— (1992) 'Preservice and inservice requirements for successful decentralization in restructured school systems', Paper presented in a Symposium on International Perspectives of Centralized and Decentralized Decision Making at the Annual Conference of the American Educational Research Association, Chicago, April.

Caldwell, B. and Spinks, J. (1988) *The Self-Managing School*, London: The Falmer Press.

—— (1992) *Leading the Self-managing School*, London: The Falmer Press.

Caldwell, B., Smilanich, R. and Spinks, J. (1988) 'The self-managing school', *The Canadian Administrator* 27(1): 1–8.

Drucker, P. (1981) *Managing in Turbulent Times*, London: Pan.

Lange, D. (1988) *Tomorrow's Schools*, Wellington, NZ: Government Printer.

Lightfoot, S. (1983) *The Good High School*, New York: Basic Books.

Macpherson, R. (1990a) 'The context, process and recommendations of schools renewal: The restructuring of New South Wales school education as genetic engineering', Paper presented at the Annual Meeting of the American Educational Research Association, Boston, March.

—— (1990b) 'The reconstruction of New Zealand education: A case of "high politics" reform', Paper presented at the International Intervisitation Programme of the Commonwealth Council for Educational Administration, Manchester, 20–29 April.

Naisbitt, J. (1982) *Megatrends*, London: Futura Press.

Naisbitt, J. and Aburdene, P. (1990) *Megatrends 2000*, New York: William Morrow.

OECD (1987) *Quality of Schooling: A clarifying report*, Restricted Secretariat Paper ED(87) 13.

Picot, B. (1988) *Administering for Excellence*, Wellington, NZ: Government Printer.

Scott, B. (1990) *School-centred education*, Report of the Management Review, New South Wales Education Portfolio.

Sergiovanni, T. (1984) 'Leadership and excellence in schooling', *Educational Leadership* February.

Thomas, H. (1988) 'Pupils as vouchers', *The Times Educational Supplement* 2 December: 23.

Chapter 9

Linking school effectiveness knowledge and school improvement practice

David Reynolds

If a Martian, that value-free creature so beloved of social scientists, were to visit the planet to take a look at its educational arrangements, the most remarkable thing that would probably strike him or her about our educational research and practice would be the lack of mesh between the enterprises of *school improvement* and *school effectiveness*. With the exception of North America which now exhibits the beginnings of links between these two disciplines or sub-disciplines, in virtually all other societies around the world there are few points of intellectual or practical contact between scholars in the two disciplines. In addition, the take up of school effectiveness knowledge not just directly into the mechanics of school improvement programmes but indirectly into school practice through influence upon the practitioner and policy maker communities is comparatively rare.

This chapter aims to outline the reasons for this overall lack of synchronization between school effectiveness knowledge and school improvement practice internationally. It surveys the two communities internationally, attempts to understand the origins and distinctiveness of the different paradigms that inform and guide the two communities, and also attempts to outline what each community could gain from an appreciation of the knowledge base of the other. Crucially, we conclude by outlining what changed practice within each of the effectiveness or improvement communities could hope to contribute to satisfaction of the knowledge needs of the other community. Examples of fruitful intellectual and practical interrelationships between the two bodies of knowledge, which represent in fact a distinctively new paradigm built on the foundations of the existing two, are then given. It is hypothesized that the further linking of these hitherto separate disciplines would advance our knowledge of how to generate high quality schools for children.

AN INTERNATIONAL SURVEY

We should start by further examining the nature of the interrelationships between school effectiveness research and school improvement practice internationally. In North America, particularly within the United States, there exists perhaps the closest of the international relationships between school effectiveness and school improvement. Over half of all American school districts are currently running improvement programmes based upon, or linked to, the school effectiveness knowledge base (General Accounting Office, 1989), although it must be noted that the knowledge base within the improvement programme is likely to be of the earlier simplistic variety of 'five factor' theories developed by Edmonds (1979) and popularized by Lezotte (1989) rather than that more recently developed from a considerably more advanced research base by researchers like Stringfield and Teddlie (Wimpelberg et al., 1989). In addition, in the United States there are the well known demonstration projects which have involved the direct, controlled transfer of research knowledge into school improvement programmes with built-in evaluation of outcomes, which have demonstrated enhanced school effectiveness (for example, McCormack-Larkin, 1985). In Canada, likewise, there are programmes which involve the utilization of school effectiveness knowledge within school improvement programmes (Stoll and Fink, 1989) and the school effectiveness knowledge base has also penetrated many other ongoing improvement projects (see reviews in Sackney, 1985, 1989).

In spite of this evident relationship between the two bodies of knowledge at the level of practice, at the intellectual level of the scholars who contribute to the respective knowledge bases there is rather little relationship or communality of perspective. In part this may be because school improvement scholars have reacted against the simplistic nature of much North American school effectiveness literature, with its focus upon merely the generation of effective academic outcomes, its simple lists of five, seven or nine factors which were said to cause schools to be effective, and its advocacy of certain school processes as effective within the existing range of school practice rather than the development of ideas in terms of what might be effective within a differently structured system (see Holly (1990) for a range of American views). Whatever the precise reasons, school improvement scholars such as Fullan, Hall, Miles, Louis and Joyce, for example, rarely base their school improvement strategies upon the work of school effectiveness researchers, judged by their own writings. Fullan (1991), for example, refers only to half a dozen school effectiveness studies from the United States, only one from the United Kingdom and to none from other societies, such as Australia, the Netherlands or New Zealand in which major school effectiveness projects have been carried out. Indeed, much of Fullan's earlier work (for example, Fullan, 1985) makes explicit his fundamental disagreements with the usefulness for school improvement of the concentration on formal organizational factors within the school effectiveness research paradigm, and outlines instead his more 'process'-oriented approach to understanding schools as organizations. Were we to take Fullan and the other improvement writers noted above, a survey of their bibliographies would suggest that only about 2 or 3 per cent of their total references are from authors commonly regarded as writing within the school effectiveness research paradigm. Were we also to take the American school effectiveness research community and look at the nature of their references, probably only about 1 per cent of total references would relate to writers conventionally located within the paradigm of school improvement.

The situation of two separate, discrete bodies of knowledge and two separate research communities that exists in North America is in evidence in most other parts of the world; indeed, in certain parts of the world separation is even more in evidence. In the United Kingdom, there has been in existence considerable mutual hostility between those in the school effectiveness and school improvement paradigms, as typified by the numerous celebrations of views of the critics of the effective schools' research, such as Cuban and Rowan, which are to be found in the writings of the school improvers, Hopkins and Holly (Reid et al., 1987). There is little practitioner take up of the knowledge base of school effectiveness (Mortimore, 1991; Reynolds, 1991), little use of the research in school improvement or school development programmes (see review in Hopkins, 1990) and little appreciation or referencing of school effectiveness material in the works of 'school improvers' (and vice versa). The British situation is further explored below.

In other parts of the world the situation is similar to that in Britain and in North America. New Zealand, for example, was the site of pioneering school effectiveness research (Ramsay et al., 1982) but there are no current signs of engagement of this knowledge base with the 'school improvement through decentralization' paradigm that has existed since the Picot Report in the late 1980s. The Netherlands now has perhaps the world's most extensive research base within the field of school effectiveness (see Creemers and Scheerens, 1989) but there is no evidence of school-effectiveness-based school improvement programmes, nor of any penetration of school effectiveness research knowledge into schools through the development planning which is now mandatory within Dutch schools. Australia, too, has a small school effectiveness research base (see Chapman and Stevens, 1989) and indeed some of this knowledge has been linked to school improvement through the school improvement model of Caldwell and Spinks (1988), but again more developmentally orientated material from Australia shows only limited take up of, or reliance on, school effectiveness literature.

Indeed, the Australian school improvement tradition relates primarily to the literature on educational management and administration, itself notable for the absence of linkages with the school effectiveness research base. Only in Israel do we see any systematic application of school effectiveness findings in school improvement programmes (Bashi et al., 1990).

THE SCHOOL IMPROVEMENT PARADIGM

Underlying the two distinctive bodies of scholarship and the separation of the two groups of scholars are two very distinctive intellectual traditions and histories. School improvement in the 1960s and 1970s had a number of paradigmatic characteristics, as shown in Table 9.1.

Table 9.1   Characteristics of two school improvement paradigms

	1960	1980
Orientation	Top down	Bottom up
Knowledge base	Elite knowledge	Practitioner knowledge or 'folk lore'
Targeting	Organization/curriculum based	Process based
Outcomes	Pupil outcome orientated	School process orientated
Goals	Outcomes as given	Outcomes problematic, to be discussed
Focus	School focused	Teacher focused
Methodology of evaluation	'Hard' quantitative evaluation	'Soft' naturalistic, qualitative evaluation
Site	Course, outside school	School
Focus	Part of school	Whole school

This early approach adopted a technological view of school improvement, in which innovations were brought to schools from outside of them and then introduced *top down*, in which the innovation was based upon the knowledge produced by persons outside the school, in which the focus was the school's formal organization and curriculum, in which the outcomes were taken as given, in which the school was the focus of the innovation more than the individual practitioner and in which the goals were learning outcomes. The whole improvement edifice was based upon a positivistic, quantitative evaluation of effects.

The worldwide failures of this model of school improvement to generate more than very partial take up by schools of the curricular or organizational innovations (see Reynolds, 1988) became established findings within the educational discourse of the 1970s. Out of the recognition of this failure came, reactively, the new improvement paradigm of the 1980s which is still reflected in much of the writing on school improvement that is current and in evidence today. This new movement has celebrated *bottom-up* school improvement, in which the improvement attempts were 'owned' by those at school level, although outside school consultants or experts would be allowed to put their knowledge forward for possible utilization. It celebrated the *lore* or practical knowledge of practitioners rather than the knowledge base of those who had conducted research. It wished to change educational processes, rather than school management or organizational features which it saw as reified constructs. It wanted the outcomes or goals of school improvement programmes to be debated and discussed, rather than accepted as given. Indeed, the process of school development was often seen by school improvers as a process of making value choices explicit rather than implicit, in which the resultant values debate aided the improvement process. The paradigm also wished to operate at the level of practitioners rather than at school level, with a qualitative and naturalistically oriented evaluation of the enterprise being preferred to a quantitative evaluation. The improvement attempt was *whole school* rather than *part of school* oriented and it was also school based rather than outside school or course based (this material is developed in Reynolds (1988)).

Lest one think that the above descriptions of the reactive, new improvement paradigm of the 1980s are oversimple, caricatured or merely the hostile counter reaction of a member of the school effectiveness research community, Hopkins' (1990, pp 185–91) description of the 14 country International School Improvement Project (ISIP), notes that 'ISIP... sees the process of setting goals as part of the improvement process', that 'quality is defined in terms of the teaching and learning process' and that the following list 'captures the spirit that pervades the working methods of ISIP...

- a concern to generate an understanding of phenomena
- a concern to focus upon the meaning human actors give to their actions
- a concern to avoid use of numerical data and to substitute verbal accounts wherever possible
- a concern to make educational accounts available to participants in the educational process'.

There is little doubt that the reactive nature of the new school improvement paradigm outlined above was deficient in terms of it actually generating school improvement, as some of its proponents began to realize. Hopkins and Holly (in Reid *et al.*, 1987) were already recognizing by the late 1980s that although schools should *own* their improvement attempts, outsiders could perform a valuable function in bringing *excellent* or *elite* knowledge to the attention of teachers in the schools. The process-oriented *journey* of school improvement was still stressed, but by the late 1980s the journey was also undertaken in order to enable schools to evaluate their processes and outcomes. Qualitative techniques were still the approved methodology for the measurement of programme impacts, processes and outcomes, but a rigour shown by a concern to check the validity of findings had now appeared in this work.

However, in spite of the signs of intellectual movement within the school improvement paradigm itself noted above, the description of the paradigm in the above paragraphs would not seem to be an unfair description of its core beliefs. Certainly there would be variation between and within countries in their reactiveness against the old paradigm, with the British sociology of education and teacher researcher movement as the most extreme (Elliott, 1980; Woods and Pollard, 1987), but overall it is clear the paradigm was substantially accepted internationally.

THE SCHOOL EFFECTIVENESS PARADIGM

The school effectiveness research paradigm has a very different intellectual history and has exhibited a very different set of core beliefs concerning operationalization, conceptualization and measurement by comparison with the approaches of the school improvers. It has been strongly quantitative in orientation with researchers arguing that the dominant, psychologically oriented beliefs in the importance of outside school factors (for example, Coleman *et al.*, 1966; Jencks *et al.*, 1971) had to be destroyed by utilization of the same quantitative paradigm rather than a more qualitatively oriented approach.

Adherents to the paradigm are concerned with pupil outcomes primarily, which is not surprising given the political history of school effectiveness research in the United States, where it has grown and built on the beliefs of Ron Edmonds and his associates that all *children can learn*. Processes within schools only have an importance within the school effectiveness paradigm to the extent that they affect outcomes – indeed, one *back maps* with the paradigm from outcomes to processes. The school effectiveness paradigm furthermore regards pupil and school outcomes as fundamentally unproblematic and as given; indeed, in the great majority of the North American effectiveness research the outcomes used are only the very limited, official educational definitions of the school as an academic institution. School effectiveness researchers, indeed, often talk of a *good* or *excellent* school as if the definition of good or excellent is unproblematic. Lastly, the school effectiveness paradigm is organizationally rather than process based in terms of its analytic and descriptive orientation, preferring to restrict itself to the more easily quantifiable or measurable. As an example, Fullan's (1985) process factors such as 'a feel for the process of leadership' or 'a guiding value system', or 'intense interaction and communication' are largely eschewed in favour of organizationally and behaviourally oriented process variables such as 'clear goals and high expectations' and/or 'parental involvement and support'. Additionally, the focus within the school improvement paradigm on the attitudinal and on personal and group inner states is replaced within school effectiveness research by a focus on the more easily measured behaviour of persons.

From the outline of the history of the two paradigms above, it can be seen that the two disciplines of school effectiveness and school improvement are coming from very different places intellectually, methodologically and theoretically. The school improvement paradigm was a reactive one from the early 1980s, reacting against the top-down imposition of elite defined knowledge in schools towards a celebration of practitioner lore, and an acceptance of the ensuing goals debate rather than an acknowledgement of predetermined school goals. In this reactive phase, school improvement is very different in its orientations to the school effectiveness paradigm which began to emerge in the early to mid 1980s, with its outcome focus, its quantitative methodology, its concern to generate truthful knowledge about schools (whether practitioners agreed with it or not!) and its concerns with reified school organizations and easily measured behaviours, rather than with the attitudes of teachers and pupils.

There is recent evidence that some of those appreciative of aspects of the school improvement tradition have realized the necessity for paradigmatic change, if only within that same paradigm, as noted earlier by Holly and Hopkins. Fullan (1991), too, in his more recent writing pays considerably more attention than before to the *recipes* of school effectiveness knowledge. Some school improvers have changed even more. In his recent writing, for example, Hopkins (1990) talks about 'the necessary synthesis between improvement and effective schools knowledge'.

Some scholars within the school effectiveness community have also argued for the interpenetration and synthesis of both bodies of knowledge in the interests of improving pupil performance and school quality. Mortimore (1991) argues for transferring 'the energy, knowledge and skills of school effectiveness research to the study of school improvement'. Elsewhere, I have also argued that school improvement attempts need to understand the complex psychological abnormality that is exhibited within ineffective schools (Reynolds, 1992), evidence of which should be taken from the effective schools literature. The mission statement of the journal *School Effectiveness and School Improvement* (Creemers and Reynolds, 1990) also argued for the still, small voice of empirical rationality being jointly utilized to assess the validity both of existing models of school improvement and the validity of our existing simplistic factor-based theories of school effectiveness. In all these respects the historical divisions between effectiveness and improvement may be considerably diminishing in importance.

HOW THE SCHOOL EFFECTIVENESS RESEARCH CONTRIBUTES TO SCHOOL IMPROVEMENT

If closer relationships between the two specialities were to be formed there is much ground for believing that both specialities could contribute greatly to the academic and practical needs of the other. To take school improvement first, the clear need is for school improvers to have knowledge of those factors within schools and within classrooms that may be manipulated or changed to produce higher quality schooling. At the moment, school effectiveness researchers are failing to generate that knowledge that is relevant to the school improvement enterprise in the following specific ways:

- There are very few case studies of the effective, or for that matter the ineffective, schools that would show the interrelationships between school process variables and which would paint a picture for practitioners of the fine-grained reality of school and classroom processes. The American study by Rosenholtz (1989) and some of the recent *mixed methodology* work from the Louisiana School Effectiveness Study of Stringfield and Teddlie (1990) are exceptions to this trend internationally. In Britain, however, there are still no in-depth, qualitative portraits of effective schools following the pioneering work of Rutter *et al.* (1979) or Mortimore *et al.* (1988).

  The explanations for the absence of rich case study data are simple, of course, since school effectiveness researchers have probably feared the identification of schools, which would follow the publication of rich descriptions, when they have customarily promised schools anonymity in the research process. The effect of this absence, though, is to reduce the practitioner relevance of the effectiveness research and to make the transfer of knowledge to the improvement community (with its qualitative orientation) more difficult.

- School effectiveness studies are deficient at the level of *processes* rather than factors, since effectiveness researchers have considerably more experience at the level of school organizational factors. School processes defined in terms of attitudes, values, relationships and climate have been neglected therefore, even though the school improvement community needs information on these factors within schools, given their centrality to the process of improvement and development.

- School effectiveness studies customarily show a snapshot of a school at a point in time, not an evolutionary and moving picture of a school over time, a neglect which hinders the usefulness of the knowledge for purposes of school development. School improvement needs to have ideas about how schools came to be effective (or for that matter ineffective) in order to replicate (or for that matter eradicate) the process, which necessitates a dynamic, evolutionary, evolving and *change over time* orientation within school effectiveness research.

- School effectiveness studies from outside North America, particularly those from Britain (for example, Reynolds *et al.*, 1987; Rutter *et al.*, 1979), neglect the detailed study of the crucial variable of the principal or headteacher. Both these early British studies of school effectiveness, for example, have few headteacher variables because the researchers had to promise their sponsoring educational authorities that they would not concentrate in detail in this area, which in the context of the professional headteacher autonomy customarily prevailing in the 1970s and 1980s was hardly surprising. When the Rutter team later sought to translate their findings about effective school factors into their schools, it is not surprising that their knowledge-deficient improvement programmes failed to generate much overall improvement in educational processes or pupil outcomes (Maughan *et al.*, 1990).

- School effectiveness studies have thus far (with the notable exception of work by Coleman and LaRoque (1991)) neglected greatly the other educational institutions, arrangements and layers above the level of the school. As Hopkins notes when discussing school improvement conducted within the ISIP model,

much thought ... was given to the way in which improvement policies are established at various levels... to the structured factors related to support e.g., external support .... Much of the effective schools literature appears to take such meso level issues as unproblematic, yet the ISIP case studies suggest that this is just not so.

(Hopkins, 1990, p. 188)

School improvement needs clearly to be informed by knowledge as to what conditions outside the level of the school are necessary to generate process and/or outcome improvement — currently school effectiveness research tends to generate knowledge only about school-level variables.

- School effectiveness research, whether of North American, British or Dutch origin, tends towards the generation of lists of organizational process factors within schools that are associated with pupil outcomes. Yet what school improvers need to know is not what 10, 20 or 30 factors may be useful enhancers of outcomes if changed, but which one or two factors should be changed. Given the difficulty of focusing upon large numbers of changes simultaneously and the importance of ordering temporally the change attempts in schools (Hargreaves and Hopkins, 1991), this need for change strategies that relates to a small and discrete number of factors is magnified by the need to alter those variables within schools which are the key determinants of other process variables. No school effectiveness study so far has attempted to isolate the direction and strength of the influences that link school process variables together.

- School effectiveness research, to compound the difficulties noted above, cannot even prove conclusively which process variables are causes of school effectiveness and which effects. If we take as an example the well established link between teachers' high academic expectations of their pupils and their pupils' good results in examinations or tests of attainment, it may be that the direction of the relationship is a positive one from academic expectations, to academic success, or that academic success may by contrast influence academic expectations since the experience of high examination passes at school level may lead to an expectation of them continuing, or there may be interactive influences. The directionality of the relationship – crucial for school improvers wishing to decide what to target for improvement – is not established within the research base for this variable and for many other groups or pairs of variables within the school effectiveness knowledge base.

- School effectiveness knowledge also misses the chance of satisfaction of the needs of the school improvement enterprise by being thoroughly dated. Improvement schemes in the 1990s need to be based on knowledge that is generated from school systems that reflect the characteristics of schools in the 1990s, not the schools of the 1970s and 1980s. At the level of what makes for effective schooling, process factors such as the assertive principal instructional leadership that was associated with effectiveness in the 1980s may not be associated in the same way in the 1990s, when demands for *ownership* by teachers may have changed the educational cultural context. Outcomes appropriate for measurement in the 1980s such as academic achievement or examination attainment may not be the only ones appropriate to the 1990s, where new goals concerning knowledge of how to learn or knowledge in mastering information technology may be necessary.

  Even those process factors associated with effectiveness in the 1970s and 1980s may not be, on their own, sufficient to generate effectiveness in the 1990s. The principal, for example, who was an effective leader in the 1980s now finds a bewildering variety of new aspects to the role in the case of British schools in the 1990s. He/she is now expected to sell the school as a product, to motivate staff without instrumental rewards, to translate the externally imposed policy agenda into internally driven programmes and to possess psychological resilience in the face of considerable anxiety, uncertainty and concern. The person able to do this in the 1990s may well not be the principal or headteacher described in the school effectiveness research of the 1980s, yet school effectiveness researchers in the 1990s are still operating within a strangely aged paradigm in terms of what school variables, and what dimensions of school variables, to collect data on (for further speculations on this theme see Reynolds (1992)).

- School effectiveness research has rarely been 'fine grained' enough to provide the school improvement enterprise with the information it needs, since the variation in *what works* by context has been a focus only of a very limited amount of recent North American work (Hallinger and Murphy, 1986; Wimpelberg *et al.*, 1989). School improvers need more than the notion of what works across context in the average school, and need more than data upon the relationships between school processes and outcomes for all schools – they need knowledge of the factors that will generate improvement in particular schools in particular socio-economic and cultural contexts. Since only a small amount of our school effectiveness knowledge base is disaggregated and analysed by context, the delineation of the precise variables that school improvement needs to target to affect outcomes is clearly impossible at present.

- School improvement researchers often find themselves working in historically ineffective educational settings yet the knowledge base within school effectiveness may not be necessarily easily applicable to those settings. Researchers seem to have worked with an implicit (and in the case of some of the earlier advocates within the school effectiveness movement, an explicit) deficit orientation towards the ineffective school, in which it is seen as not possessing the factors that make other schools excel. The possibility, which is my own view (Reynolds, 1992), that the ineffective school may possess variables at the level of interpersonal problems, projections, defences and the like, which in turn do not exist in the effective school, seems to be rarely considered by researchers. The knowledge of these areas, of these *ghosts* or *shadows* on the change process that improvers of the ineffective schools would naturally need, will not be found in a school effectiveness paradigm in which the good practice of effective schools is simply *back mapped* on to the ineffective schools and then assumed to be sufficient to help the ineffective improve.

HOW SCHOOL IMPROVEMENT COULD HELP SCHOOL EFFECTIVENESS RESEARCH

At its simplest level, school improvement strategies provide the ultimate test for many of the theories posted within the school effectiveness research enterprise, since the change in school outcomes identified by research as being linked to school processes is the way of testing whether there is a causal link between processes and outcomes. School improvement schemes and strategies based upon the school effectiveness research communities' identified characteristics are therefore of crucial importance to the development of school effectiveness research.

A number of further tasks for school improvement practitioners to facilitate the further development of school effectiveness research also suggest themselves:

- School improvement studies all too rarely measure the impact of changes in improvement programmes upon the outcomes of pupils or students. Part of the explanation for this may be the historical tendency of school improvement to celebrate certain styles of professional practice because of its association with the training needs and desires of the teaching profession within schools, and part of the explanation may be the reluctance of many within the school improvement paradigm to be explicit about what the nature of the school outcomes or the educational goals of their programmes really are. The absence, though, of these data as to programme effects restricts the ability of those within the school improvement paradigm to help the school effectiveness research base expand in terms of further understanding the possible relationships between school processes and school outcomes.

- School improvement programmes need to cease their *grapeshot-* or *multiple-factors*-based approach to school development and change, since changing more than one school factor at a time (which is what most attempt) makes it impossible for school effectiveness researchers to judge which of the factors concerned may be those factors accounting for any sources of increased pupil outcomes. The school effectiveness knowledge base is again clearly impoverished by an inability to elucidate what, or what not, at the level of the processes of the school has an impact upon outcomes.

- School improvement programmes need urgently to pay attention to the implications of multi-level modelling procedures for their programmes. The evidence from effectiveness research that schools can have differential effects upon their pupils (Nuttall *et al.*, 1989) and that schools effective for some groups of pupils may actually be ineffective for others, has wide ranging implications for school improvement, since these results imply that improvement attempts need urgently to move away from the much vaunted whole-school strategies towards more finely targeted programmes that may vary within the school in terms of their focus and their target group. By focusing improvement at the level of boys/girls, high ability/low ability pupils, and pupils from ethnic minorities/pupils from *host* cultures it would be possible for school improvement persons to generate more appropriate school change strategies, but most importantly it would be possible for school improvement to generate evidence about differentially effective school processes as the effects of their change attempts were targeted within schools, an area where school effectiveness knowledge has been historically non-existent.

- School improvement research needs to refocus its activities away from the level of the school to that of the classroom if it is to generate the possibility of increased school outcomes and if it is to generate knowledge of use to the school effectiveness research enterprise. A considerable volume of research now exists that shows teachers' focal concerns to be with the content of their curricular and instructional practices rather than with the wider area of the school, yet school improvement rarely has an instructional focus (see, for example, Fullan, 1991). Without centring itself upon the instructional level, school improvement runs the risk of manipulating variables only at the level of the school, which in most recent research explain much less of the variation in student outcomes than do those variables at the instructional or classroom level (see, for a review, Creemers, 1992). School improvement also runs the risk of not helping the development of school effectiveness research by not manipulating, and giving information about, the characteristics of the instructional level.

CONCLUSIONS

We have seen in this chapter that there are wide divergencies in the orientation, methodology and theoretical approaches of the specialisms historically known as *school effectiveness* and *school improvement*. These differences are the result of the historical nature of each group of scholars' and practitioners' development, with school effectiveness researchers desirous of remaining within a positivistic framework to disprove the findings from positivistic educational psychology and with school improvement practitioners reactively moving to a qualitative, appreciative stance rather than an evaluative one because of the nature of their reaction against the failed improvement paradigm of the 1960s and 1970s. We noted, however, some movement by both groups towards a blending of what had been seen as oppositional approaches.

We have continued by arguing, though, that there is much that school effectiveness researchers can do to develop the school-based knowledge base which school improvers need in their possession as they relate to their schools, and we have concluded that there is much that school improvement attempts can do to improve the validity and reliability (and in fact the transferability) of the school effectiveness knowledge base into schools, by means of testing the findings of school effectiveness research and their resulting propositions within schools.

All our discussions so far assume, though, that the intellectual and practical enterprises of school improvement and school effectiveness remain separate, yet that separation in itself may be undesirable, when compared with the potential benefits for knowledge and practice of an integrated, coherent and coordinated intellectual and practical enterprise that would be concerned jointly with research and practice on school effectiveness and school improvement. There are currently a number of examples in embryonic states of development which show what this integrated enterprise might look like.

First, the 'Improving the Quality of Education' project at the Cambridge Institute of Education (Hopkins, 1992) represents a useful blend of approaches and methods which have until now only been used exclusively in either effectiveness or improvement initiatives. It is pupil outcome orientated, involves measurement of programme success or failure at outcome level but is also concerned with the within-school study of school processes from a qualitative orientation. In the school improvement knowledge base that is to generate and inform practice and professional development, there is space for both the *elite*, research-determined knowledge concerning school effectiveness and instructional effectiveness research, and in addition there is space for the results of professional collaboration, reflection and education to influence the chosen improvement strategies in a blend of research and practitioner knowledge.

A second example is the series of school improvement programmes run by the Halton Board of Education in Canada (Stoll and Fink, 1989) noted earlier.

These began as an inspired attempt to bring the results of school effectiveness work done within one culture (Mortimore *et al.*, 1988) into the schooling practices of another, but it soon became clear to the programme operators that there were major problems involved in the implementation of the effectiveness programmes that had to be resolved by the adoption at school level of organizational and planning arrangements from the school improvement literature. The result was a blend of the effectiveness knowledge base about effective practices, and the improvement-generated knowledge base about successful school-based planning and change. There was simply a major philosophical shift within the enterprise and a commitment to make the Halton schools more effective for all students through the blended application of school effectiveness and school improvement research.

Our third and final example of a fruitful blending or synthesis of perspectives from what had hitherto been regarded as *school effectiveness* and *school improvement* is perhaps our own school improvement attempts at Cardiff (Reynolds *et al.*, 1989b). Our school effectiveness knowledge base, derived from British work on the topic, was blended with grassroots practitioner *lore* as to what made for effectiveness at school level, and the knowledge base was applied within schools by utilizing the improvement methodology characteristic of the Organization Development (OD) or change agent variety (for example, Schmuck and Miles, 1971). Our focus was upon changing pupils' school outcomes but we also attempted a full appreciation of the importance of studying school processes as they were changing. The emergent improvement programme was a blend of quantitative and qualitative methodologies, of elite and professional knowledge, of effectiveness and improvement scholarship, and of behavioural, school outcome-based approaches together with appreciation of the attitudinal and *deep structural* components of schools' and teachers' individual and institutional dynamics.

All three examples above represent a blend of what have hitherto been regarded as mutually exclusive orientations, theories and methodologies. All three approaches suspend existing commitments to present disciplinary purity and to the historically constructed bodies of so-called *normal science* and accepted practice, in favour of the adoption of an approach which is problem, pupil and school centred. All three approaches adopt not an either/or orientation but are concerned to ensure both school effectiveness and school improvement are joined together in an intellectually creative and practically productive new wave of educational studies. It will be both interesting and instructive to see if further examples can follow.

REFERENCES

Bashi, J., Saff, Z., Katzir, R. and Margolin, I. (1990) *Effective Schools: From Theory to Practice*, Jerusalem: Nevo Publishing.

Caldwell, B. and Spinks, J. (1988) *The Self-Managing School*, London: The Falmer Press.

Chapman, J. and Stevens, S. (1989) 'Australia', in D. Reynolds, B.P.M. Creemers and T. Peters (eds) *School Effectiveness and Improvement*, Groningen: RION.

Coleman, J. *et al.* (1966) *Equality of Educational Opportunity*, Washington, DC: US Government Printing Office.

Coleman, P. and LaRoque, L. (1990) *Struggling to be Good Enough*, Lewes: Falmer Press.

Creemers, B. (1992) 'School effectiveness and effective instruction – the need for a further relationship', in J. Bashi and Z. Saff (eds) *School Effectiveness and Improvement*, Jerusalem: Hebrew University Press.

Creemers, B. and Reynolds, D. (1990) 'School effectiveness and school improvement: A mission statement', *School Effectiveness and School Improvement* 1(10): 1–3.

Creemers, B. and Scheerens, J. (eds) (1989) 'Developments in school effectiveness research', A special issue of *International Journal of Education Research* 13(7): 685–825.

Edmonds, R.R. (1979) 'Effective schools for the urban poor', *Educational Leadership* 37(15–18): 20–4.

Elliott, J. (1980) 'Implications of classroom research for professional development', in E. Hoyle and J. Megarry (eds) *World Yearbook of Education 1980*, London: Kogan Page.

Fullan, M. (1985) 'Change processes and strategies at the local level', *Elementary School Journal* 85(13): 391–421.

—— (1991) *The New Meaning of Educational Change*, London: Cassells.

General Accounting Office (1989) *Effective Schools Programs: Their Extent and Characteristics*, Gaithersberg, MD: General Accounting Office.

Hallinger, P. and Murphy, J. (1986) 'The social context of effective schools', *American Journal of Education* 94: 328–55.

Hargreaves, D. and Hopkins, D. (1991) *The Empowered School*, London: Cassells.

Holly, P.J. (1990) 'Catching the wave of the future: Moving beyond school effectiveness by redesigning schools', *School Organization* 10(2): 195–202.

Hopkins, D. (1990) 'The international school improvement project (ISIP) and effective schooling: Towards a synthesis', *School Organization* 10(3): 129–94.

—— (1992) 'School improvement in an era of change', in P. Ribbins and E. Whale (eds) *The Issue is Quality*, London: Cassells.

Jencks, C. *et al.* (1971) *Inequality*, London: Allen Lane.

Lezotte, L. (1989) 'School improvement based on the effective schools research', *International Journal of Educational Research* 13(7): 815–25.

McCormack-Larkin, M. (1985) 'Ingredients of a successful school effectiveness project', *Educational Leadership* March: 31–7.

Maughan, B., Ouston, J., Pickles, A. and Rutter, M. (1990) 'Can schools change 1: Outcomes at six London secondary schools', *School Effectiveness and Improvement* 1(3): 188–210.

Mortimore, P. (1991) 'School effectiveness research: Which way at the crossroads?', *School Effectiveness and School Improvement* 2(3): 213–29.

Mortimore, P., Sammons, P., Ecob, R. and Stoll, L. (1988) *School Matters: The Junior Years*, Salisbury: Open Books.

Nuttall, D., Goldstein, H., Prosser, R. and Rasbash, H. (1989) 'Differential school effectiveness', *International Journal of Educational Research* 13(7): 769–76.

Ramsay, P.D.K., Sneddon, D.G., Grenfell, J. and Fort, I. (1982) 'Successful vs unsuccessful schools: A South Auckland study', *Australia and New Zealand Journal of Sociology* 19(1): 272–304.

Reid, K., Hopkins, D. and Holly, P. (1987) *Towards the Effective School*, Oxford: Blackwell.

Reynolds, D. (1988) 'British school improvement research: The contribution of qualitative studies', *International Journal of Qualitative Studies in Education* 1(2): 143–54.

—— (1991) 'School effectiveness in secondary schools: Research and its policy implications', in S. Riddell and S. Brown (eds) *School Effectiveness Research*, Edinburgh: HMSO.

—— (1992) 'School effectiveness and school improvement in the 1990s', in D. Reynolds and P. Cuttance (eds) *School Effectiveness*, London: Cassells.

Reynolds, D., Creemers, B. and Peters, T. (eds) (1989a) *School Effectiveness and Improvement*, Proceedings of the First International Congress, London, 1988, Groningen: University of Groningen, RION.

Reynolds, D., Davie, R. and Phillips, D. (1989b) 'The Cardiff programme: An effective school improvement programme based on school effectiveness research', in B.P.M. Creemers and J. Scheerens (eds) *Developments in School Effectiveness Research*, A special issue of the *International Journal of Educational Research* 13(7): 800–14.

Reynolds, D., Sullivan, M. and Murgatroyd, S.J. (1987) *The Comprehensive Experiment*, Lewes: Falmer Press.

Rosenholtz, S. (1989) *Teachers' Workplace*, New York: Longman.

Rutter, M., Maughan, B., Mortimore, P. and Ouston, J. (1979) *Fifteen Thousand Hours: Secondary Schools and their Effects on Children*, London: Open Books.

Sackney, L. (1985) 'School district imperatives for effective schools', *The Canadian School Executive* 16(2): 2–13.

—— (1989) 'School effectiveness and improvement: The Canadian scene', in D. Reynolds, B. Creemers and T. Peters (eds) *School Effectiveness and Improvement*, Groningen: RION.

Schmuck, R.R. and Miles, M. (eds) (1971) *Organization Development in Schools*, Palo Alto, CA: National Press Books.

Stoll, L. and Fink, D. (1989) 'An effective schools project: The Halton approach', in D. Reynolds, B. Creemers and T. Peters (eds) *School Effectiveness and Improvement*, Groningen: RION.

Stringfield, S. and Teddlie, C. (1990) 'School improvement effects: Qualitative and quantitative data from four naturally occurring experiments in phases 3 and 4 of the Louisiana school effectiveness study', *School Effectiveness and School Improvement* 1(2): 139–61.

Wimpelberg, R., Teddlie, C. and Stringfield, S. (1989) 'Sensitivity to context: The past and future of effective schools research', *Educational Administration Quarterly* 25: 82–107.

Woods, P. and Pollard, A. (eds) (1987) *Sociology and teaching: A New Challenge for the Sociology of Education*, London: Croom Helm.

Chapter 10

Leadership, school-based decision making and school effectiveness

Judith Chapman

THE CONCEPT OF SCHOOL EFFECTIVENESS

The concept of *school effectiveness* is central to much educational discourse about the management of schools and school systems. Given this centrality, some might suggest it is remarkable that there exists no uniformly accepted definition of the term. But this is hardly surprising, for no definition of this highly value-laden notion can exist uncontested. It has been argued elsewhere (Chapman, 1991a) that *school effectiveness* is a term that exhibits all the characteristic features associated with what Gallie (1964) called 'essentially contested concepts'. All that one can be certain about in discussion involving such terms is that people will disagree in their understanding and use of them.

Words or concepts such as school effectiveness are not single uncontroversially definable entities. Rather they are best understood as contested moves in that set of *language games* that give them their meaning and power; in this respect they only function within a whole set of complex interwoven fusions of theory and practice, fact and value, descriptions and evaluations, framed in the context of the institutions and contexts that give such words, concepts and conceptual networks meaning, purpose and applicability.

In many countries attention has been focused in various ways on researching the effectiveness of schools, some of this research taking account of such complexities, some not. Much research, regrettably, particularly in earlier times, has tended to use narrow definitions and measurements of effectiveness, concentrating on a select number of school objectives and generally only those that could be stated in measurable terms.

The so-called *scientific* approach to understanding school effectiveness, particularly that emanating from the positivistic paradigm and relying heavily upon the quantitative mode of elaboration, is replete with methodological and conceptual problems of various kinds (Chapman, 1991b). These difficulties are so fundamental that there is much to commend the suggestion that the empiricist basis of that paradigm calls into question much of the enquiry based upon it.

One of the basic tenets of empiricism, according to Quine (1953), is the positing of an absolute divide between the *neutral, factual* and *value-free* statements held to be characteristic of mathematics and the natural sciences, which are thus treated as paradigms of objectivity, and those of other such theoretic domains as ethics, politics and psychoanalysis, which are held to be non-factual, value laden and irredeemably subjective.

In opposition to the thesis of empiricism, the main burden of recent arguments on this issue has been to show that there is no such distinction between fact and value. For Quine and many others more recently all language and all enquiries are inescapably and *ab initio* theory laden, far from value free, and a mixture of both descriptive and normative elements. Such arguments are used powerfully by Evers and Lakomski (1991) to argue for a new science of educational administration, one based on a much broader view of science: namely, science justified on coherentist criteria not narrow logical empiricist criteria. Evers and Lakomski see this new science as embracing values, human subjectivity, politics, psychology and so on.

Chief among the most important aspects of schooling are those that are unamenable to quantification. Such aspects may only be discerned in the qualitative and organic changes that education brings about in the individual, the school and in the community. Proponents of this view would follow Wittgenstein's (1922) dictum regarding supreme matters of value: 'Some things cannot be described. They can only be shown. They are what is continually being made manifest.'

In education these manifestations are for us discerned in the effective educational practices of the institutions of schooling – in the ways in which individuals are so transformed as to become the bearers of the values, attitudes and beliefs held to be important by society and by the institutions in which they find expression.

Wittgenstein's metaphor of 'the rope' (1958) is helpful in explaining this idea more fully. In one long piece of rope, he explained, there is no single fibre that runs the whole length; neither are there two distinct fibres, running from each end and meeting in the middle. What one has instead is a complex interweaving of a myriad of small separate fibres, that criss-cross and overlap for the length of the rope and thus together constitute the one visible whole. So it is with the qualitative and quantitative aspects inherent in the concept of school effectiveness, in which whole layers of meaning are cross-woven and intertwined to give it the complex character it possesses.

In light of the foregoing, the OECD in its activity *The Effectiveness of Schooling and of Educational Resource Management* (Chapman, 1991c) has been prepared to offer, not a *definition* of school effectiveness, but only a broad working framework for elucidation of what might be meant by school effectiveness. Such a framework may then serve to lay the basis for negotiation as to what constitutes school effectiveness within the key particular political, social, economic and educational contexts in which this idea functions and has value.

This framework includes consideration of:

- the nature of the goals of schooling and the achievements obtained (this relates to such values as the relevance, academic standards and desirable social effects of the achievements);
- the means by which objectives are obtained (having to do with such matters as the economy of effort, time, and resources expended on the task/process);
- the criteria used in the measurement of the objectives obtained (as regards the range, depth, comprehensiveness and totality of cover).

It will be clear from the foregoing that a knowledge of the multi-level range and complexity of the objectives of a school forms a crucial part of any attempt to understand, make intelligible, manage and assess *school effectiveness*. Given the extensive range of school objectives, processes and outcomes, the difficulty of providing any comprehensive set of guidelines – much less injunctions – that will unambiguously show the way towards effective leadership as a precondition of enhancing school effectiveness becomes clear.

It is important to realise that in a field as complex as school effectiveness the processes of decision making and leadership must be highly articulated, evolutionary and always subject to review. In such a field it will be important to note that:

- the process of change has no terminal point;
- the pace of change at times will be slow and not uniform;
- a problem solved in one area is likely to generate a problem elsewhere;
- there will almost never be a point at which one may confidently say that the evidence is all in and a so-called rational decision can be made.

Leadership in such a field cannot be simply explained by a purely rationalist model of decision making. Such an approach would fail to be adequate, for the reason that there also needs to be considered the extent to which intangible factors arising from human conscious and unconscious purposes and drives will exert determinative effects on the processes of organizational functioning and change.

Yet, despite this complexity, the need for improving the effectiveness of schooling cannot be escaped. Moreover, a major role will be assigned to the school leader in ensuring that the school fulfils its responsibility in each of the substantive areas outlined above. In such areas the extent of direction and control emanating from central or regional authorities will vary from country to country and the degrees of freedom available to school leaders will alter accordingly. Common to all countries, however, will be the responsibility of the school leader to create and sustain the moral–political and the psycho-social climate in which such issues can be, within organizational constraints, addressed, and expectations relevant to performance met.

UNDERSTANDING SCHOOL EFFECTIVENESS IN THE AUSTRALIAN SETTING

Within Australia much of the recent thrust for considering school effectiveness has emanated from the Commonwealth Government. The Commonwealth has, in the view of one recent Minister for Employment, Education and Training, John Dawkins, a legitimate interest in schooling. It falls under two areas of Commonwealth responsibility and concern: economic adjustment, and social equity and the quality of life for all Australians. Improving the effectiveness of schools is seen as a way of addressing both economic and social adjustments. In a speech to the first conference of the National Board of Employment, Education and Training (NBEET) held at Coffs Harbour in November 1990, Dawkins spoke of the need which he saw as driving the major educational reforms proposed by the Commonwealth Government:

> to use our intelligence and wit to cement the processes of change and to secure and improve our place in the world. This involves working better and smarter, scuttling mediocrity for quality and distinction ... with a respect for achievement, a passion to succeed and with a will to be innovative and successful.
>
> (Dawkins, 1990a)

He proceeded to identify the need for Australia's schools to contribute in a major way to the development and expansion of the Australian economy to enable the country to compete with her neighbours and economic competitors, particularly major trading nations in Europe and the Pacific Rim. Underlying his position is the belief in a straightforward causal relationship between high educational standards and national economic success.

In countries against which Australia is competing in the international economic environment school retention rates have been much higher, many more students have entered for public examinations, national systems of testing have been seen to have a direct relationship with high educational achievement and the proportion of students going on to higher education, and the successes of schools in producing a cadre of high quality graduates for work in leading goods and services industries have been viewed as enabling them to take leading positions in world comparative economic terms. The resultant economic imperative is clear.

Alongside this economic concern, however, the Commonwealth Government in its educational policy is also committed to concerns that have been traditional ideals for Labour: the extension of social justice, equity and welfare provision, to make it possible for all citizens in a productive democracy both to contribute to the production of the commonwealth to the best of their ability, and to seek to capitalize on the realization of the creative potential of all individuals without reference to class, wealth or social status. Schools, Dawkins has argued, have a responsibility for opening up to as wide a range of classes as possible the means of individual improvement, some form of success, and the ability to work out a satisfying pattern of life options for themselves based on information and the freedom to make real choices without the constraints that poverty, distance, social marginality or institutional inefficiencies had imposed on them. This argument is espoused in one of Dawkins' speeches:

> The provision of education is more than simply an economic exercise. It is a basic tenet of Labor's philosophy that since a good education enriches the lives of all individuals all should be entitled to experience such an education. To the extent that education provides important skills, develops critical awareness and is a necessary condition for understanding individual and group rights then it is of great importance to the less privileged that these have equal opportunities to obtain an education which provides these benefits.
>
> (Dawkins, 1990b)

Some of the barriers and inefficiencies preventing the achievement of such goals have, in Dawkins' view, been made even more rigid and coercive by what he sees as gross dysfunctions arising from the large-scale differences in educational structures and systems of organization, and modes of delivery and methods of testing achievement between the states, which have led to disparities in the range and type of subjects studied, the levels of achievement worked for, and transferability of credit for achievement between state systems.

From the Commonwealth perspective, these and other local practices have militated against the achievements of harnessing the nation's resources to produce a coherent and coordinated set of national education goals that would make Australia a *clever* country and enable it therefore to answer the two challenges of economic efficiency and competitiveness and social justice and equity which face it.

THE INTERNATIONAL CONCERN FOR SCHOOL EFFECTIVENESS AND IMPLICATIONS FOR SCHOOL-BASED MANAGEMENT

Concern regarding the effectiveness of schooling, the quality of education, the relationship between education and international economic competitiveness, continuing financial stringency and competing community, and social demands for public funds have forced educational authorities in most countries to reassess the goals, provision and assessment of education in schools and school systems. In most countries consideration of ways to improve the effectiveness of schools has tended to be based around policies or rationalized budget allocations and accountability. In most instances the concern has been, if not how to achieve effectiveness at a lower cost, at least how to achieve effectiveness in the most cost-efficient manner (Chapman, 1991c).

Restricted budgets have led to increased attention to efficiency and effectiveness in the public service. In some countries this emphasis has been associated with a change in the very concept of public service and thence to fundamental changes in styles of public administration. The new model of public administration in countries such as the UK tends to be more consumer and market oriented, based on the assumption that effectiveness is generated and promoted by competition among institutions.

Not all countries are following this trend, however. In France, for example, there is an awareness of the limitation of the consumer approach to the full range of values, representations and expectations vested in the public education system. Elsewhere, in Scandinavia for instance, there has been an emphasis on rolling reforms, based not on changing the nature of the public service but on improving the quality of that service by a range of internal mechanisms, including the improvement in human resources through professional development.

No matter what the orientation of the reforms, however, most countries have directly addressed management in their educational reform efforts and in most instances this has involved a changed relationship between central administration and schools. In the new arrangements, most countries have tended to place an increased emphasis on the responsibility of the centre to determine objectives and monitor achievement, whilst at the same time providing for more implementation and resource management decision making at the level of the individual school site.

Contemporary analysts have pointed to the paradoxes inherent in this approach to reform. Furthermore, as Cuban (1989) has argued, it is frequently the school leader who is expected to resolve the paradoxes inherent in seemingly contradictory trends. What is perhaps most interesting to observe is the tension between the reality of increasing bureaucratic centralism and the rhetoric and professed desire to vest management and control of schools within the local community.

Regarding the UK, for instance, Aspin (1992) has observed the paradox that policies of a 'minimalist radical anarchist' kind may be discerned lying beside the increasingly centralizing powers of national government. Furthermore, in countries such as Australia and New Zealand, he notes, policies are emerging that exhibit not only the paradoxes of the UK experience, transported in line with the internationalist managerialist trends of education, but the larger paradox of such policies working under the aegis of governments of the Left.

In such a setting, he argues, the difficulty of government is to promote and secure the twin goals of increasing international economic competitiveness through education while at the same time extending social justice in a time of economic restraint. This has committed the government to educational policies, the requirements of which do not always sit well together: trying to address traditional Labour concerns for social justice and emancipation of all constituencies simultaneously with trying to operate education on more corporatist business lines.

Such a business mentality is based on competition and the norms of profit-and-loss budgeting, with far less reference to the social values of caring, compassion, support and assistance to the underprivileged and needy, which have traditionally been associated with Labour governments. Aspin argues that the problem with the corporate managerialist approach to educational administration currently being adopted by governments ideologically driven from both the Left and the Right is:

> the sheer logical fallacy of postulating an analogy between the nature and purpose of public service institutions such as education and those of business. One aim of education is preparation for the world of work but education is far more than that. It also requires the induction into the cognitive and affective worlds that enable human beings to live a life of quality. This involves a young person becoming the bearer of the human traditions of critical and creative thought not a mere container of packages easily prepared and digestible for human consumption.
>
> (Aspin, 1992)

Another problem with the managerialist approach is the professional paradox that people responsible for management run the risk of losing the skills that laid the basis for their selection in the first place. For school leaders, faced with the demands of balancing budgets and competing for clients in the educational marketplace, the danger of the potential costs to their substantive professional and educational expertise is clear.

It has long been established, of course, that educational reform will come about as much from the reflection of the political and economic environment of the day, as it will from a response to the needs, interests and concerns of students and educators; and the resulting reforms will be facilitated but also limited by the interplay of both these factors.

In her elucidation of the causes of the decentralizing trends in educational management in Sweden and the USA, Eliason (1992) has argued that, while emphasising the participatory advantages of current reform efforts, national policy makers have in reality engaged in a form of compensatory legitimation. Lacking the means to buy off voters by expanding public programmes they resort to procedural means to legitimate policy. They can endeavour to mobilize broad support for their policies in the name of local control and public choice, but in the meantime other real policy objectives such as making cut-backs in funding can be accomplished without high political costs.

It is the ambiguity of decentralization which makes it politically useful in a highly politicized policy making environment. Despite the rhetoric of decentralization the government can still steer educational policy through its much more tightly held purse.

(Eliason, 1992)

Moreover, as Grantstron (1992) has argued, decentralization to the school implies a high degree of competence in new decision-making arenas not only for the school leader but for all members of the school community. For this reason, school-based personnel, without the requisite knowledge and theories regarding organizational structure, power distribution or planning, and without the language appropriate to the discussion of aims, goals and teaching strategies, will still run the danger of falling victim to hierarchical thinking. These factors, combined with the potential for collective regression in response to unprecedented, confusing or inherently contradictory change efforts, then work to hinder the development of productive, innovative effort at the school site.

SCHOOL-BASED DECISION MAKING IN AUSTRALIA

In Australia during the 1970s and 1980s school systems in each of the states and territories, faced with the need to respond to a broad range of social, political, economic and management pressures, attempted to decentralize administrative arrangements and devolve responsibility to the local level. In view of the states' attempts to bring about this change it became necessary for policy makers, system-level and school administrators, and representatives of teachers' and parents' associations to address the considerable tensions that began to emerge between the bureaucratic concerns for hierarchy, impersonality, consistency, economy and efficiency that had previously characterized traditional state approaches to education, and the concern for participatory decision making and increased local autonomy which had begun to characterize the pluralist society of Australia in the latter half of the twentieth century. Many of the initiatives for these changes emanated from Commonwealth policies and the increasing involvement in educational matters of the Commonwealth Government.

As Australia entered the 1990s, despite the momentum that developed during the previous two decades towards more democratic school-based structures and processes, state bureaucracies continued to be seen as indispensable requirements for the administration of education. It was generally agreed that schools and regional administrations should increasingly involve teachers, parents, students and administrators in local site-based management, but it was also widely acknowledged that such decision making should be subject to constraints within the boundaries of government policies and guidelines. The major issues addressed, therefore, tended to revolve around such questions as how much control state authorities should retain and how much should be granted to regions and schools. The various and differing understandings and interpretations of the proper and desirable boundary line between state and local responsibility held by the various constituencies having an interest in what they saw as desirable outcomes of educational processes contributed to the difficulties being experienced by all such interest groups in their attempt to address this issue. The impulse was towards increasing democratization of education within government constraints, conditioned by concerns for equity and distributive justice.

In the current context, the educational debate in Australia is still pervaded by a discourse that employs the language of decentralization and school-based management. In observing this phenomenon we may believe we discern, at least superficially, a straightforward connection or evolution from those earlier trends just described. But closer examination reveals fundamental shifts in ideology and political direction, both of which combine to make the debate much more contentious than one merely between proponents of central control – whether that be defined as centred at state or national level – and those supporting the cause for overriding autonomy and determinative involvement to be given to representatives of the local community in the management of their local school.

The New Right, for instance, clearly appears, as part of its response in Australia to international trends such as those in evidence in the United Kingdom, to have adopted and indeed taken over much of the language and the rhetoric centred around notions of school-based management. In this context, however, school-based management rests on an application to education of the values of diversity, competition and the marketplace: a clear example of simplistic rhetoric leading to gross conceptual confusion.

THEORY AND RESEARCH RELEVANT TO THE FIELD

Since the 1950s the field of educational administration has been strongly influenced by behavioural science and the human relations school of management, with an emphasis on observable behaviour and process. The emphasis on process has been reflected in major policy initiatives, such as those in the 1980s associated with school improvement.

Such initiatives have been based on the assumption that the way to improve schooling is to improve the processes of decision making, an inherent aspect of which was the enhancement of the capabilities of people at the school site. In so doing, this approach advocated and adopted a long-term solution to the issue of school effectiveness.

In the 1990s, however, there is pressure for more immediate and direct responses to the problem of improving schools, focused as much on substance and outcomes as on process and technique. In this context the mainstream body of theory and research informing the academic study and practice of educational administration has been found increasingly to be deficient. A re-examination and re-integration of theories and a more coherent approach appears to be required.

In the specific area of school effectiveness and leadership, for example, the most recent reviewers of the existing literature (Leithwood *et al.*, 1990) challenge the past emphasis on mere factual description of behaviours and call for research exploring relationships between external influences and internal states based on a coherent and more embracing set of theoretical considerations.

As Leithwood and his colleagues have shown, results of research concerned with school effectiveness and school improvement have consistently ascribed importance to school leadership. Building their account on an extensive review of research conducted between 1974 and 1988 they have been able to illuminate the nature, causes and consequences of what school leaders do in contributing to the effectiveness of schools.

In summary, their synthesis reveals:

- *Impact:* that school leaders are capable of having a significant influence on the basic skills achievement of students. In addition, that school leaders are capable of influencing teachers' adoption and use of innovative classroom practices and teachers' job satisfaction.
- *Practices:* with respect to goals, highly effective school leaders have been found to demonstrate high levels of commitment to goals for the school, especially instructional goals. Such leaders articulate an overall multi-faceted vision for the school. Effective school leaders, the research reveals, set relatively high professional standards for goal achievement and actively work towards the development of widespread agreement concerning such standards. The research thus confirms the central role of goals – their nature, sources and use – in explaining effective practice on the part of school leaders.

   Research on patterns or styles of practice confirms that effective school leaders operate in distinctly different ways. It has been found that participatory decision making is used selectively but frequently by effective school leaders depending on their assessment of the context.
- *Influences on practices:* Obstacles standing in the way of school leaders providing instructional leadership are often raised by teachers in the schools (for example, lack of knowledge about new practices, lack of motivation to change, uneven professional development); and constraints on programme decision making arising from collective bargaining and union contracts.

The ways in which several features of the school leader's role function also appear to provide further obstacles. These include: ambiguity (for example, unclear expectations) and complexity (for example, number of people to consider).

Obstacles associated with the system, such as hierarchical structures, rigid and time-consuming policies and practices, inadequate resources and the conservative stance of central administration to school-initiated change, are also identified as problems. Aspects of the community (for example, pressure of special interest groups) are also seen as obstacles, although it is interesting to note that obstacles associated with the system tend to be most dominant, especially in more recent studies.

At the completion of their review, Leithwood and colleagues point to the following deficiencies in the existing research:

- Research has tended to concentrate on only a limited set of student outcomes.
- Research which looks at the relationships between external influences and internal states is conceptually and methodologically limited.

Little of the research is guided by a coherent theory. Leithwood *et al.* (1990) conclude that:

> There is arguably a greater need for research exploring these relationships than there is for more descriptive research on effective practice (there is a need for a) ... better understanding of principals' (school leaders) internal mental processes and states; the rational aspects of those processes, such as the content and organization of knowledge structures, as well as the non rational elements such as beliefs, attitudes and values. (p. 22)

This echoes the claims made by Reynolds (1990) that the most important and damaging isolation of all for school effectiveness research is that from the disciplines of psychology and psychiatry, without which we have failed to understand the 'deep structure' of the ineffective school. Reynolds maintains that:

> We have concentrated, to put it simply, upon the first dimension of schooling – the formal, reified, organizational structure – without looking in enough detail at the second, cultural and informal world of values, attitudes and perceptions, which together with the third dimension of the complicated web of personal relationships within schools will determine a school's effectiveness or ineffectiveness.

> (Reynolds, 1990)

The body of knowledge pertaining to school effectiveness within the rational–empirical paradigm may well be past its shelf life, concludes Reynolds. Multi-paradigmatic approaches are identified by Reynolds as a way forward.

In the final section of this chapter some of the deficiencies in the literature as identified by Reynolds are addressed by postulating a new framework for understanding leadership and school effectiveness. New dimensions for analysis are suggested, drawing on the insights derived from the disciplines of psychology and psychiatry. Such insights are offered, not in line with Reynolds' call for multi-paradigmatic approaches, but in the quest to develop a more integrated or coherentist approach to leadership, school-based decision making and school effectiveness, in line with current developments at the cutting edge of theory development in the field of educational administration.

TOWARDS A NEW FRAMEWORK FOR UNDERSTANDING LEADERSHIP, SCHOOL-BASED DECISION MAKING AND SCHOOL EFFECTIVENESS

The capacity to lead and manage a school or school system effectively is not only a function of administrative and judicial freedom and autonomy; it is also a function of the qualifications of the leaders and the nature of the relationship that exists between leaders and those with whom they interact in the accomplishment of the work of schools. The pertinent question here is this: in the context of a changing political, social, economic and technical environment, in which there is increasing emphasis on school effectiveness, but in which altered patterns of educational governance have brought about changes in the decisions to be taken at different levels of the school system, what is required of those people now responsible for educational leadership at the school site?

In answering this question it is claimed that visionary and creative leadership and effective management in education require a deliberate and conscious attempt at integration, enmeshment and coherence: the enmeshment of the qualitative and quantitative concerns of schooling, the linking together of substance and process, an external and an internal view, a strategic and an operational perspective simultaneously. This integrative or coherentist approach to educational leadership mirrors approaches proposed in the broader field of public administration and business by theorists such as Gilmore and Krantz (1991).

Gilmore and Krantz argue that the approach to revitalizing organizations in the post-industrial period necessitates an integration of the substantive concerns of the organization with the operational tools, processes and techniques necessary for the achievement of the organization's mission. Drawing conceptually from the work of the Tavistock Institute, Gilmore and Krantz claim that the current moves towards the splitting of the functions of leadership and management arise from the anxieties inherent in attempting to administer complex organizations and serve as a defence to diminish, evade or trivialize the deep changes and sophisticated attention to primary task or mission that are required.

What is needed much more, according to these authors, is a deliberate and conscious integration of leadership and management in a way that fuels the insights and skills of both roles and functions. As Gilmore and Krantz argue:

> At the boundary line between any unit and its wider organizational context, or alternatively, at the boundary between the enterprise and its wider environment, a leader integrates the unit's mission or strategic orientation with the tools and means for accomplishing it. It is specifically the function

of leadership to weave the two ... to articulate an appropriate mission which the resources of the unit can realistically achieve and to deploy its resources efficiently in the service of its primary tasks.

(Gilmore and Krantz, 1991)

To extrapolate from this literature, the substantive leadership required to revitalize or develop schools in the turbulent environment of post-industrial society would require people who are prepared to:

- grapple with the complex realities of their current situation and confront the difficult substantive issues of education and schooling;
- enable all members of the school community to work through difficult dilemmas over issues of direction and purpose;
- sustain the capacity for continuous organizational flexibility, adaptability and renewal;
- enter into responsive relationships with partners across the traditional boundary of the educational enterprise;
- acknowledge each person's interdependence in the school setting and handle the anxieties inherent in collaborative work relationships;
- link new and visionary ideas in education with the organizational tools, methods and apparatus to realize them, and
- continually struggle with the value-laden issues underlying their technical expertise.

This approach to school leadership is a challenge to the frequently held distinction between leadership and management, which Gilmore and Krantz see as associated with the segmentalist culture that inhibits innovation and adaptation. It draws strength from recent work exploring new meanings of educational change in which Michael Fullan (1991) stresses the need for more holistic and deeper understandings in the undertaking of educational change efforts.

But the difficulties of exercising such an approach to leadership are profound. Leithwood *et al.* (1990), for example, have commented upon the obstacles to leadership and school effectiveness which have been identified in the existing body of literature based on a rationalist–empirical paradigm. In addition to this, more fundamental difficulties may be identified at the level of what Reynolds calls *deep structure*.

As one of the major barriers to organizational effectiveness, for instance, we may note with Zaleznik (1989) the cleavages which occur as executives subordinate the 'real work' challenges to the demands of psycho-politics – to balancing the rational and irrational expectations of others – as a result of which process and politics, coordination and control, receive more attention than substance and outcomes.

The complexity in human nature – especially our conflicting tendencies to cooperate and go it alone – leads managers to spend their time smoothing over conflict, greasing the wheels of human interaction, and unconsciously avoiding aggression, especially aggression that centres on them and their role.... People can focus their attention only on so many things. The more it lands on politics, the less energy – emotional and intellectual – is available to attend to the problems that fall under the heading of real work.

(Zaleznik, 1989, p. 60)

It is important at this point to emphasise that this approach to leadership is not one that is insensitive to human concerns. Rather it is based on the belief that the humanizing benefits of social satisfaction, independence and maturity emerge when all people in the workplace are freed to use their talent *to do their substantive work well*. This is a vital responsibility of leadership. Zaleznik (1989) concludes:

Leading with substance requires maturity not only to tolerate others' aggressiveness but also to direct it to substantive issues ... the politicization of work and human relationships is not an inevitable consequence of people being people. Rather it goes hand in hand with reactive and defensive behaviour. (p. 64)

The existence of defences in the workplace, however, is not isolated to the individual. Menzies (1979) has demonstrated that individuals develop and use in concert, organizational means for dealing both with real difficulties and dangers and with highly personal anxiety situations that are projected into them. Individuals thus collaborate over the erection of a system of socially structured defences arising from personal and common sources.

This socially constructed defence system crucially affects the competence with which the institution or the work group performs its task and adapts to innovation and change: the more primitive and powerful the defence system the less effective the institution or the work group will be. This parallels the system in the individual. Some of the difficulties in bringing about social change, Menzies suggests, seem to stem from the need to maintain these social defence systems.

An understanding of the defensive aspect in both the individual and the work group is thus an important diagnostic and therapeutic tool for the leader in working with social organizations such as schools and in trying to affect school change. This has clear implications for leadership and school effectiveness. In particular it highlights the need for a psychologically informed leadership which possesses an awareness of the personal, group and social factors which might interfere with the accomplishment of the primary tasks of schools and the creation of healthy social systems.

Of course, some social systems seem to be more healthy for the individuals in them than others. Main (1977) attributes this to the culture, the human folkways by which the system operates, the quality of human relationships inside the social structure, what Reynolds has called deep structure.

Hinshelwood (1987) identifies the following as relevant to the development of healthy systems:

- the psychodynamics of responsibility, that is responsibility is located in the right place;
- the allocation of human resources, qualities and responsibilities to enable all staff to share in being healthy, knowledgeable, kind, powerful and active;
- the use that members make of the social system, that is the ways that the social system is used by members to protect themselves from personal suffering, defensive manipulation of the work and the institution;
- the rigidities in the organization in which 'both the accretion of bits and pieces of organization and the clinging on to every aspect of the old structure (rigid bureaucracy and ossification) contribute to a phenomenon in which complexity relentlessly increases ... there is too much doubt to allow questioning and adaptation to develop' (Hinshelwood, 1987, p. 201).

IMPLICATIONS FOR THEORY DEVELOPMENT AND FURTHER RESEARCH

The number and complexity of all the foregoing kinds of considerations, as well as their inchoate nature and their recalcitrance immediately to under-standable characterizations, underline the difficulty, if not the impossibility, of locating concepts such as school leadership, school-based management and school effectiveness under any rationalist rubrics. For the plethora of consider-ations rendering such concepts amenable to articulation ensures that rationalist accounts of them are likely to be no better than at best partial, and at worst grossly deficient in highlighting their most important aspects. Such rationalist accounts are fraught with the dangers of dubiety and incompleteness.

As a consequence it may seem reasonable to support Reynolds' suggestion that multi-paradigmatic approaches may be the way to proceed in school effectiveness research. However, Reynolds' references to the possibility and utility of a multi-paradigmatic drawing of the cognitive map of such concepts is itself flawed.

Reference to paradigms immediately privileges the notion of Kuhnian versions of scientific advance and appears to offer at least *prima facie* a scientific plausibility. But what Reynolds tries to do is in fact a contradiction in terms, for, as Kuhn shows, the notion of multi-paradigmaticity is logically im-possible; paradigm shifts occur as between paradigms and in linear progression only. They occur from one to another because of breakdown. Reynolds may find greater plausibility, therefore, in the Hirstian notion of the explicability of school effectiveness and other such concepts by applying a Hirstian *fields of knowledge* approach.

But, as Evers and Lakomski (1991) and others have shown, there is little to be said for the notion of knowledge as partitioned into discrete sets, from which different forms of illumination can be focused upon problems, topics and issues and then be brought to bear upon practical application. Knowledge does not have that discrete and partitioned rationality: it is much more Protean in character.

Better and more plausible is the notion to which reference has already been made: the idea that knowledge in educational administration, leadership and management is, like any other cognitive enterprise, a complex web of belief, formed of different elements that interweave and form, in their separate parts, a coherent whole. The notion most helpful here, and one frequently used by Quine, is that of Otto von Neurath: the theory of educational administration is like a boat crossing the sea, which, because of the continuing stresses and strains upon it, has continually to be repaired and rebuilt even as it crosses the ocean, while it is still on the move, so to speak – and in a way that will, while still giving overall coherence to the whole, make for a vessel that, at the end of the enterprise of theory building, is fairly radically different from that 'theoretical vessel' upon which the journey began.

What is critical to this enterprise of theory/vessel building and repairing is the need continually to look at other plans, theories and forms of cognitive transport, in the attempt to see how well they manage to convey their passengers and their intellectual impediment in the subject, and to subject them to critical scrutiny, appraisal and comparison, to see what elements of utility, fecundity and felicity might be drawn from them and applied to our own theoretic purposes.

This is then the nature of our enterprise. Neither extreme objectivism, such as that emanating from rationalism and positivism, nor ethnomethodological subjectivism, nor doctrinaire Marxism will do as single or would-be comprehensive theories to account for all the phenomena and features constituting the bases and interstices of the subject of leadership and school effectiveness. Rather, we need to go beyond objectivism and relativism and enhance and facilitate discriminatory theory construction and comparison and so make our own theories meet for application, modification and repair at every stage of our intellectual journey.

Even in this undertaking, an integration of the kind I have here outlined will only be a preliminary stage in the launching of our coherentist theoretical vessel in which, like Odysseus, we embark upon what is still, 'the boundless and never-ending sea'.

Acknowledgements

This chapter draws upon work undertaken by the author on behalf of OECD, Paris, and contained in the OECD General Distribution Document: J. Chapman, *The role of school leadership in enhancing the effectiveness of schools and developing a capacity to innovate and change*, OECD, Paris, 1992.

The author acknowledges the assistance provided by Professor David

Aspin, Dean of the Faculty of Education, Monash University, and Dr Stanley Gold, Department of Psychological Medicine, Faculty of Medicine, Monash University, in the preparation of this chapter.

REFERENCES

Aspin, D.N. (forthcoming 1992) 'The liberal paradox', in W. Boyd, J. Chapman, R. Lander and D. Reynolds (eds) *Quality, Equality and Control: International Responses along the Centralization–Decentralization Continuum*, London: Cassells.
Chapman, J.D. (1991a) *Making Australian schools more effective. Australian schools in international perspective*, A Report to the Australian Commonwealth Department of Employment, Education and Training.
—— (1991b) *School effectiveness and management: The enmeshment of the qualitative and quantitative concerns of schooling*, A keynote address presented at the International Congress of School Improvement and School Effectiveness, Cardiff, Wales.
—— (1991c) *The effectiveness of schooling and of educational resource management: A conceptual–analytical report*, OECD, Paris.
Cuban, L. (1989) *Effective schools: Policy, research and practice*, A keynote address presented at the conference Enhancing School Quality, organized by the Delta School District, Vancouver, Canada, November.
Dawkins, J. (1990a) *A clever country: Australian education and training in perspective*, A keynote address presented at the first national conference of the National Board of Employment, Education and Training, Coffs Harbour, NSW.
—— (1990b) *The impact of Commonwealth issues on education*, The Macarthur Lecture Series, University of West Sydney.
Eliason, L. (forthcoming 1992) 'The many meanings of centralization', in W. Boyd, J. Chapman, R. Lander and D. Reynolds (eds) *Quality, Equality and Control: International Responses along the Centralization–Decentralization Continuum*, London: Cassells.
Evers, C.W. and Lakomski, G. (1991) *Knowing Educational Administration*, Oxford: Pergamon.
Fullan, M. (1991) *New Meanings of Educational Change*, New York: Teachers College Press.
Gallie, W.B. (1964) 'Essentially contested concepts', Ch. 8 of his *Philosophy and the Historical Understanding*, London: Chatto & Windus.
Gilmore, T.N. and Krantz, J. (1990) 'The splitting of leadership and management as a social defence', *Human Relations* 43(2): 183–204.
Grantstron, K. (forthcoming 1992) 'Decentralization and teachers: Professional status cannot be granted – it has to be acquired', in W. Boyd, J. Chapman, R. Lander and D. Reynolds (eds) *Quality, Equality and Control: International Responses along the Centralization–Decentralization Continuum*, London: Cassells.
Hinshelwood, R.D. (1987) *What Happens in Groups: Psychoanalysis, the Individual and the Community*, London: Free Association Books.
Leithwood, K.P., Begley, J. and Bradley Cousin, J. (1990) 'The nature, causes and consequences of principals' practices: An agenda for future research', *Journal of Educational Administration* 28(4): 5–31.
Main, T. (1977) 'The concept of the therapeutic community – variations and vicissitudes', reprinted in M. Pines (1983) *The Evolution of Group Analysis*, London: Routledge & Kegan Paul.
Menzies, E. (1979) 'Staff support systems: Task and anti-task in adolescent institutions',

in R.D. Hinshelwood and N.P. Manning (eds) *Therapeutic Communities*, London: Routledge & Kegan Paul.

Quine, W.V. (1953) *From a Logical Point of View*, Cambridge, MA: Harvard University Press.

Reynolds, D. (1990) *School effectiveness and school improvement in the 1990s*, A keynote address given at the International Congress of Effective Schools, Jerusalem.

Wittgenstein, L. (1922) *Tractatus Logico–Philosophicus* (trans. C.K. Ogden), London: Routledge & Kegan Paul.

—— (1958) *The Blue and Brown Books* (trans. G.E.M. Anscombe), Oxford: Basil Blackwell.

Zaleznik, A. (1989) 'Real work', *Harvard Business Review* 67 (Jan-Feb): 57–64.

Chapter 11

School-based management, school improvement and school effectiveness
Overview and implications

Raymond Bolam

The purposes of this chapter are twofold: first, to provide a summary overview of the earlier chapters in the book by highlighting and analysing some of their principal themes; and second, to consider some of the main implications for policy, practice and research. Some concluding remarks are made in the final section.

SUMMARY

The studies presented in this book are all on related themes but they are, nevertheless, diverse. For the purposes of this section, they are, somewhat arbitrarily, summarized under four headings: school-level studies; system-level studies; studies of a single technique; international analyses.

Three research studies at school level

Hallinger, Murphy and Hausman report on a qualitative study of professionals' expectations of restructuring, based on interviews with 14 teachers and 15 principals in elementary, middle and high schools in three states. They present their findings under four headings: general conceptions of restructuring, potential impact of restructuring, prerequisites for implementation and changes at the school and classroom levels. Most of the respondents supported restructuring but reservations were expressed about the system's capacity to change and about the practical implications of restructuring. It was expected to lead to more teacher participation, to a reduction in the power of principals, and to student learning gains, although not necessarily ones that were testable; scepticism was expressed about parental involvement. Clarity about restructuring, collaborative decision making, training, accountability mechanisms and budgetary support were seen as essential to implementation. The respondents wanted a more coherent curriculum, more student-centred activities and more flexible scheduling. Principals tended to be sceptical about teachers' capacity to develop a curriculum and they generally had a more coherent view of the need for professional development than did the teacher respondents.

The authors make three concluding observations: that, somewhat surprisingly, the respondents saw little connection between restructuring and improved teaching and learning; that teachers were more likely than principals to support increased teacher participation in decision making, a finding which was not consistent with some earlier research; and, finally, that principals were more likely than teachers to stress the importance of clarifying accountability for the outcomes of participative decision making.

Hord and Poster present comparative case studies of the restructuring strategies adopted in two multi-ethnic, primary schools – one in England and the other in New Mexico. The English case deals with the adoption by the headteacher, and subsequently by the staff, of a generic, problem-solving, management technique – GRASP – and its application to the management of a radically innovative approach to the involvement of the school's community in the educational process – the Just School Project. The New Mexico case deals with a principal developing the role of instructional leader and changing his own views and values as teachers increasingly participated in decision making and leadership with him. The study charts these developments over a six-year period and highlights the substantial changes that have occurred in these management processes. The findings from both cases are seen as consistent with the conclusions from earlier research that five main factors are associated with effective principals: visioning, translating the vision, providing a supportive environment, monitoring, and intervening both to reinforce and to take corrective action. In addition, both leaders exercised patience, provided time and arranged training – all seen as central to effective leadership and to effective change.

Leithwood and Steinbach report on a study of the generic, problem-solving processes used by elementary school principals who were engaged in implementing British Columbia's new Primary Program. Data from the 12 principals and all 44 primary teachers in the sample of schools were analysed using a conceptual framework with four dimensions: leadership style; problem-solving constructs; outcomes; demographic variables. These four dimensions distinguish between four leadership styles (focused on interpersonal relationships, student achievement, task achievement and building management); six problem-solving constructs (interpretation, goals, values, constraints, solution processes and feelings); three types of outcome (teachers' ratings of principals' helpfulness, school culture and teacher development); and four demographic variables (gender, experience, school size and school district).

Three of the four leadership styles were observed in the school improvement practices used by the 12 principals. Substantial differences in the use of problem-solving processes were also evident, and these tended to follow from the differences in the initial interpretation of problems. Only moderate support was found for any relationship between principals' patterns of practice and the three outcomes. The analysis based on demographic characteristics suggests a strong interaction effect between gender and district-level socializ-ation and selection processes. The authors conclude that the principals did use different leadership practices and problem-solving processes to tackle the same school improvement problem – how to implement the new Primary Program – and that the way they initially interpreted that problem (for example, as an opportunity or a blur of confusing demands) significantly influenced their subsequent actions.

Two system-level case studies

Cuttance describes the background to, and the operation of, a framework for reviewing school effectiveness and auditing management performance in South Australia from his perspective as Director of the responsible Education Review Unit. This framework addresses performance at all organizational levels (individual school, school support units, central and area directorates, and the system as a whole) and includes five types of review (school develop-ment plans, effective practices in schools, the effectiveness of educational programmes and policies, the implementation of state requirements and the performance of directorates and units).

Caldwell reviews the changing role of the school principal in Australia and New Zealand in the light of substantial restructuring aimed at increasing quality and cost effectiveness. In Australia, the most recent trend has been towards school-site management (for example, for budgeting) and increased community involvement, within the framework of a state-wide curriculum, state-level strategic planning and strict accountability. In New Zealand, the changes have been in a similar direction but have gone further and faster. A concern for equity in public policy is said to underpin the use of certain outcome indicators (for example, an increase in student retention rates) and the acknowledgement that schools should have sufficient resources to achieve this, for instance by using resource allocation procedures based on student numbers. Two arguments used to support the shift to school-based manage-ment and the reduced or changed roles of both central authorities and external support agencies are, first, that schools are more responsive to changed needs than central authorities and, second, that they can make better judgements about priorities and whether or not to purchase external support in a time of financial restraint or budgetary crisis. The empowerment of parents and the community as well as of teachers are also features of these trends.

Thus, school principals now require strategic planning skills to operate within these frameworks, especially in relation to the curriculum and student learning and they also have to operate collaboratively with teachers, parents and the community. Self-management is offered as a unifying concept. The self-managing school is accountable to a central authority for the way it uses the following resources: knowledge, technology, power, material, people, time and finance. This involves managing the ongoing cycle of goal-setting, needs identification, policy making, priority setting and programme planning, budgeting and evaluation. In addition, it involves a leadership role with four facets: cultural, strategic, educational and accountability. Beyond this, certain 'megatrends' are identified and the overall implications for the professional development of principals are considered.

Three international reviews of a single technique or concept in relation to school-based management

Knight analyses the relationship of delegated financial management to school effectiveness. He distinguishes between three reasons for, and approaches to, delegated financial management: managerial efficiency and effectiveness; empowerment of teachers, parents and community; and as one means of creating a competitive market economy for schools. Schemes in various countries differ in their scope, administration, structure and implementation. Schools are said to be affected by, and to respond to, these schemes differently, according to their individual circumstances (for example, headteacher's values, the views of staff and governors, the school's current financial position and its perceived needs).

Research findings so far are of limited value because they mainly arise from pilot schemes and lack a quantitative dimension. Thus, it is unclear what the impact of financial delegation is on headteachers, on the senior management team, on department heads, on governors, on time and workloads, on staff participation, on school development planning, on administrative loads and roles, on the efficient use of time as a resource, on the school's capacity to innovate and on accountability. It is also unclear whether delegation leads to more or less funds for schools and whether the allocation is more or less equitable between schools and between phases and whether community education is enhanced. There do seem to be gains in terms of increased flexibility of decision making at school level, particularly over the internal allocation of funds; increased choice over the purchasing of central services and in-service training (where such arrangements exist); increased use of information technology. Perhaps most significantly, although those who have experienced it are convinced that it has a positive impact on school processes, there is no evidence that financial delegation has improved school outcomes.

The author concludes by speculating that, carried to its logical conclusion, subsidiarity could lead headteachers and governors to contract with departments to deliver a curriculum service, perhaps in competition with external providers, and thus to examine the cost effectiveness of alternative teaching and learning strategies within a framework of outcome-led financial management.

Dimmock examines the relationship between school-based management and the curriculum, arguing that the two main forces driving towards improved quality – the educational or school effectiveness force and the economic or political one – are both enhanced by, and depend upon, school-based management. The main features of the latter are said to be: autonomy; flexibility and responsiveness; planning by the principal and the community; adoption of new roles by the principal; a participatory school environment; collaboration and collegiality among staff; and a heightened sense of efficacy for principals and teachers. The school effectiveness research identifies certain characteristics of management which correlate with learning outcomes (for example, strong leadership from the principal; school planning; monitoring and evaluation of school activities) but there is no hard evidence that these are features of school-based management in particular.

The concepts of linkage and 'loose coupling' are explored to answer the question: 'How can school-based management nurture a quality curriculum?' Eight analytic dimensions of coupling (between individuals, sub-units, organizations, levels, the organization and its environment, ideas, activities, and between intentions and actions) are applied to school management. The discussion is then extended to deal with four critical variables which influence, or link with, school outcomes: learning; teaching; school climate; curriculum structure and content. The author concludes that the features of school-based management need clarification, that the links between features and the curriculum and student learning outcomes should then be researched, and that coupling, or linkage, offers a fruitful conceptual framework for such research.

Campbell-Evans adopts a values perspective in order to address issues surrounding the principal's role in school-based management and school effectiveness. Leadership style, vision, aims, priorities and culture are all said to be reflections of values and to be both interactive and mutually reinforcing. Values are personal and are exhibited through words and actions. Decision-making processes, which involve interpretations of facts and choices between possible alternative courses of action, are influenced by, and filtered through, value systems. Decision makers with access to sound factual information and the capacity to clarify and resolve value conflicts operate on the 'high ground'; those who are not in this position operate in the 'swamp'. Leadership is stipulatively defined as including two components: first, those functions, tasks and skills which are more routine, predictable and quantifiable; second, those aspects of the role which involve influencing people's behaviour and beliefs and are, therefore, concerned with value transmission and transformation. Vision expresses a view of what is desirable and can inspire and motivate people: it is a public statement of individual and collective values, and may take the form of a development plan which expresses the vision in terms of priorities. Culture is analysed along two dimensions (bureaucratic and professional domains; personal or shared motives for action) to produce a four-cell typology of schools – ineffective, efficient, classroom effective, school effective – in which tight and loose coupling are central concepts. Core values are said to be the touchstone of effective schools. In school-based management, participation and collaboration are core values: they are integral to decision making, to leadership style, to vision, and thus to the culture of the school. Centrally imposed restructuring, with competition as a core policy value, is said to be at odds with the policy process – school-based management – which is most likely to ensure its effective implementation. School leadership in future will require 'people' skills (for example, interpersonal communication and team building) and skills related to value clarification and conflict resolution. The implications for the professional development of school leaders are said to be considerable.

Two international analyses of the broad field

Reynolds describes and analyses the lack of connectedness between research and practice in two fields: school effectiveness and school improvement. For example, although some practitioners in the USA and Canada have attempted to use the research findings from both fields, school improvement researchers in the two countries rarely cite school effectiveness research and vice versa. This is still more true of other countries where even the practitioner usage is less evident. School improvement is described as a paradigm which, in the 1960s, was characterized by, for example, top-down, pupil outcome and quantitative approaches to improvement and, in the 1980s, by, for example, bottom-up, process-orientated and qualitative approaches. The school effectiveness paradigm is said to have the following characteristics: strongly quantitative in orientation; concerned with pupil and school outcomes, which are regarded as essentially unproblematic; concerned with school processes only as a means to these ends; uses organizationally and behaviourally oriented process factors and criteria which are more easily measurable and quantifiable.

There is some evidence that the two traditions are coming together but much remains to be done. For example, school effectiveness researchers are recommended to concentrate more on 'data-rich' case studies of effective schools; on studies of process factors like climate and attitudes; on longitudinal studies; on the role of the headteacher; on the influence of external, local system factors; on studies of particular key factors which practitioners can then utilize; on the directionality of causal factors; on the problems of contemporary schools; on what works in most contexts; and on studies of ineffective schools. School improvement researchers should measure the impact of programmes on students; improve one rather than many factors at a time; aim at more specific target groups (for example, high- and low-ability students); and concentrate more on classrooms and instructional improvement. Three examples are outlined to support the conclusion that the two enterprises should adopt an integrated approach to research and practice.

Chapman also advocates a more integrated approach for understanding leadership, school-based decision making and school effectiveness but from a rather different standpoint. She argues that the reason there are so many definitions of effectiveness is that the concept is highly value laden and, therefore, is inevitably contested. Hence, it is unfortunate that school effectiveness research has placed such emphasis on measurable outcomes, quantitative methodology and the positivistic paradigm because important aspects of schooling are not amenable to such approaches. She proposes an approach to educational administration which embraces values, human subjectivity, politics and psychology. A rational model of decision making and leadership is inadequate because the leader is also responsible for the moral–political and psycho-social climate, working within particular national constraints.

In this spirit, an ongoing OECD project has agreed a framework for, not a definition of, effectiveness which pays regard to national context, the goals of schooling, the means available for achieving them and evaluation criteria. For example, in Australia, the Labour Government is trying to improve school effectiveness for two reasons: economic advancement and social equity; whereas, in the UK, the government has implemented a new concept of public service which is more consumer and market oriented and assumes that effectiveness will result from increased competition between schools. In most countries, attempts are being made to improve effectiveness within policies of restricted budgets, accountability and cost efficiency; to emphasise the role of the 'Centre' in determining objectives and monitoring achievement; and simultaneously to allocate more discretion over resource management decisions to the school level. These developments are often linked with the adoption of business management techniques and have been interpreted by some commentators as devices for legitimating budgetary cuts. Moreover, they pose contradictory demands, especially for governments of the Left, for example in Australia, where the notion of school-based management has, in practice, become inextricably bound up with the application of market values to schools.

Finally, following a summary review of recent theory and research, the author offers a new framework for understanding leadership, school-based decision making and school effectiveness. In the changing context outlined above, effective leadership requires: vision and creativity as well as managerial competence; the integration of quantitative and qualitative measures of performance; a concentration on 'real work' or substance in order to reduce the pressures and demands of organizational and psycho-politics; and the simultaneous adoption of an operational and strategic perspective. A multi-paradigmatic approach to research into school effectiveness is criticized on logical grounds and rejected in favour of a more pragmatic approach in which theories are constructed, trialled, compared and modified in the light of experience.

ISSUES AND IMPLICATIONS

It is evident from this summary that there are many issues and themes which

are either unresolved or which warrant further consideration and investigation. They are discussed below under four thematic headings: conceptual
issues; policy issues; technical issues; and research issues. In reality, the themes
intertwine and overlap but the headings do provide a convenient structure for
the discussion.

Conceptual issues

The three central concepts in this book are school-based management, school
effectiveness and school improvement. While the latter has, according to
Reynolds, shifted its operational meaning somewhat over recent years, it is a
less problematic concept than the other two although, as discussed below,
some of its technical and policy implications are insufficiently understood and
taken into account by practitioners and policy makers. The other two are more
problematic, though for somewhat different reasons.

Operational definitions of school-based management differ according to
national, regional and state contexts. Thus, as Hallinger, Murphy and Hausman demonstrate, in the USA it has become inextricably associated with the
broader notion of restructuring, a concept which is itself highly context bound,
sometimes according to school district (Elmore, 1990). In Europe, discussions
about school-based management are bedevilled by different national traditions, practices and beliefs about the extent to which decision making and
control over key aspects of educational policy and management are and should
be centralized or decentralized. In passing, it is perhaps worth observing that
most countries in both the developed and developing world organize their
education systems on relatively centralized lines and thus that many of the
ideas and practices discussed in this book would be seen as unfamiliar and, in
some cases, inimical by educationists and policy makers in those countries.

Several of the authors (for example, Dimmock, Knight and Caldwell) point
to the distinctive configurations of school-based management in different
countries. The key variables appear to be:

- the **task areas** over which decision-making discretion or autonomy is
  exercised (for example, school aims and policy; curriculum content; teaching methods; finance, budgets and resource allocation; staff appointments,
  deployment, salaries, development, appraisal, promotion, discipline, dis-
  missal and retirement; student recruitment and selection; purchase of
  supplies and support services, including training);
- the **level** at which decision-making autonomy or discretion is exercised (for
  example, national government; state or regional government; local government; school headteacher or principal; teachers; parents; local community,
  commerce and industry);
- the **degree** of discretion or autonomy over decision making which is

exercised and the extent to which it is constrained by regulations, examinations, inspections and other forms of external control and accountability.

The ways in which these variables operate in particular national situations appears to be as much a function of political and professional ideology as it is of practical experience or research evidence. Three examples may be cited in support of this proposition. First, school-based management is not necessarily linked to the introduction of a quasi or regulated market in which schools compete with each other for student numbers and income as part of a process in which parents behave as consumers and choose the schools to which they send their children; yet several governments (for example, New Zealand and the UK) are making this connection, primarily because of their political beliefs. Second, school-based management does not necessarily require local education authorities to be decoupled from schools nor to be stripped of most of their powers yet in the same two countries this, too, appears to be happening for largely political reasons, with the paradoxical corollary, in the UK at least, that more powers have had to be taken to the centre in order for the system to work. Third, school-based management does not necessarily require a collaborative and collegial leadership style, nor the participation of teachers, parents and community in decision making (as indicated by the behaviour of managers, customers and shareholders in successful, and unsuccessful, private companies), yet professional opinion in many countries is clearly in support of teacher empowerment and several governments are empowering parents and the community, in both cases, for reasons which are largely based on values and political beliefs rather than empirical evidence.

The concept of school effectiveness is problematic for two sets of reasons. First, as Reynolds demonstrates in his chapter, the technical questions associated with measuring effectiveness are complex and both the questions and the answers have changed over time, all of which confirms and compounds the problematic nature of the concept. Second, and as Chapman argues, the underlying cause is that perceptions of effectiveness are unavoidably rooted in values and hence the concept will always be contested. In practice, governments impose their own definitions of effectiveness via examinations, testing systems and other approved performance indicators. For example, the British government is pressing for schools to be judged by parents on the basis of published test scores and examination results in their 'raw' form and rejects the alternative, which is supported by researchers and professional associations, of weighting the results to take account of student intake characteristics in order to obtain a 'value-added' measure of effectiveness.

The contested nature of the concept is compounded further by the fact that apparently many, and possibly most, teachers and headteachers do not have explicit, agreed criteria for judging the effectiveness of their own schools, preferring to use subjective, implicit criteria related to student satisfaction and internal school processes rather than 'hard' outcome data (Bolam et al., 1992).

The technical complexity associated with the concept is confirmed by the growing evidence that subject department scores on examinations vary considerably within and between individual schools (Fitz-Gibbon, 1992).

Policy issues

Key questions facing national policy makers with respect to school-based management are, as indicated above, to decide which tasks to delegate, to which level and to what degree. Knight offers three reasons for the adoption of delegated financial control to schools – empowerment of teachers and the community, as a means of creating a market in schooling and to increase managerial efficiency and effectiveness yet, as argued above, the first two are by no means necessary features of delegated budgetary control. The third reason is probably the most powerful and the evidence which is available so far from the UK, mainly based on practitioner reports, indicates that the profession, and certainly the headteachers, do regard it positively. However, Knight is correct to point out that there is no evidence as yet that this leads to increased managerial or school effectiveness. Interestingly, the teachers in Hallinger *et al.*'s study did not expect restructuring to lead to improved teaching and learning, while Leithwood and Steinbach found only moderate support for any link between the principal's behaviour and school outcomes.

Moreover, there is little reliable evidence about what these changes will actually mean in practice. The fears mentioned by Knight that delegated budgets are a way of disguising budgetary cuts are very real, especially in the current, prolonged recession. Certainly, there is impressionistic evidence from the UK that discussions about the interpretation of the funding formulae can lead to struggles between primary schools and their traditionally more powerful, and better-funded, secondary neighbours over access to the limited available resources. There are also indications from the UK that delegated financial control, especially in a context where resources are severely restricted, leads to school governors having increased powers and LEAs steadily reduced powers, a situation which could produce some unfortunate decisions. For example, will lay governors faced with hard budgetary choices have the experience, knowledge and vision to spend their limited resources on training and development? Are they not more likely to spend them on, say, improving the student–teacher ratio, on books or on urgently needed repairs to the fabric of the building? And won't many headteachers and teacher governors, perforce, adopt a similar stance? Such outcomes are entirely probable, especially in small primary schools and especially if LEAs are no longer able, as they are at present, to ensure that training and development are priorities.

In order to resolve these and similar policy issues about tasks and levels of delegation, governments must first be clear about their answers to certain more fundamental political questions. As Campbell-Evans argues, such questions must necessarily be addressed in particular value frameworks and the answers can only be understood if analysed from a values perspective. It is striking, for example, that both Caldwell and Chapman stress the importance attached by the Labour Government in Australia to equity as a basic policy goal, and of school-based management as one means to this end. The same could certainly not be said of the Conservative administration in the UK where the emphasis is upon customer (that is, parent) choice as a means of raising educational standards.

The concern to improve educational quality, standards and effectiveness is, of course, pretty well universal. However, in order to understand those recent policy initiatives, including school-based management, which are intended to achieve these aims in particular countries, three sets of values have to be considered. One is associated, as Chapman indicates, with the belief that industrial and commercial management techniques are worth adopting in education. Examples include such practices as: decentralized financial control to cost or profit centres and branches within large firms; accountability for achieving prescribed or agreed objectives within a given resource framework; customer- or client-led approaches to all aspects of working practice, including the adoption of charters, total quality management and the creation of provider and customer relationships between different sections of the same organization.

A second set of values is held by those who assert that the market mechanism is the best available for ensuring that goods and services are provided as cost effectively as possible and for promoting improvements in both their overall quality and delivery. Influential advocates of this position (for example, Hayek, 1976) reject the idea that social justice can be rationally allocated, accept that inequalities are an inevitable feature of market-based economies, and argue that the result is a net gain for everyone, even for the least well off, because the overall standard of living is higher under this system than it would be under, for example, socialism or social democracy. Accordingly, equity is not a goal of social policy for those who believe in the market mechanism in its purest form. Furthermore, they believe that any hindrance to the free operation of the market, including regulations, controls and trade union power, should be reduced or, wherever possible, eliminated.

Unquestionably, the relationship of a market-oriented approach and equity in education is the most important policy issue thrown up by the contributions to this book. In the heat of political debate it is, of course, grossly oversimplified. For example, in practice, the UK system of a national curriculum, national testing and approved inspectors represents a regulated or quasi, rather than a pure, market and it is criticized for being so by the far Right. Moreover, the issue of the market approach has been conflated with those related to the introduction of school-based management and the reduction of LEA powers. Nevertheless, the introduction of competition between schools for students and the linking of budget allocations to student numbers is virtually certain to result in the reintroduction of student selection and the creation of a hierarchy of schools. It will also almost certainly disadvantage those parents and students who live in remote rural areas and deprived urban areas, in neither of which can the 'choice by parents' process meaningfully operate. The key policy questions for those who are unconvinced by the Hayekian arguments, therefore, are:

- Will the market approach lead to selection in schools, both at the point of entry and during the processes of schooling?
- Will it lead to improved quality all round or to greater social injustice?

However, for those who broadly accept the Hayekian position and thus who hold both sets of values, a third set follows quite logically: that successful management techniques from industry and commerce, together with the market mechanism, should be applied to as many aspects of public sector services as possible. Thus, they believe that the health, housing, welfare, social and prison services should all be radically restructured in order to introduce these features and education, as a major and expensive public service, should naturally be subject to the same changes.

The impact of these three sets of ideas on political beliefs and policies is evident in several countries, notably Australia, New Zealand and the UK, but also, for example, the Netherlands and Denmark. The three sets of beliefs are mutually reinforcing but, although they probably originate with the 'New Right', it would be simplistic not to recognize that support for them is more broadly based along the political spectrum. Thus, for many years they have, to a greater or lesser extent, underpinned the approaches adopted by influential international agencies like the World Bank and OECD. Second, the collapse of communism in Central and Eastern Europe has generated enormous support for them, support which cuts across traditional political categories. Third, the Left in Europe and elsewhere, the principal source of ideas for radical social change in the post-war period, is in intellectual disarray and, in consequence, no coherent or convincing alternative strategy has been forthcoming.

All of this has had its impact on public sector professionals in general and educationalists in particular. In the UK, for example, the education profession has, albeit reluctantly, adopted a reactive rather than a proactive role in the period of the current reforms. This is partly because it is reeling from the constant stream of changes flowing from central government, partly because it has been virtually disempowered by a government which holds it responsible for the current, perceived ills of the system, partly because it regarded some changes (for example, the introduction of a national curriculum) as more acceptable than others (for example, national testing and the market mechanism), but fundamentally because it had no coherent response to the government's radical, comprehensive and sustained assault on its established and taken-for-granted beliefs about what constituted an effective educational system and process.

In this context, the response of the professionals to two important features of school-based management – teacher and parent/community empowerment – deserves careful scrutiny. Hallinger et al. found that teachers were more likely than principals to support increased teacher participation in decision making while earlier American research indicates that teachers vary in their views about this according to their gender and age, the age-range of their students and whether their school is urban or rural. Although much of the research on effective schools suggests a positive correlation with participative leadership, the evidence is not robust, as Leithwood and Steinbach's findings also indicate. Moreover, professional traditions and expectations differ considerably from country to country: in France, teachers expect to be responsible only for teaching their subjects; in the UK there is a long tradition, now being challenged, of headteacher autonomy at school level and of teacher autonomy at classroom level; in Spain, teacher participation in school decisions is a legal requirement, to the point that school principals are elected by the teachers for a specified time period. Once again, policies adopted here are likely to reflect values rather than research data. Certainly it is understandable that teacher associations in the UK, for instance, are enthusiastic in their support for teacher participation, especially in the present climate.

Equally, it is unsurprising that they and the headteacher associations are much more sceptical about parent and community participation in school policy decisions. Although there is probably a greater degree of professional consensus about this across countries, the reasons for this scepticism are taking a particular form in those countries which are introducing market mechanisms and industrial-style management organization and methods. Essentially, this is because these approaches are designed to empower the parents as customers on the one hand and to encourage parents to take ownership of decision making, albeit at the expense of professional autonomy, on the other hand.

Technical issues

It is evident that the key policy issues outlined above can only be resolved in the specific setting of a particular education system. Nevertheless, the various contributions to this book offer valuable insights into the factors associated with the implementation of an approach to school-based management which will lead to school improvement and more effective schools.

First, it is essential that the aims, nature and scope of the particular configuration of school-based management being implemented should be as clear as possible at the outset, as required by the teachers in Hallinger et al.'s study. Beyond this, however, the research on implementation consistently concludes that complete and final clarity cannot be achieved at the outset: change is a process which takes place over time and during which all participants deepen their understanding of the innovation and learn how best to implement it as part of the experience of implementation itself. Hence, a central task of leadership is to ensure that the implementation arrangements are ones which will enhance the likelihood that such learning is productive and effective. All three school-level studies confirm this approach. Moreover, both highlight the importance of the problem-solving strategy adopted by the leader in achieving successful implementation, although whereas Hord and Poster focus on collaborative problem solving, Leithwood and Steinbach conclude that the way in which the principal construed the problem at the outset was crucial.

Cuttance provides an admirable and detailed account of another crucial piece in the school-based management jigsaw puzzle. As several of the authors point out, review and accountability mechanisms are essential at all levels – classroom, department, school, LEA, region or state and national – if school-based management is to be credible and effective. The South Australian model was constructed in a specific cultural setting but it offers a framework against which other approaches can be assessed. One major difference in the emerging British approach is that schools will be required to be inspected every four years and to buy the inspection from a list of approved inspection teams: thus, the extent to which a market-oriented approach to accountability is adopted will have significant implications for its operation. It is also becoming increasingly apparent in the UK that the role of governors, including parent governors, in school management and accountability is problematic: the complexity of their tasks and the heavy demands on their time have led to resignations and recruitment problems. The implications of this are, as yet, unclear but it will be interesting to see if other systems of community involvement encounter similar problems.

Running through most, if not all, of the contributions is the conviction that the principal or headteacher is central to the successful implementation of change, to school-based management and to effective schools and several of them summarize the main features of successful leadership. Caldwell's conceptualization and operationalization of the self-managing school appears to offer a productive way forward, though it probably pays insufficient attention to the practical and value-based dilemmas facing those managing schools in a competitive market context. What is apparent from his account is that everyone involved in the self-managing school – headteachers, teachers, parents and governors – will require ongoing training, development and support. As indicated above, it is unlikely that a market-driven training and support system would meet this need in anything other than a minimalist fashion. National systems, like the UK, which are adopting this approach, ought to beware. Furthermore, since systems of management training and development for headteachers and teachers are, in most countries, at a very early stage of development (Bolam, 1992), a great deal remains to be done if these new approaches to school management are to be adequately supported and implemented.

Finally, on the technical front, it is important to recognize that politicians appear to be prevented by the nature of their roles from being able to act upon, and in some cases accept, the now well established findings from research on the implementation of change. Changes of the kind discussed in this book are essentially long term and their success will depend on the provision of ongoing support and resources over several years. This is particularly true of changes which challenge deeply held beliefs and values, as many of those under discussion undoubtedly do. Practitioners as well as researchers need to be aware of this and to take whatever steps they can to convince decision makers about its practical import.

Research issues

Reynolds is quite right to highlight what is probably the most important substantive research issue in the book: the need for the two traditions of school improvement and school effectiveness research to come together. Furthermore, his recommendations for a strategic plan of action and integration are generally practical and feasible. The technical problems will, of course, continue to be daunting ones, as Reynolds acknowledges. The underlying conceptual and values problems, discussed by Dimmock, Campbell-Evans and Chapman, are of equal complexity and difficulty. These several problems can only be satisfactorily addressed by careful and sustained work of the kind exemplified in, for instance, the studies by Hord and Poster and by Leithwood and Steinbach, both of which draw upon, and are the product of, a series of research studies and of two long-standing research programmes.

The funding implications of such sustained programmes are obvious enough and so, too, are those for the strategy advocated by Reynolds. The difficulties encountered by researchers in seeking to influence policy decisions and of policy makers in making use of research findings are also now well known. What is of particular concern at present is that those policy makers who are ideologically committed to a market-oriented system are apparently unable to countenance the funding of research which would investigate the approach independently. Hence, in those countries where this situation exists, one can only be pessimistic about the possibility of obtaining the funding needed for the integration of the two improvement and effectiveness traditions to research those questions which are of most urgent, practical importance. Fortunately, not all countries are in this position.

CONCLUSION

This overview chapter has tried to clarify and distinguish between some of the main features and issues generated by the contributions to this book. Specifically, it has argued that there is no necessary connection between several of these features and, moreover, that the arguments for adopting some of them are more ideological than empirical. The latter is not necessarily a bad thing and, indeed, in many aspects of public affairs it is unavoidable. Hence, one need have no qualms about advocating school-based management and a collaborative approach to leadership and decision making within that framework. Both are broadly consistent with the social democratic tradition which is well tried and accepted. Similarly, many of the techniques arising from industrial and commercial management are worth trialing in schools, provided that they are sensibly monitored and evaluated and that appropriate action is then taken.

The critically new factor which has recently emerged in several of the countries described in this book, is that of the introduction of a consumer-led and market-orientated culture in education in general and in schools in particular. If one could be confident that it would be treated as a limited, social experiment to be studied and evaluated and then either extended, modified or dropped, depending on the outcomes of the experience, one would feel more sanguine. Regrettably, because it is apparently being driven by ideological and political conviction rather than by rational argument and research, one can only be pessimistic about its impact upon schools and children. In those countries where this is the case, the best hope is that the features which go to make up the regulated or quasi market, like the national curriculum and approved inspections, will prevent the worst excesses of an unregulated, free market. Those countries which have not yet done so would be well advised to consider carefully before choosing this particular route to school improvement and effective schools.

REFERENCES

Bolam, R. (1992) 'Administrative preparation: In-service', in T. Husen and T.N. Postlethwaite (eds) *The International Encyclopedia of Education*, Oxford: Pergamon.

Bolam, R., McMahon, A., Pocklington, K. and Weindling, R. (1992) *Effective Management in Schools*, Bristol: NDCEMP, School of Education, University of Bristol.

Elmore, R. and Associates (eds) (1990) *Restructuring Schools: The Next Generation of Educational Reform*, Oxford: Jossey Bass.

Fitz-Gibbon, C. (1992) 'School effects at A level: Genesis of an information system?', in D. Reynolds and P. Cuttance (eds) *School Effectiveness: Research, Policy and Practice*, London: Cassell.

Hayek, F. von (1976) *Law, Legislation and Liberty* (Vol. 2), London: Routledge.

Index